YOU WON—NOW WHAT?

How Americans Can Make Democracy Work
from City Hall to the White House

Taegan D. Goddard

and

Christopher Riback

A LISA DREW BOOK

SCRIBNER

A LISA DREW BOOK/SCRIBNER
1230 Avenue of the Americas
New York, NY 10020

SCRIBNER and design are trademarks of Simon & Schuster Inc.
A LISA DREW BOOK is a trademark of Simon & Schuster Inc.

Set in Walbaum Monotype
Designed by Brooke Zimmer

Manufactured in the United States of America

1 3 5 7 9 10 8 6 4 2

Library of Congress Cataloging-in-Publication Data

Goddard, Taegan D.
You won—now what?: how Americans can make democracy work from city
hall to the White House/Taegan D. Goddard and Christopher Riback.
p.   cm.
"A Lisa Drew Book"
Includes bibliographical references and index.
1. Bureaucracy—United States. 2. United States—Officials
and employees. 3. United States—Politics and government.
4. Democracy—United States. 5. Government productivity—
United States. I. Riback, Christopher. II. Title.
JK421.G55 1998
352.3'0973—dc21   97-37469
CIP

ISBN 0-684-83411-1

To Sara:

You are the center of my life
and my inspiration.

—TDG

To Karen:

Each time I think
I couldn't love you more,
I find out I'm wrong.

—CR

Acknowledgments

As we began to write *You Won—Now What?*, a television news executive posed a straightforward, sincere question: Why did we want to write a book? The answer was simple. After years of debate and reflection on how government worked, we thought we had some ideas to make it better and wanted to share them with others. The television executive was unimpressed. Sitting in his well-groomed office, which overlooks a Barnes & Noble, he pointed to the four-storey superstore and asked what apparently was the pertinent question: "Have you been across the street? Have you seen all the books that go unsold?" It was then that we grew to greatly appreciate words of support, which (along with actions of support) we kindly acknowledge here.

If our book's premise is that today's public officials can learn lessons from those who have done it before, we figured the same was true for book writing. Walt Bogdanich is the nation's finest investigative reporter, a Pulitzer Prize winner and an accomplished author. Stephen Goddard is a former journalist and congressional aide, a gifted writer and editor, and though he doesn't list it on his résumé,

Taegan's father. Bogdanich and Goddard helped nurse the idea that became this book from its earliest stages. They each read every chapter, exposing holes in logic and prose. They were stern, caring, and as only true friends can be, direct. We owe them more gratitude than we could ever repay.

It was a stroke of luck to meet our literary agent, Jane Dystel. We couldn't imagine a more tenacious representative. She believed in our message and hunted for an editor who would do the same. She connected us with Lisa Drew, the most insightful and talented editor in the business. Her enthusiasm for this project inspired and encouraged us to keep writing during many late nights and weekends. We can think of no one better to work with. Lisa's assistant, Blythe Grossberg, endured repeated phone calls and e-mails and kept us on track as the book moved from draft to its current form.

Many people debated our ideas, read chapters, or lent moral support. They include: Scott Alexander, Jimmy Altman, Wilbur and Lucy Baugh, Larry Bernstein, Ron Bernstein, Diane Brady, Sherry Brown, Sarah Bua, Rick Carnell, Dick Cavanagh, Michele Cavataio, Jennifer Donaldson, John Eadie, Gil Gaul, Steve Greenbaum, Jim Griffin, Steve Harris, John and Alison Hockenberry, David Hoffman, David and Lilly Icikson, M. T. Joseph, Joan Konner, Frank Koughan, Robert Krulwich, Ray LaRaja, David Mammen, Chris Parker, Alvin Patrick, Robert Rodriquez, Melissa and Lawrence Rosenbloom, Stephanie Saul, Forrest Sawyer, Lisa Thiesfield, Whitney Todd, Josh Quittner, Mike Wallace, Hugo Young, and Frank Yu. We also thank our colleagues at CBS News and Connecticut's treasury department for understanding that the faraway look in our eyes had nothing to do with our day jobs but with our night jobs.

Our parents deserve special thanks—quite literally, this book could not have been written without them. They taught us at an early age to follow our dreams and gave us confidence that we could make a difference. Our love and respect for them could not be greater.

Family members were excited from the start, reading chapter drafts written so badly only proud parents, grandparents, and siblings could like them (or pretend to). Our biggest supporters include: Patricia Goddard, Karen and Michael Fox, Donatella and Frank Riback, Lucy Waring, Julie Schwartz, Brad Goddard, Chelsey Goddard, Melissa Riback, Brandon Liss, Randy Riback, Nicollo Riback, Virginia and Burt Abrams, Julie Riback, and Philip and Francis Blaney. They were such good liars we sometimes believed their flattery was

Acknowledgments

true. One of the best liars was Chris's father-in-law, Ron Schwartz, who died suddenly just before the book was completed. His spirit will live forever.

Take the contributions of all the people listed above, add them together, then multiply them by some really big number, and it still wouldn't match the level reached by our best friends, our wives. Sara Goddard and Karen Riback, having made the mistake of marrying us, paid in full through months of late nights at work, missed vacations, and incessant phone calls. As if that weren't burden enough to bear, we decided to start families during the process and our wives gave birth to—and this is totally objective—the two most beautiful boys ever, Chase Goddard and Emerson Riback. Having Sara's and Karen's love means everything. Happiness is sharing life with them.

Contents

YOU WON—NOW WHAT?

Introduction

This is not your typical political book. Here you will read stories about
politicians, yet see nothing about campaign strategy, tracking polls, or
negative advertising. You will get an inside look at American government, yet this is not a kiss-and-tell memoir by some disgruntled
staffer or disgraced political consultant. You will learn how top officials get things done, yet there is little about their pursuing public
office.

Instead, this book focuses on what happens after the campaign is
over. It is about the government takeovers, hostile and friendly, that
occur after each election.

We wrote this book because we're alarmed. Instead of getting
more done with less, as so many public officials promise, less seems to
be getting done with more. More people. More time. More money.
Complaints about government abound: Political contributions pervert
the system, campaigns last too long, and scandals are everywhere.
From talk radio to newspapers to Internet web sites, dissatisfaction
bombards us from every point on the political spectrum. Cynicism is
at an all-time high.

What concerns us most, however, isn't so much the problems but the proposed solutions. People talk about reinventing or reengineering or revitalizing government. A whole industry of consultants and politicians and writers has been built on buzzwords that promise to fix government.

We offer something different. In all the talk of supposed solutions, one extraordinarily important fact gets left out: Americans entrust their government to novices. Every November they elect a bunch of people who have never done this before. And each newly elected official brings unseasoned political appointees to head agencies, direct divisions, or serve as staff aides.

The system has great benefits. New people bring new ideas and new direction. By design, our government reinvents itself each election day. But this strength of American democracy has become a major weakness. Much of today's cynicism is rooted in public officials' inability to do what they promised. It corrodes confidence when candidates win on great promises, four years pass, and everything seems worse. It leaves the public frustrated, with fewer citizens willing to serve their governments.

This book's premise is straightforward: To take over government successfully, public officials must first learn how to govern. Instead of reinventing government or turning to the latest management fad, new public officials must learn how to succeed in a world unlike any other. They must show voters that their election day choices really matter. They must follow through on their promises.

For only through better governing will America get better government.

To attack the problem, this book draws lessons from real successes and real failures of today's public officials. It speaks to the newly elected state treasurer who comes to office with little management background, or the appointed deputy human services commissioner who takes over suddenly when his boss retires, or the mayor's staff aide fresh out of college. It speaks to those who govern and those who hope to someday. Most important, it speaks to any citizen who is concerned about government's condition.

The book is organized in two parts. The first part (chapters 1–3) establishes our theme: that much of the cynicism in politics today originates during the takeover. Many new public officials swept into office are novices who stumble along trying to get things done. Unable to accomplish their goals, these newcomers declare government broken and blame everyone but themselves. It's a bad joke played out hundreds of times over the last century at the state and federal levels. And the joke's on us. Instead of reinventing government, we must reinvent our government officials.

The second part of the book (chapters 4–11) provides answers. It describes, in depth, the eight traits of effective government officials. Each chapter examines a single trait by profiling novices during the takeover, unearthing valuable lessons for new public officials who want to govern and for citizens who want improved government. The examples bring to life problems faced by any new government executive—from motivating career civil servants to understanding political tradeoffs. The stories address a new official's more personal concerns, such as dealing with the ghost of one's predecessor and staffing an office after the takeover. Each chapter describes officials' triumphs and tragedies and uses analysis to segue from one example to the next. The reader will finish each section with specific ideas to apply to his or her own situation. To conclude, we provide a "takeover checklist" summarizing the traits of effective governing.

Though each public official's experiences might seem unique, we show that managers at all levels of government face similar obstacles. We do this not by parroting today's conventional wisdoms but by challenging them. We confront widely unquestioned ideas, such as the common belief that government should be run like a business or that a public official should tackle just one goal at a time. We challenge real public officials, praise them when they're right, and criticize them when they're wrong. Succeeding in a government takeover means resisting the lure of the status quo.

THE PATHS that led us to write this book could not have been more different.

Taegan Goddard is a government insider. He has served in federal and state government: at the Federal Reserve Board and U.S. Senate Banking Committee in Washington, D.C., and for a governor and state treasurer in Connecticut. He has experienced government takeovers firsthand, from walking into an office just vacated by the guy who lost the election to preparing confirmation hearings for new presidential appointees. He helped draft legislation to rescue an insolvent federal bank insurance system, designed a new economic development strategy to pull Connecticut out of recession, and directed the largest public pension fund restructuring in history. He is also a rarity for an appointed official, having worked for Democratic, Independent, and Republican politicians.

Chris Riback is a government outsider. He's an investigative journalist whose closest brush with government service was on jury duty. As a journalist he has observed and reported on government from the outside—domestically for *60 Minutes* and ABC News and internationally for the Associated Press. As a broadcast and print reporter, he has asked the questions that make public officials squirm. Riback has grilled federal officials on drug control strategy, terrorist bombings, and racketeering charges; state officials on prison conditions, lax health standards, and questionable job-creation programs; and foreign leaders on trying to turn their communist jungles into capitalist fairylands. He has reported from the middle of violent political uprisings, the shores of devastated floodlands, and deep in the heart of tobacco country.

Goddard is a Connecticut Yankee, Riback a Midwesterner from the Land of Lincoln. Our paths have brought us, separately, to California, Washington D.C., New York, and Bucharest, Romania. But at one point years ago, our paths crossed. And at that juncture, the thought that became this book first bloomed. That place was Harvard's John F. Kennedy School of Government.

The Kennedy School's personality depends partly on who's *not* in the White House. It harbors Republicans when Democrats are in control and Democrats when Republicans rule. It has been home to many once and future public officials, from Republican Bob Dole's former chief of staff Sheila Burke to 1988 Democratic presidential candidate Michael Dukakis. It's a place that evokes strong opinions. *Time* magazine's Margaret Carlson (a former Kennedy School Fellow) called it "the Betty Ford Clinic for washed-up politicians." And that was one of the gentler comments.

For us, the Kennedy School provided two years to concentrate solely on what has become our prime concern: how to make government work better. We did this through the mundane (regression analysis and economic problem sets), the entertaining (hearing Ross Perot, then a businessman virtually unknown to the political world, tell us how "simple" it was to fix government), the serious (listening to presidential candidates and cabinet secretaries explain their proposals for a better America), and the absurd (drinking whiskey and eating old sausage with Russian army generals until 1 A.M., only to get up five hours later and run with them along the Charles River. They outdrank us, but we outran them). The joke was that if you couldn't make it to your professor's office hours, you could always watch him on *Nightline*. For us, who—almost literally—ate, slept, and drank public policy, it was an exciting time.

However, our real-world experiences taught us more about government than any class or professor. As a result, our book is more about what they don't teach at Harvard's Kennedy School of Government than what they do. Despite all our research papers, problem sets, and lectures, it wasn't until after graduation that we understood what made an effective public official.

From the Senate floor or behind a TV camera, we saw some public servants succeed brilliantly and others quickly fall from grace. We saw the cynicism that slowed many new public officials and completely paralyzed others. We saw how citizens no longer believed that their choices at the polls even mattered after election day. We saw too many public officials fail to achieve their goals once in office. Most important, we shared a commitment to find the solution.

During this journey—and through the extensive research that went into this book—we discovered eight basic traits to being successful in government. We show what others have done. We bring their stories together, organize them, analyze them, and find common themes. These are the rules of effective governing, rarely passed down from one generation of public servants to the next. This is the unwritten code of getting something done in government (and possibly making the history books). Yet because it was unwritten—until now—many of today's public officials struggle needlessly.

In every sense of the term, the book is coauthored. We each wrote and rewrote every chapter. We interviewed, corresponded with, and read memoirs of hundreds of current and former public officials. We spent hours on the phone and days on the Internet, argued about examples, and challenged each other's research. Each chapter was rewritten so many times that it is difficult to remember who wrote what first. The result is a book that is truly a collaborative effort and speaks with one voice.

We believe government can make society better. So while we join critics who say government is the problem, we also believe that government is the solution. Through this book, we hope to show how elected and appointed officials can succeed at taking over their governments. We show how public officials overcome obstacles and change government in the way they promised during the elections. Finally, this book helps anyone who cares about government understand how to make it work.

We discuss not political philosophy but practical methods for getting something done. This is not an argument for a permanent ruling class. We relish the vitality and freshness that can come only from new public officials. But since voting to change our leaders is the central feature of our democracy, this book focuses on the takeover and the rookie public servants thrust into new positions of authority after each election.

Our hope is that, through this book, we will help make democracy work the way it was designed.

1

A Government of Novices

You cannot bring inexperienced men into the government and expect the government to run well.

> —*Clark Clifford, U.S. secretary of defense and later counsel to the president*

First Day on the Job

On January 4, 1995, investment banker Chris Burnham arrived at his new job and found the offices empty. Desks were cleared out, computer files erased, pictures taken from the walls. Burnham's predecessor had even stripped the carpet off the floor, leaving the unfinished wood exposed. Down the halls, 225 employees sat anxiously awaiting their new leader's directions.

Yet Burnham was a stranger to their business. The previous afternoon, he became the chief fiscal officer of an organization with a $9 billion budget and the sole trustee of more than $13 billion in investments. But his predecessor had never briefed him on what the investments were.

This was Burnham's first day as Connecticut's state treasurer.

By 9 A.M., his senior aides had already been at work for two hours. Of his four top staffers, only one had previously served in government. Excited and nervous, they filed into Burnham's sparse office

and sat in blue cloth chairs, about the only comforts the former treasurer didn't take with him.

The five had first met as a group just the day before, immediately
after the swearing-in ceremony. They could become friends later.
Now it was time to get to work. Seated in a circle, with Burnham at
twelve o'clock, the new treasurer turned to his crew and asked, only
half joking, the question they all were wondering: "What do we do
now?"

IN DOZENS of agencies across Connecticut—and in thousands across
the country—similar meetings were taking place and the same question was being asked. That's because every November, Americans
elect a government of novices. Hundreds of bankers and teachers and
lawyers take over public office, their predecessors swept out, either
voluntarily or by voter mandate.

Americans pluck new government officials from all walks of life,
many of which seemingly make no sense: a farmer wins election as
Louisiana's governor; a university professor gets named U.S. secretary
of labor; a real estate consultant becomes Los Angeles parks commissioner. Frequently these people are lost upon entering public service.
What made them successful in their other endeavors—growing corn,
teaching students, or rehabbing shopping malls—holds little value in
government.

Others may have government experience but in a completely different arena. Americans regularly elect presidents, governors, and
mayors who served in a legislature or on a city council. Yet despite the
usefulness of understanding the legislative process, most legislators
have none of the skills needed to become effective chief executives or
agency heads. Many have managed no more than a handful of aides
and a small office budget.

As a result, many public officials find themselves in charge of
multimillion-dollar operations, yet have never managed anything of
significance in their careers. Many are lawyers who have only managed other lawyers. Some are academics who have had little or no
management experience at all. Many others with management experience come from the business world, but find that running a government is not the same as running a factory or showroom floor.

American democracy is based on the belief that extraordinary
possibilities exist in ordinary people. Yet many new public officials

spend their terms struggling to understand how government works and find it impossible to achieve anything of significance.

Only in government are such takeovers normal, where upper layers of management routinely get swept in and out. If the top managers of Microsoft or McDonald's or General Electric regularly left their posts—only to be replaced by neophytes whose last business experience might have been as a Young Entrepreneur in high school—investors would have a fit. Companies would slide into bankruptcy. No one would ever suggest implementing this model of replacing executives in the business world.

American government, however, is founded on repeated takeovers, hostile or friendly: An incumbent governor retires, voters "throw the bum out," or "the bums" are forced out through term limits. And a newcomer frequently takes over. As voter-imposed term limits grow more popular (70 percent of the public supports them) so will government housecleaning. Today, forty governors and nearly twenty thousand mayors, legislators, and city council members face term limits. It's a succession of novices.

Furthermore, most top public managers are appointed, from a president's cabinet to state agency commissioners to young staff aides. And even the youngest staffers have great responsibility, typically much more than their private-sector counterparts. Still, these appointed officials often serve even less time than their elected leaders before moving on. A midterm staff shake-up, major scandal, or just plain fatigue causes many appointed officials' tenures to be short.

"You get burned out very quickly," said Stuart Eizenstat, then an aide to President Jimmy Carter. "You can sprint one hundred yards, but you can't sprint a mile. And these jobs are all sprints."

Meanwhile Congress, acknowledging the federal government's past failures, is passing responsibility to state and local governments. Yet local officials are as unprepared as their federal counterparts for so many new duties. As power devolves to state and local governments, even more novices are in charge of even more government functions. If the federal government couldn't complete the tasks it now pushes to the state and local levels, is there any reason to expect that public officials with less training—and with less media scrutiny—will be able to?

States and localities now are asked to solve the intractable problems of welfare, affordable housing, and other social ills. As the devolution of power continues, more will be asked of the millions of public officials who serve in these governments. Voters will expect action, but many of the officials will not be ready.

Of course, continual turnover of public officials carries fantastic benefits. Fresh minds bring fresh ideas. Investment banker Chris Burnham, as Connecticut state treasurer, brought a new approach to managing the state's money and turned America's worst-performing pension fund into one of the best. Real estate consultant Steve Sobo-roff, as Los Angeles parks commissioner, knew how to motivate his employees, who maintained the same public grounds his own children used. Carolyn McCarthy, whose husband was killed during a mad gunman's shooting spree on a New York commuter train, developed a passionate commitment to gun control and transitioned from Long Island housewife to U.S. representative. These newcomers bring much-needed energy and excitement to tired bureaucracies. They have also lived as "regular citizens" and know firsthand how government policies affect average citizens.

But since the days of the Founding Fathers, concerns over a government of novices have run high. In the *Federalist Papers*, James Madison worried that no public official could serve competently without knowing the current issues. Sure, part of that knowledge could come from private life, he wrote, but "another part can only be attained, or at least thoroughly attained, by actual experience in the station which requires the use of it." In other words, only experienced people need apply.

Yet today Americans regularly elect people with little relevant experience for their jobs. Legislators confirm appointees to head agencies with little more than the president's or governor's recommendation. And each new public official frequently recruits an inner circle of staffers that matches his own inexperience.

As a result, few new public officials know how to steer the vehicle of government in the direction they promised. After the elections, these newly elected and appointed leaders waver like drivers lost in an unfamiliar neighborhood during a rainstorm, trying to interpret the blurry signposts put up on election day. Few succeed in reaching their destination.

The blunt message of this book is that American democracy is in trouble. Behind the reassuring facade of elections that promise a new government every few years, many of our public officials drift aimlessly and never complete what they promised. Some barely get started.

But it doesn't have to be that way. This book, for citizens and public servants alike, is a road map to effective government.

As THE 1994 elections groaned to a close, Mark Goodin, wiped out from months of political battle, rode in a van from one nameless campaign stop to another and reflected. Goodin served as campaign manager in Ollie North's failed attempt to unseat Virginia Senator Chuck Robb. It was a nasty, bitter campaign, the kind that has turned people off politics and helped spread cynicism among voters.

"Getting people elected unfortunately has a lot to do with dividing, setting up bases of support, and fracturing off those that—you know, it's like busting a big rock," Goodin said. "That is different than what it takes to govern. Because what it takes to govern is all about ·finding consensus on different issues and bringing people together, people who don't always agree, under some sense of common purpose. And we are obsessed with getting people elected and we are obsessed with the show. . . ."

Hundreds of books and thousands of hours of airtime are devoted to busting the big rocks, the primary objective of political campaigns. Preelection discussion centers on the easy stuff—the horse race, the daily tracking polls, the talking heads who follow bad predictions with worse. Where will the candidate spend money? Should he have "gone negative" so early? Does she have the best political consultants? Debates are less about bold ideas to shrink unemployment lines than finding opportunities to drop punch lines. Then, once the election is complete, pundits and voters alike complain about (choose one): the dearth of good candidates, the shortage of ideas, or the length of the political season.

But almost nowhere does discussion focus on the campaign's true purpose—how will this person govern once in office? Politics runs as if the first Tuesday in November is the finish line instead of the starting gate, the final lap instead of the starters' gun. As soon as one election ends, political commentaries almost immediately focus on the next election and who will run, rather than the hard work of governing that lies ahead. On Election Night '96, much of the coverage centered on the possible Al Gore–Jack Kemp presidential race in the year 2000. Voters are sick of this practice, and politicians and journalists pretend to be. Still, it never ends. Everyone seems to understand that campaigning is not governing. But while many talk about it, few practice it.

"The only problem with running for office is, once you are elected you have to serve," remarked J. Marshall Coleman wryly after his election as Virginia's attorney general. Watch many public officials in action today, and it appears they agree.

"We campaign in poetry, but when we're elected, we're forced to govern in prose," said former New York governor Mario Cuomo. Added Louisiana senator John Breaux: "There are very few people who love to serve in [government] and at the same time love to campaign. Most people like one or the other."

"To be elected to public office requires no qualifications," Ed Eilert, the mayor of Overland, Kansas, observed. But while no formal experience requirements exist, voters do make judgments when choosing the best official on election day. To make democracy work, more attention must be paid to how the candidate will govern once in office.

The focus must also include appointed public officials: the commissioners, chiefs of staff, or assistant state treasurers who are the right-hand men and women of our elected representatives. Political appointees normally get their jobs for a variety of reasons: they advocate the right policy position and promote those ideas articulately; they remain loyal to the elected official or served well or contributed financially to a campaign; or they add diversity to an administration by representing a specific demographic or interest group. Rarely is managerial background or competence the primary reason for choosing a political appointee.

In other words, simply running for office or getting appointed to a top government position does not, by itself, ensure a person will get the job done. Unless new public officials learn fast, they become the problem instead of the solution.

"The first duty of any campaign is to be smart and win," said author James Fallows, "but politicians become hacks when they think of winning as their ultimate duty."

THE DECAYED condition of American democracy is undeniable. Only twenty-five years ago, three quarters of the public said they had confidence in government; today less than a quarter do. When ABC News polled citizens in 1993 on whether they would "rather be president for four years or spend a week in jail," the majority said they'd rather go to jail. Even at Harvard's John F. Kennedy School of Government—which trains students for public service careers—only a third of the graduates take jobs in government.

It's just as bad at the voting booth. In 1996, fewer than half of all eligible citizens even voted for president. In off-year elections, many municipalities are lucky to get a 25 percent turnout. This occurs despite extraordinary amounts of money and hoopla generated every four years to attract people to the polls.

"There is a very deep public frustration with the political class," says Everett C. Ladd of the Roper Center for Public Opinion Research. "People want politicians to say what they mean, mean what they say and keep their promises."

In short, citizens want public officials who know how to get the job done.

Yet from the Sunday morning television shows to newspaper op-ed pages, pundits pin the blame for growing cynicism on everything but the government of novices. The three most talked-about causes of cynicism are money in politics, modern campaign strategy, and scandals.

Few disagree that campaign financing is a problem. Money in politics is everywhere. When Democratic fat cats donate $100,000 to sleep in the Lincoln bedroom or Republicans pay big bucks to golf and dine with senators on a Florida junket, evidence grows that government is for sale. Money is "the mother's milk of politics," noted the late House Speaker Thomas P. (Tip) O'Neill Jr.

Campaigns also breed cynicism. From negative advertising to the length of the campaign season, the public is tired of the way we select our top officials. Stories about political consultants and their prostitutes or dirty campaign tricks are plastered on the front pages. Many public officials now run perpetual campaigns to keep potential challengers away. When campaigning becomes indistinguishable from governing, cynicism swells.

And then there are the scandals. From Watergate to Iran-Contra to check-bouncing congressmen to Whitewater, the public is no longer shocked. Each new episode is met with a mixture of disgust and indifference. Cynicism runs that high.

The pundits are right. Each of these problems deserves attention. They all represent the effect of public officials wandering off course and stand as monuments to the basic fact that our government frequently doesn't do what it's supposed to do. The ignored problem is that many public officials do not know how to govern.

As a result, many citizens have simply given up on a government that cannot solve today's urgent problems. Elections seem pointless, no longer connected to what happens once they are over. For many citizens, elections are about setting a direction for their government. But when government takes off in a different way than voters pointed, as often occurs, cynicism increases.

"The basis of effective government is public confidence," President John F. Kennedy recognized. But instead of confidence, Americans' distrust spreads like a computer virus, from one system to another, transferred by casual contact and, frequently, unnoticed until it's too late.

"This country faces all kinds of problems that politicians are afraid to address honestly," wrote Anthony Lewis of *The New York Times*. "But underlying the particulars is a peculiar condition of our democracy: disaffection from the very idea of government. Disaffection is really too weak a word. The American public seems to hate government, most of all the Federal Government."

Former Clinton administration defense official Joe Nye left his post after the terrorist bombing of an Oklahoma City federal building—the ultimate expression of hatred for government—to become dean of Harvard's Kennedy School of Government and search for solutions to the problem.

"There is a difference between healthy skepticism and mistrust so great that it breeds cynicism and paranoia," Nye said. "The worry is that low trust may tend to be cumulative. If it becomes the conventional wisdom that government can't do anything right, and that is repeated time and again by politicians and by the press, people begin to believe it. And that may reduce the effectiveness of government, which in turn will lead to lower and lower trust."

Government, however, can do remarkable things. It instituted child work laws, built the interstate highway system, fought civil rights abuses, and sent man to the moon. Still, today's conventional wisdom is that government can't do anything right. It is repeated time and again by politicians and the press. And people believe it.

The idea that public officials are inept has become so absurd that one fellow running for Congress in Arkansas aired a television advertisement that boasted of his never having held elective office. The ad extolled the man's past as a farmer and businessman. Amazingly, he had previously served as an elected city councilman and just didn't want to admit it.

To compensate for the void of effective government, people grasp wildly for quick fixes. Throughout American history, voters have flirted with everything from the Communist Party to Ross Perot. They have elected racist governors in the South and Socialist mayors in the North. More recently, they elected Republican George Bush in 1988 and then Democrat Bill Clinton in 1992. Unhappy with Clinton, in 1994 they yanked control of Congress away from Democrats for the first time in forty years and signed on to Newt Gingrich's Contract with America. But two years later, the contract was broken, and Clinton easily won reelection.

If most citizens still believe their election day choices are not about putting a party in power but setting a direction for their government, then the extreme swings in recent years suggest that voters are desperate to put candidates in office who can do the job. So when someone swears to "get under the hood and fix it" like Ross Perot or carries a can-do attitude like Colin Powell, the promise is very appealing. The cynicism of today's electorate begets respect—and creates opportunity—for any outsider who promises to get the job done.

But this urge can be dangerous for democracy. Frantic searches for a would-be messiah could entice voters to gloss over candidate's obvious flaws. Voters may one day opt for someone who, at any cost, can simply make the trains run on time.

"Everybody believes in democracy until he gets to the White House, and then you believe in dictatorship, because it's so hard to get things done," an aide to President Kennedy once said.

Despite the regular changes in government, despite the widespread citizen dissatisfaction, rarely does the search for answers focus on what happens after the elections.

"If the political process keeps running down government," asks Harvard's Nye, "how do you get good people to run the government that is elected? Unless you are an anarchist, somebody's got to run it."

"The most difficult job is being a manager in government," Philadelphia mayor Ed Rendell, a former lawyer, recognized after taking over city hall in 1991. "But too many of our public leaders simply do not know how to get the work of government done."

Most attempts to improve government management concentrate on changing government's structure. Would-be reformers establish blue ribbon commissions or publish scholarly reports that show what the perfect government looks like but ignore how to achieve it. Most efforts to improve government attempt to create the perfect organizational chart. That's no solution.

"The right people can make a poor organizational structure work well, and poor people will make the best possible organizational structure work miserably," observed former secretary of defense Donald Rumsfeld. "People are the key."

And that is the root of today's cynicism. Throughout American history, new public officials try to "reinvent government" without looking at the real reason government doesn't work—themselves. Instead of trying to rearrange bureaucracy (or, horrors, add to it), the focus should be on what these new government officials must know to do their jobs. Government labors on with mostly well-meaning souls who have little background in the jobs they undertake.

To run their government, Americans elect more than half a million people, from the town sheriff to the president. Millions more are brought into government by elected officials as appointed top managers. Indeed, more Americans now work in government than in manufacturing. There are thirty-nine thousand governments in America, with nearly twenty million public employees. (More than three million civilians work for the federal government, five million for state governments, and eleven million for local governments.) And millions more are involved in government from the outside, as contractors, political activists, or members of public-interest groups.

Making matters worse, Americans ask today's government to do more than ever. Agencies that have endured through the years have gained more duties, not fewer. The U.S. Department of Agriculture, for example, began life in 1862 under President Lincoln, as the "people's department." Back then, 90 percent of Americans were farmers, and many needed help growing their crops. But now, in addition to handling farm duties, the Agriculture Department runs the food stamp program and the National Forest Service. Who would have guessed that more than a century after Lincoln's death, the USDA's most famous employees would be Woodsy Owl and Smokey the Bear?

And even when significant job cuts are made, they frequently occur because agencies simply contract out, or privatize, the work. Nearly every federal agency has dozens of contracts with private vendors that do the nuts-and-bolts work for them. For example, although NASA runs the national space program, it hires contractors to build the space shuttle. But while public officials can sometimes contract out work, their responsibility and oversight remain. A particular agency may not employ as many people as before, but it hasn't really shrunk either.

More important, voters still want the services government provides. Anyone who doubts this should follow the logic of the *National Journal's* Jonathan Rauch:

Imagine a small dinner party—say, four men—at a restaurant. Everyone is going to pay an equal share of the tab. Each person soon notices that if he orders a $10 dessert, he gets to eat the whole thing while paying only a fourth of the cost. So he indulges.

The trouble, of course, is that everyone else makes the same calculation. And so everyone orders dessert. And wine. And appetizers. Soon the bill is high and everyone is distressed. So the four diners talk to one another and decide that from then on, they'll make do with less. End of problem.

Now imagine the same dinner, but with one change. This time there are, say, 10,000 people around the table—so many that any conversation between them all is impossible. So many, indeed, that no one diner can know the intentions of any but a few of the others. Now the problem is greatly magnified, in two ways.

First, the incentive to over-order is much larger. Each diner now pays only one ten-thousandth of the cost of his or her extra dessert. Others may not even notice. Second, there is now no ready solution. You may give up your dessert, and persuade the person next to you to do the same. But how can you have any confidence that others will not merely take advantage of your sacrifice to order more chocolate mousse for themselves?

Lacking someone who can construct and enforce a joint agreement, it's always rational, from any one diner's point of view, to order as much food and drink as he or she can get away with. It is also always rational for the diner to oppose any attempt to take food off his or her own plate. The very large dinner party is like a society of people and groups who receive, and lobby for, benefits from government.

It's doubtful that Americans will change their dining habits. Certainly they won't change overnight. Rauch sees two possible solutions for this problem of American democracy—find a great leader or create a better-informed electorate. In effect, he suggests either employing a better chef or improving diners' tastes.

But another possibility exists: Get better waiters and waitresses. Get servers who don't just plop a menu in front of ravenous eaters and say "choose," but instead suggest different nightly specials, offer substitutes, or recommend which side dish goes best with which main course. By focusing on the individuals who interact with the kitchen and the diners, the complete experience—from ambience to after-dinner drink—will improve.

In other words, create better public officials. Make sure our elected and appointed leaders—the ones directly accountable to voters—have the skills that graduate school or business doesn't provide. Recognize that the way our democratic system staffs itself invites disaster. And fix it. This is the hard work needed to rescue America's democracy from cynicism. It is a daunting task, but no more so than many previous challenges overcome by the American people.

Put into office public officials with the abilities to fulfill their promises and magical things will happen. The debilitating cynicism that prevents progress will dissipate. The void of qualified candidates will begin to fill. The government of novices will begin to work like a government of experts.

No perfect public official exists. Take any of the officials featured in these pages, and one finds human beings, imperfect figures succeeding, perhaps, in one area of management, and failing, perhaps, in several others. But weave together the lessons this book examines and, like a Polaroid photo, the picture of a complete public official slowly develops. Implement this commonsense approach to government—focusing on the officials most directly accountable to the people they serve—and that hypothetical Polaroid can become reality.

2

Reinventing Government Again
(and Again)

When I walked the state 25 years ago, an old cracker told me the walk
would get me elected senator—but he wanted me to always remember that "Government don't work." I've puzzled this over the years.
Now I know he was right. Government don't work. Government can't
work. People work. Government is the framework through which people work.

> —*Lawton Chiles, U.S. senator and*
> *later governor of Florida*

Hail to the Chief

The warm September day welcomed several dozen congressmen and
nearly every cabinet secretary to the manicured White House Rose
Garden. "Hail to the Chief" sounded in the background as President
Bill Clinton and Vice President Al Gore stepped briskly onto the
White House lawn and stood behind a dark blue podium embossed
with the presidential seal. The setting was regal—except for two
large yellow forklifts piled high with reams of government paperwork.

"Mr. President, if you want to know why government doesn't
work, look behind you. The answer is at least partly on those forklifts," Gore said in introductory remarks. "Those forklifts hold copies
of budget rules, procurement rules, and the personnel code. The personnel code alone weighs in at over 1,000 pounds. That code and those
regulations stacked up there no longer help government work, they
hurt it; they hurt it badly. And we recommend getting rid of it."

After a shaky nine months in office, a time of failed presidential nominations and unsatisfying policy victories like "Don't Ask, Don't Tell," the new administration declared the federal government broken. Now they wanted to fix it, and the unveiling of the National Performance Review was their attempt. The project's nickname was "Reinventing Government," or "ReGo" for short. To emphasize its importance, Clinton tapped the vice president to lead the effort in drafting 168 pages of recommendations to make government "work better and cost less."

"For too long government has been an obstacle to change," Gore said. "But if government is powerful enough to block change, then it is powerful enough to bring change."

The Clinton agenda was on the line. Although the president had promised to "focus on the economy like a laser beam," his budget passed the Democratic-controlled Congress by only one vote and an economic stimulus package failed. As a candidate, Clinton also pledged to change the welfare system, revamp health insurance, and reduce crime by putting more police on the streets. None of these had yet occurred. In his inaugural address, the word *change* appeared eleven times. Yet little had changed except the faces at cabinet meetings. The "Putting People First" program he ran on was stuck in first gear.

"To accomplish any of these goals, we have to revolutionize the government itself so that the American people trust the decisions that are made and trust us to do the work that government has to do," Clinton remarked. "The entire agenda of change depends upon our ability to change the way we do our own business with the people's money. That is the only way we can restore the faith of our citizens."

Government would be remade: agencies reorganized, bureaucrats cut, and red tape slashed. More important to Clinton, the review promised to "rebuild the confidence of the American people in this great public enterprise."

It was a direct attack on cynicism. America's government, at long last, would do the people's work in an efficient and businesslike manner.

OBSTRUCTED by the glow of that sunny September afternoon but discernible to anyone willing to look closely was evidence that Clinton's plan to fix government was doomed. The president's team ignored the chief reason government doesn't work well: Many new officials taking over their government do not understand how to make it work. Indeed, it was much less painful for Gore to argue that these new officials weren't the problem.

"We have excellent, hardworking, imaginative workers trapped in bad systems," Gore told the president at the unveiling ceremony. "We need to help get them free of those systems."

One could almost hear the collective "whew!" from the dozens of administration officials in the audience relieved to know that "I'm OK; you're OK." To continuous applause, Gore threw jabs at "the government," blaming it, and not themselves, for the cynicism swelling across the nation.

"It's old-fashioned, outdated government," Gore said of the government he led. "It's government using a quill pen in the age of WordPerfect."

However, the vice president's comment itself was outdated, not an effective attack on government. For it was already the age of Microsoft Word, which had recently topped WordPerfect as the best-selling word processing software package.

Gore's remark symbolizes the problem facing any new administration, whether at the federal, state, or local level. Citizens' views change frequently, often as quickly as new software packages are introduced. At election time, and sometimes before, they demand that their public officials "upgrade" their government with new features or eliminate the "bugs" that cause the system to crash.

How Americans vote to "manage" government reflects their changing and often inconsistent views on precisely what their government should or should not do. Governing successfully starts with accomplishing what citizens ask for in elections. When new public officials fail, they typically do what Clinton and Gore did—blame "the government" and promise to reinvent it. Once again, it's the system's fault, not the fault of people who run the system. This stokes cynicism, because the system keeps changing, but the results remain the same. No one is accountable.

Another way the National Performance Review fueled cynicism was the way it portrayed citizens.

"We can treat taxpayers like customers," Gore said at its unveiling.

Citizens, however, are not customers of government. They are its owners. And as government's shareholders, they had received no dividends.

The difference is great. Customers look first at what they can reap from government. If citizens think of themselves as consumers, they will shop for candidates who give them the most services now for what they spend. In contrast, owners tend to take a longer-term view. They look to make government work better, hiring public officials who can achieve the common goals expressed during the elections. Citizens were frustrated not with the government but with the management they put in place to run it. The Gore report tried to shift the focus. Yet it was an unsustainable strategy.

The National Performance Review also missed its mark by overstating claims of making government more efficient. The General Accounting Office didn't believe the effort would save the $118 billion Gore claimed. In fact, the administration's budget director, Leon Panetta, reportedly found the announced savings so questionable that he refused to sign off on them.

For all his talk of streamlining government, the vice president's own office looked like a textbook example of government excess. Gore had five taxpayer-financed offices: one in the West Wing of the White House; one nearby in the Old Executive Office Building; one in the Capitol; one in the Dirksen Senate Office Building, and even one in his home state of Tennessee, although he served a national constituency. In contrast, the president had only one.

Peter Drucker ridiculed the Gore effort in an *Atlantic Monthly* article: "In any institution other than the federal government, the changes being trumpeted as reinventions would not even be announced, except perhaps on the bulletin board in the hallway. They are the kinds of things a hospital expects floor nurses to do on their own; that a bank expects branch managers to do on their own; that even a poorly run manufacturer expects supervisors to do on their own—without getting much praise, let alone extra rewards."

For example, as proof of "radically changing government," with great fanfare the vice president released a report trumpeting that government workers could now buy a stapler for $4 (instead of the $54 it cost in the past) or send a three-pound FedEx delivery for $3.62 (instead of $27). These changes, while tremendously embarrassing to administration officials if not implemented, could hardly be considered radical. Citizens, the owners of government, expect no less.

Rightly, Americans never gave the administration much credit for the antibureaucratic crusade launched on the White House lawn. In the administration's first two years, opinion polls indicated that the number of citizens who felt the government was too intrusive had risen from less than half in 1992 to more than three quarters in 1994. When asked if the Clinton administration had made progress in making government more efficient, 78 percent of respondents said "just a little or none." And of course, in the 1994 midterm elections, Democrats lost not only the Senate but also control of the House of Representatives for the first time in forty years.

Sensing that the political winds had shifted, Gore changed tack.

After just fourteen months, it was time to reinvent the reinvented government. Specifically, Gore refocused his effort to match the Republican rhetoric about turning over control of many government programs to the states. Rather than make the tough administrative changes in Washington, D.C., Gore passed the buck to the nation's governors and mayors.

"We will stop making so many decisions in Washington that would be better made by state government, local government, or individual citizens," Gore said at a news conference two months after the midterm elections. "And we will replace Washington interference with local opportunity."

The reinvented National Performance Review, or ReGo II, as Gore staffers called it, would shift the responsibilities for many programs to the states by giving block grants. Other functions, such as air traffic control, would be privatized entirely. After nearly two years of claiming that agency management needed improvement, Gore now focused on abolishing some programs forever. How could times have changed so quickly?

Surprisingly, Gore never looked in the mirror. Perhaps government was not working because the people responsible for fulfilling the voters' wishes—the elected and appointed officials brought into office with the new administration—were not delivering on them. Perhaps the problem was not with "the government," but with the government officials.

In fact, the inaction of the president's own appointees was in large part to blame. A 1996 GAO report reviewing Gore's progress suggested that many innovations coming from "reinvention labs" in the agencies were resisted by top administration officials. If there was a more efficient way to do something in government, Gore wanted agencies to seek waivers from the standard government procedures. But waivers from rules and procedures were frequently denied by Clinton administration officials at the Office of Management and

Budget, Office of Personnel Management, and the General Services Administration.

Some top officials simply disagreed with the president's diagnosis that government was broken.

"I don't buy the notion that government is not working and that government is the problem," former deputy treasury secretary Roger C. Altman said. " 'Reinventing government' is just a political phrase of the day. You can say 'make it better,' but that just doesn't resonate."

One Gore report declared that the "history of reinventing government" started on March 3, 1993, when Clinton issued an executive order initiating the National Performance Review. But the demand for a leaner, more efficient government is nothing new and began long before Clinton's administration.

Every new public official must understand this lesson from history: Reinventing government is an old story. It's been told hundreds of times in the last century at all levels of government. And as the saying goes: Those who ignore the errors of history are doomed to repeat them.

Let the Games Begin

The first real attempt at reinventing American government came not in 1993 but 1881. Charles J. Guiteau, who had been turned down for a government job after working on the presidential campaign, was not terribly happy with how the hiring process ran. A "spoils system" ruled, where people received and kept jobs based almost solely on whom they knew. Fifty-three thousand employees were regularly replaced after presidential elections. And if to the victor go the spoils, Guiteau lost. He got no job.

Instead, he took the opportunity to single-handedly reinvent American government: He shot dead President James A. Garfield. A bit crude, but it worked. "The crime," an editorial at the time stated, "acted on public opinion like a spark on a powder-magazine." Congress reconvened after the state funeral and in 1883 President Chester Arthur signed the law establishing the federal civil service system, which sought to replace favoritism with objective standards for government hiring.

But while the civil service system created a professional, permanent class of government servants, it did nothing to prevent the abuses still rampant in the political appointment process. After the 1888 presidential election, Benjamin Harrison was shocked to find that he could not even choose his own cabinet, because Republican party leaders had given away the best positions to the highest bidders.

"When I came into power, I found that the party managers had taken it all to themselves," Harrison said. "I could not name my own Cabinet. They had sold out every place to pay the election expenses." The Harrison administration's future was for the political machine to decide.

Since that time, government's scope has grown and the civil service has expanded. As the twentieth century began, reformers moved to control government's inner workings, ending the era of Boss Tweed and replacing it with the era of bureaucracy. They hoped the shift from politics to professionalism in government would put an end to corruption and favoritism. But while the new bureaucratic system cleaned up many abuses, it also created a whole new set of management problems.

The Era of Management

The next phase of reinventions, in the early 1900s, focused on improving public management. But the broad goals of each were really not much different than Al Gore's reinventing government effort. Administration after administration, struggling to make government do what the voters wanted, promised to fix the government without looking to improve the people who ran it.

President Theodore Roosevelt tapped Assistant Treasury Secretary Charles Keep to head the Keep Commission (1905–9), the first national commission to seek gains by improving management. It meticulously reviewed the entire federal bureaucracy. And though the report put political appointees in charge of agencies, it annoyed many members of Congress, who considered their role to actively oversee most executive branch functions. The plan went nowhere.

Under President William Howard Taft, the President's Commission on Economy and Efficiency (1910–13) proposed creating an overall budget for the executive branch and recommended that the president do more to set a national agenda. Once again, however, Congress resented this infringement on its turf. With congressional leaders resisting, it wasn't until 1919 that legislation passed allowing the president to submit individual agency budgets.

President Warren Harding had his own reinvention scheme. The idea that the president could actively manage the federal government first came from Harding's Joint Committee on Reorganization (1921–24), in response to an increased number of public service programs. The plan grew during Franklin D. Roosevelt's second term, when the Brownlow Committee (1936–37) argued that the executive branch had "grown up without plan or design like the barns, shacks, silos, tool sheds and garages of an old farm." Congress had produced this haphazard structure by creating a new agency every time it introduced a new program.

To correct the problem, the Brownlow Committee created the first organizational chart for the executive branch, designing clear lines of authority to the president as top manager. In the committee's view, a strong democracy needed "a responsible and effective chief executive as the center of energy, direction, and administrative management." To help put the chief executive at such a center of activity, the report also recommended creating an Executive Office of the President, where top policy and management decisions for the government would be made.

When the committee finished its work in 1937, Roosevelt summed up the state of federal government at the time: "Our struggle now is against confusion, against ineffectiveness, against waste, against inefficiency. This battle, too, must be won, unless it is to be said that in our generation national self-government broke down and was frittered away by bad management."

If FDR's words still sound relevant more than sixty years later, one wonders what other American presidents and their political appointees have been doing since. A clue: making a lot more changes to government's organizational chart.

Déjà Vu All Over Again

If the bureaucratic system worked at all in the early 1900s, it was because government handled just a limited set of tasks. Yet as FDR's New Deal increased demands, new problems developed. As government grew larger, fresh management challenges loomed. Still, public officials kept looking for answers in the same old places. And more commissions were formed to reinvent government yet again.

After World War II, former president Herbert Hoover led the first extensive study of every administrative aspect of the federal government. The Hoover Commission (1947–49) recommended that political appointees be given legal authority to manage their departments. Previously, most authority was reserved for lower-level officials. The change clarified who was in charge and was expected to solve many of government's problems.

Government, however, had not been fixed; four years later, President Dwight D. Eisenhower commissioned another Hoover Commission. Like most sequels, however, Hoover II (1953–55) hardly advanced the storyline and, indeed, repeated the plot played out in Hoover I. It attempted to pare down the functions of the federal government, targeting some programs for elimination.

During the Kennedy and Johnson administrations, a variety of commissions came up with the same not-so-radical recommendation: Improve government efficiency without focusing on the top officials. President John F. Kennedy's budget director led an effort to root out problems in government contracting. President Lyndon B. Johnson launched a reorganization task force that recommended creating five new departments to handle his new Great Society programs. As he dramatically increased the scope of government, Johnson installed planning and budgeting systems to seek greater productivity, declaring it "a very revolutionary system so that through the tools of modern management the full promise of a finer life can be brought to every American at the lowest possible cost." Of course, government only got more expensive.

Richard M. Nixon decided that what really needed to be done to government was to run it like a business. Nixon tapped industrialist Roy Ash to head the Ash Council (1969–71), which, remarkably, concluded the same thing that FDR's Brownlow Committee had thirty-four years earlier: Government was woefully inefficient, and the executive branch needed a major restructuring. Ash recommended a massive assault on fragmented government, suggesting that smaller departments be subsumed by larger ones with broader mandates. But it was just another reordering of the bureaucracy, and as Watergate engulfed the White House, the Ash Council recommendations landed, for the most part, in the dustbin.

Next, Jimmy Carter promised massive change in the way government conducted its business. The President's Reorganization Project (1977–79) attempted a bottom-up reshuffling of the entire executive branch. With a staff of more than three hundred, it became the largest effort to date to revamp the government. Carter's "zero-based budgeting" plan was the key (does this sound familiar?) to greater efficiency. "It's simple and it works," Carter said. "It will make sure that the money that is allocated goes further."

But Carter's effort did little to give the president greater control over the government. After Nixon's resignation, Americans were increasingly wary of a strong president. So Congress placed "inspectors general" in executive branch agencies to keep watch on administration officials. In the next decade, more than twelve thousand auditors penetrated federal agencies to root out waste. Though beneficial from a watchdog standpoint, the move accomplished the exact opposite of Carter's goals—it made government bigger.

In 1981, Ronald Reagan took his turn. In his inaugural address, the Gipper declared that "Government is not the solution, it's the problem." So it was no surprise that his Grace Commission (1982–84) would try to win one by targeting major government functions for elimination. Headed by industrialist J. Peter Grace, Reagan promised the commission would "work like tireless bloodhounds, leaving no stone unturned in their search to root out inefficiency and waste of taxpayer dollars."

The commission itself, though, was overstuffed. It comprised 161 corporate CEOs and more than 2,000 loaned executives who suggested the federal government be run like a large corporation—with top-down control. But for all of their brave talk, the Reagan crowd soon discovered that government was not a corporation. Citicorp's John Heilshorn served as one of the Grace Commission executives.

"We were part of the problem—the major part," Heilshorn recalled. "We were on an ego trip. Here we were, a bunch of business leaders coming to Washington to fix the problems with government. As soon as we took credit for developing a recommendation, that was the kiss of death. The culture of Washington buried us."

Finally, George Bush tried a plan of "rightsizing government." It was a modest effort once again modeled after corporate America. "I honestly believe that this is the only way to get the size and spending of government under control," Bush said. But as the economy slid into recession, deficits increased, and voters sent Bush into early retirement.

Then Bill Clinton stepped up to the plate. He promised to reinvent government by initiating the boldly named National Performance Review. It was the largest and most visible management review of the federal government in history.

"Make no mistake about this," Clinton said at its unveiling. "This is one report that will not gather dust in a warehouse."

Thirteen presidents, thirteen reinventions. Each one promised a better government but left citizens still wanting. And it wasn't much better at the state and local levels.

States of Despair

The Clinton administration's second attempt at reinventing government, ReGo II, promised to shift control of many programs down to the states. After years of having the big boys in Washington bungle things, state and local governments got the chance to run more programs on their own. Responsibilities for welfare and housing, for example, were pushed down to governors and mayors.

In many ways, the challenge for state officials is greater than for federal officials. Limitations on the president's power were primarily established by statute. But at the state level, limits on the governor's authority are much more complicated. Suspicious of executive power, the founders of the original thirteen states restrained governors with explicit constitutional provisions. For example, early state executives were granted few powers, and their terms were typically limited to one or two years and sometimes to a single term. Most states that later joined the union followed this trend.

The nineteenth-century reform movement diluted state chief executives' power even further. These reforms increased the number of independently elected executive branch officials, such as the state treasurer, attorney general, secretary of state, comptroller, auditor, and, in some cases, a state education chief.

For example, the treasurer may be a state's chief fiscal officer, but often he reports to the people and not the governor. In nineteen states, the lieutenant governor is elected separately from the governor. These checks on chief executives' power slow governors and their appointed officials from accomplishing their agendas, because they must rely on other independently elected officials for assistance. They also add exponentially to the number of possible reinventions that can take place. The governor could reinvent one aspect of government, while an independently elected state comptroller might reinvent another, each using different philosophies.

"It was different being in the legislature or city council," said Martha Whitehead, former Texas state treasurer. "In the city council there were shared goals, and we would celebrate the successes as we reached them. But as state treasurer, my agenda might be 180 degrees from the governor's. And the governor's might be 180 degrees from the lieutenant governor's. That frustrated me."

Further complicating matters, state legislatures were even more vigilant than Congress at limiting the executive branch's power. Legislatures often refused to allow the governor to run newly created programs, instead forming new boards and commissions to oversee them. In addition, legislatures usually reserved authority for appointing members, further keeping control from the governor. So states like Louisiana and Georgia grew to have three hundred agencies, yet the governor lacked influence over most of them. In North Carolina, the governor didn't even get the right to veto laws passed by the state legislature until 1997. While these checks on executive power ensured that nothing terrible would happen, they prevented much good as well.

Over the past 75 years, more than 170 attempts were launched to reorganize state governments and eliminate overlap, waste, and inefficiency. The majority of these attempts were introduced with great fanfare and then defeated, either dying in the state legislature or failing in implementation. The Council of State Governments found that for the twenty-one successful state government reorganizations completed between 1965 and 1979, the average "germination time" was a staggering forty-five years. Few public officials besides record-setting eight-term U.S. Senator Strom Thurmond can wait that long to implement an agenda.

But like the comedian's plea of "stop me before I strike again," this notion of reinventing state governments is bad humor. Most important, like their federal counterparts, these state-level reinventions suffered from the same problem—they sought to fix government without focusing on the government officials responsible for making it work.

By the 1990s, state-level reinventions picked up steam, starting with the Texas Performance Review in 1991. The Texas management study helped launch dozens of copycats across America, including the

Clinton effort. After a wave of new governors took office in 1995, the National Academy of Public Administration found that forty-one governors had announced plans to "reinvent government." The reinventions cut across party lines and took different approaches, but their objectives were the same: to make their state governments deliver what was promised. For example:

- In California, Republican governor Pete Wilson began his second term with an assault on government, the same government he had already headed for four years: "When a family goes shopping . . . they look for the best quality at the lowest price. Common sense for California families should become common practice for state government. We should not spend tax dollars hiring state employees to do work the private sector can do as well or better for less money."

- In Maryland, Democratic governor Parris N. Glendening declared: "We can make our government work smarter and leaner."

- In Missouri, Democratic governor Mel Carnahan promised his first budget "cuts obsolete spending, and it focuses on ways to make government more efficient and less wasteful."

- In North Dakota, Republican governor Edward T. Schafer pledged a more responsive government: "Above all else, citizens said they want a government that places a premium on efficiency. They want a government that works for them, not against them. They want a government that is accountable and responsive to their needs, not to the needs of the bureaucracy. . . . Now it is our term to deliver."

- In Maine, Governor Angus S. King, an Independent, promised his election would once and for all change the direction of state government: "Is this all that can be done to make government more efficient, effective, and affordable? [Are these] all the programs that should be considered for cuts or consolidations? Certainly not. The ship of state won't stop on a dime, but let no one doubt that as of today, we've changed the course."

- And in Indiana, Democratic governor Evan Bayh challenged his citizens "to let us build a government that is not only off our backs but on our side. Let us recreate a government that is both smaller and more just. Let us insist upon a government that not only does no harm but a government that once again becomes a force for positive change and the greater good."

From the federal government to many state and local governments, the reinvention craze continued. Democrats, Republicans, and Independents agreed that government was not working the way it should. But in most cases the problem was not with the government; it was with those who ran it.

IMPROVING government has never been easy. That's why efforts are repeated year after year, administration after administration. History shows the constant tensions between good politics and good government. It shows the struggle between the executive and legislative branches seeking to change government. In fact, new administrations try to reinvent government so often, they run out of new ideas. Many recommendations carry over from report to report, some for more than fifty years.

For example, Vice President Gore's suggestion to close more than one thousand Department of Agriculture field offices where farms no longer exist, such as in cities and suburbs, was first made during the Eisenhower administration. Many of Gore's other specific cost-saving initiatives were proposed a decade earlier by the Grace Commission.

These commissions often promise the impossible, such as running government like a business or boosting workforce morale while cutting workers. While politically popular at first, these promises fuel cynicism when they never materialize. Instead of becoming manageable, government grows more complicated and more inefficient—and more disliked.

The Grace Commission's John Heilshorn saw little reason for each successive administration to launch a brand-new management review of government. "I had no idea what went on in government when I started. I made a lot of mistakes," Heilshorn admitted. "Nobody reads history. We made so many mistakes that do not need to be repeated. Others can learn from us, if only they wanted to. But nobody read our reports."

Governor William J. Janklow of South Dakota sees the problem in simpler terms. "Reinventing government is nonsense," he said. "The original invention had nothing wrong with it. We don't need to go out and reinvent government. What we need to do is step back and look at what it is that we honestly, politically want our government to do."

Elections occur so that voters can decide the answer to exactly that question. But new public officials have trouble delivering on their promises. Despite repeated efforts to reinvent government, the same maze of issues continues to vex public officials. It's little wonder that Americans are cynical.

The problem is not that all of the ideas are bad ones. Lots of good ideas simply never get implemented. Public officials often seem paralyzed when instituting solutions. And while many people might be tempted to blame all of government's problems on partisan gridlock, plenty of commissions have failed during periods of one-party rule.

Indeed, most government functions, from trash collection to road repair, are not ideological battlegrounds. Agreement on solving many public dilemmas is possible. As New York mayor Fiorello La Guardia once said, "There is no Republican way to collect garbage."

The real problem is that many newly elected and appointed officials have little relevant previous experience. And even for those who have served, managerial competence usually is ignored when staffing top positions.

"Al Gore talks about reinventing government," said Chap Hurst, the administrator of Lancaster County, South Carolina. "You don't have to reinvent it; you've just got to manage it to start with."

Yet too many public officials don't even try. "Many elected officials, even those unleashing their barrages on government programs, take no steps to make the programs efficient and well managed," noted former New York City comptroller Elizabeth Holtzman. "Such efforts are tedious and unglamorous. Why bother? What practical or political benefits accrue from doing so?"

The reason frequently given for this stunning record of nonaccomplishment is "resistance by the bureaucracy." In fact, most reinvention efforts have focused on the wrong people. The faceless bureaucracy, not the top public officials themselves, gets blamed for government's problems.

Of course, many inefficiencies are intentionally built into government that make it hard to accomplish anything, such as the balance of control between the legislature and executive branch.

Furthermore, public officials entering government service from the private sector are often shocked at the rules and procedures they must follow. The democratic process has developed dozens of ways to tie its leaders' hands.

Some inefficiencies are probably a good thing. Not all public officials use their powers honestly and consistently with the public's desires. There will always be need for a system of checks and balances to limit and oversee an executive's power. Inefficiency is the price citizens pay to blunt any evil lurking in public servants. Very little gets done that is extremely bad—or extremely good.

Gore wisely suggested that government's proper role is to "steer and not row." Unfortunately, this requires that captains of government know how to work a tiller. Many do not. As a result, their governments float endlessly in no particular direction or, worse, crash on the rocks.

Most government reinventors attack government for not working but seem to expect the bureaucracy to fix itself once a report outlines the problems. Only the top officials have the authority to make changes. Yet as soon as a commission has made recommendations, many leaders are on their way out, only to be replaced by another batch of novices. The unaccountable bureaucracy grows larger and more powerful.

In retrospect, John Heilshorn agreed that this was an oversight by Reagan's Grace Commission. "Right at the heart of the whole thing is accountability. Government officials don't do enough to be accountable," Heilshorn said. "That is where most inefficiencies come from in government. There isn't anybody who accepts responsibility for the end result. Everyone pushes the responsibility onto someone else. To be successful in government, I'm convinced you can't hide from accountability."

Because politics and policymaking are typically more interesting and easier than good management, many new public officials have little interest in managing their agencies. Others may have an interest but little aptitude. Still other public officials may have interest and aptitude, but limits on their time, energy, and resources prevent significant results. Management skills are largely ignored by voters when electing new leaders. And newly elected leaders too often ignore management skills when appointing agency heads.

"Whenever people get frustrated with substance," said former congressman Dan Glickman, who later became Clinton's agriculture secretary, "they tend to want to move boxes around [that is, to reor-ganize]."

Full of frustration, these public officials then try to reinvent government. But that's been done hundreds of times through special commissions and blue-ribbon panels. It also gets done, in a sense, each election day. What these new public officials really must reinvent is themselves.

3

Reinventing Government Officials

> While all other sciences have advanced, that of government is at a standstill—little better understood, little better practiced now than three or four thousand years ago.
>
> —*John Adams, U.S. president*

Bumper-Sticker Governing

With its old-fashioned smokestack industries and staid Midwestern values, Michigan is not especially known as a home for trendsetters. But like many other governments, Michigan's has been victimized by the passing fancies of public officials who ecstatically embrace the latest management fads.

At the state's Department of Natural Resources in the early 1990s, the craze was Total Quality Management, or TQM, the macarena of its day. The concept is based on a team approach to success, where individual rewards and achievements take a backseat to the squad's. And the Michigan department was sold. Said Steve Sliver, an environmental engineer also trained as a TQM facilitator: "They threw tons of staff time and money at TQM."

Then, of course, it went out of fashion. Suddenly, TQM was O-U-T, replaced by its near opposite: performance-based pay. Now, government workers would be judged on their individual performance rather than that of team. Said Sliver: "I was naïve in thinking that this was going to be a new philosophy."

Sliver was not alone. In fact, Michigan was not alone. The list of fly-by-night government management trends is so long, and changes so quickly, that one almost needs a scorecard to keep track. For even the most powerful public officials, management fads are all the rage.

After the 1992 election, President Bill Clinton organized a bonding weekend at Camp David for his new cabinet, complete with facilitators to build trust among the group. (Secretary of State Warren Christopher reportedly shared his enjoyment of jazz and piano bars.) On becoming Speaker of the House in 1994, Newt Gingrich issued a reading list to fellow revolutionaries that included books by management gurus Peter Drucker and Alvin and Heidi Toffler. And to heal his wounds after losing control of Congress the same year, President Clinton invited motivational speakers Anthony Robbins and Stephen Covey to Camp David for private inspirational sessions.

"In the 1960s politicians who wanted to appear with-it talked about science," observed *The Economist.* "These days the hip subject is management theory."

The latest theories were listed in a *Governing* magazine article appropriately titled "Fad Mad." The article described governments embracing "TQM, managing for results, benchmarking, reengineering, value engineering, rightsizing, strategic planning, downsizing, flattening, privatizing, competitive contracting, virtual organizations and systems management. . . . Some call this phenomenon 'management by bestseller' or 'management flavor of the month.' Some of the more frayed career employees simply call it 'BOHICA,' for 'bend over, here it comes again.' "

Unfortunately, many of these management theories are contradictory. For example, "reengineering" demands that managers tear apart an organization and piece it back together more efficiently, while TQM preaches continuous, incremental improvement over time. "Downsizing" views lower-rung workers as expendable, while TQM sees them as incredibly valuable. The theories are incompatible, yet many government officials switch between them like channel-surfing couch potatoes.

About the only thing these trends have in common (besides failure) is a love for buzzwords, a virtual Esperanto understood by no one without a secret dictionary. It's as if each management technique's viability gets judged not on potential results but on the number of catch phrases it incorporates. Mix buzzwords with politics and you'll get today's public-sector approach to management: bumper-sticker governing. This is nothing more than snappy slogans—"reinventing government" or "run government like a business"—proclaiming big changes in the way government works.

How absurd have the buzzwords become? A whole industry has been built around them. For example, KPMG Peat Marwick, one of the largest government consulting firms, commissioned a poll to choose "the right words for change." It recommended which buzz-words public officials should use, examining focus group reaction in five states to "privatizing," "rightsizing," "reforming," "reinventing," "streamlining," and "reengineering."

The report's bottom line: "In states where a 're-' initiative is underway, voters are more positive about the governor and the state direction."

Buzzword overload is one reason these management trends—and the books bought by millions that describe them—will not fix government's problems: Nobody really knows what they mean.

BUZZWORDS are just the beginning of the problem. Most of the latest management fads are simply repackaged private-sector theories sold as new by P. T. Barnum-like hucksters to unsuspecting public officials, who adopt them without reconciling what makes government fundamentally different from business.

The government of novices put into power on election day faces unique challenges for which there is no private-sector analogy. Citizens set their government's course at the polls, yet many officials find themselves bewildered once in office. With dozens of private-sector elixirs offered as a cure, there is great temptation to find the perfect management trick that will mystically fix government's problems.

Some of these tricks became well known from *Reinventing Government* by David Osborne and Ted Gaebler, a 1992 offering firmly embraced by the Clinton administration. The book contains interesting ideas and stories, but many public officials are still lost when they finish it. The authors describe perfect worlds of "competitive government," "customer-driven government" or "enterprising government," but offer little guidance on how to get there.

Ultimately, *Reinventing Government* is simply an amalgam of private-sector theories poorly adapted for very different public-sector problems. (In fact, the book was named after John Naisbitt's 1985 business best-seller *Reinventing the Corporation.* Its working title had been *In Search of Excellence in Government,* after the 1982 business classic *In Search of Excellence* by Tom Peters and Robert Waterman.) *Economist* editors John Micklethwait and Adrian Wooldridge, whose book *The Witch Doctors* destroys the myths of management black magic, wrote that "the problem with Osborne and Gaebler's book is that, for all the details, it is really about recycling old ideas rather than creating new ones."

One need not read beyond the book jacket to see that *Reinventing Government* missed its mark. In bold letters the publisher claims that the book "focuses not on what government should do, but on how government should work." But in reality, while citizens may set a general course, public officials do need to think about what functions government should perform. Moreover, though the book discussed how government *should* work, it gave little insight into how to *make* it work.

Vice President Gore's reinventing government task force—and the book on which it was based—were flawed from the beginning because they ignored the most basic difference between government and business. Like so many other management fixes, Gore's effort merely rearranged the building blocks of bureaucracy while doing nothing to ensure that the builder had the right construction skills.

But to isolate Osborne and Gaebler for criticism is unfair. They are simply the most famous of the public-sector management gurus. Encouraging more public officials to consider management was itself a success. Yet even today, nearly every management fad tried by government overlooks the most basic feature distinguishing our democracy from other forms of government or business: the rookie managers who are regularly swept into jobs unlike any other they have held. These would-be guides describe the way government ought to be ("market-driven," "decentralized," "catalytic"), yet ignore the lessons officials need to learn to achieve it.

It's no different at the state level. In 1996, California governor Pete Wilson introduced with great fanfare a report titled "California Competes," his solution to government's problems. "It reads like the Cliffs Notes version of *Reinventing Government,*" wrote *Governing* magazine, which reported a major oversight: "It doesn't mention anything about California's sweeping TQM initiative, which the gover-

nor announced by proclamation two years ago and which was supposed to be the key statewide management initiative. Rather, the
booklet lays out a veritable smorgasbord of management trends and
theories guaranteed to inspire any lower-level manager or front-line
employee to reach for the Tums and hunker down."

On the other side of the country, Connecticut's economic development commissioner Joseph McGee declared his department reinvented when he introduced "one-stop" service in 1993 for businesses
seeking answers to their questions. This was accompanied by a
nationwide advertising campaign with the slogan "The State That
Thinks Like a Business." In reality, the "one-stop" initiative simply
meant phone calls were answered rather than being lost in endless
transfers from one bureaucrat to the next.

The public-sector management fads—from reinventing to
reengineering to downsizing—are not merely unhelpful; they hurt
government. They leave government worse off than it was before. For
each time some poor public official holds up one of these plans as the
magic tonic to save government, people believe. And each time
they're disappointed.

So WHAT does it mean to reinvent government officials?

Though our democracy thrives from the fresh input of new public servants, it seems to wilt soon after they take office. It makes little
sense that we keep putting people into public office—from presidents
to city managers—who struggle as soon as they are sworn in. Seeking
the latest management fad or launching a management task force
only postpones the reckoning that each new public servant must face.

"Most government managers know what good government looks
like," one General Accounting Office report said. "They just can't put
it into practice."

This persistent problem can be overcome. Sick governments and
government agencies can be cured in spite of complicated civil service restrictions, election year politics, and numerous other obstacles.
But governments don't get well by themselves. There is always a committed public official making it happen.

New public officials can learn from those who have already
served. While some officials have proven unfit for public office, others
have risen to the occasion and left a legacy of remarkable accom-

plishments. By analyzing these successes and failures, common elements of success emerge.

Government officials succeed because they:

- *Recognize government is not a business.*
  This concept, of course, runs contrary to nearly everything said, written, or thought about government today. Officials at all levels of government and from both major political parties drink from this Holy Grail of political theory. However, forcing government managers into private-sector thinking causes more problems than it solves.

- *Rethink government's main purpose.*
  If a government function can be run like a business, maybe it should be one. Many new public officials find themselves heading agencies where the day-to-day work goes beyond what they expected. With dozens of management teams swept in and out over the years, most agencies perform tasks they should not. Some government functions are more appropriate for the private sector, some overlap with those of other agencies, and some are simply no longer relevant. By using up time and energy, these excesses keep officials from doing their best job.

- *Know what they want to accomplish.*
  Little could sound more obvious. After all, who would run for office or accept appointment to an important government position without having a clear vision of what to achieve or how the department should perform? Yet many do.

- *Change the old guard, the old culture—or both.*
  Putting one's stamp on a government agency—making it one's own—is never easy. Staff positions must be filled with people who share similar goals, even when too few vacancies are available. And new positions are difficult to create. The pay typically runs lower than for comparable private-sector jobs, and new public officials—lacking any similar experience—must negotiate the political appointments minefield, especially when higher-ups put on pressure to take their unqualified cousin for that last vacancy.

• *Take control of the bureaucracy.*

Empowering bureaucrats is today's conventional wisdom in making government work. It is also wrong. Instead, top new public officials must learn to empower themselves. They must liberate themselves from the multiple layers of bureaucracy and arcane rules that block their ability to take control of their agency.

The permanent bureaucracy, originally designed to prevent abuse, now insulates public officials from the people so that empowering bureaucrats actually decreases government's accountability. The elected or appointed public manager is most directly accountable to the citizens and, as a result, should have the most responsibility.

• *Juggle many balls at once.*

If there is one supreme lesson of which nearly every public official wishes he or she had been reminded before taking office, it's that time is short, and much of their time is taken by juggling crises. The crises can develop slowly, such as recessions that decrease government revenues; or they can appear out of nowhere, such as scandals plastered on the front page of the morning newspaper. But make no mistake—they will come.

• *Manage their message.*

A government official's communication skills are frequently overlooked. They're not taught in public-administration programs or business schools, nor are they mentioned in the so-called management books. Yet regularly they make the difference between success and failure in public-sector initiatives. If public officials do not manage their message, it will be managed for them.

Without a clear and understandable message, a leader cannot motivate staff. An official will lack public support to make critical decisions. Indeed, public outcry can jump-start—or kill—the proposal that's been pushed for months. Whether a public official has direct media access, like a big-city mayor, or must work through backdoor channels, like a staff aide, the message must get out.

The skill is difficult, because the question "Whose information is it?" is not as simple as it first might appear. Certainly, information belongs to the public. Little could be worse than a society where the public does not have access to government information. At the same time, few would argue that throwing open a file drawer and inviting people off the street to take a look would be an effective use of time. Public officials must understand how to control access and the way information is presented.

• *Seek feedback from citizens.*

American democracy, like most democracies worldwide, has evolved into a system called "representative government," which, in plain language, means, "Elect me. I know better." But times have changed. No longer is it sufficient to take office and check back four years later to see if you've done a good job.

Technology has changed government. Feedback is so easy to get, from constantly whirring fax machines to the lightning-quick responses of e-mail, that no public official can ignore it. Officials have a responsibility not just to put information out but to get input in return. The concept of representative democracy has evolved, and officials ignore the public at great risk.

Ultimately, this book is about responsibility. Public officials call for personal responsibility every day—from welfare mothers, from recovering drug addicts, from average citizens. Yet rarely do they take personal responsibility for their own jobs. They blame the bureaucracy. They blame the press. They blame citizens for voting the wrong way.

THE EXAMPLES in public life are endless. In 1996, Speaker Newt Gingrich blamed just about everyone for the congressional ethics investigation against him, and only when he was finally caught misleading his colleagues—handing in "inaccurate, incomplete and unreliable" information, in his words—did he confess to wrongdoing. President Clinton addressed his party's fund-raising fiasco similarly, saying "mistakes were made." The problems are always a function of "the system," or caused by someone else. Unless this shirking of responsibility stops, the vibrancy of America's democracy will continue to decline.

Taking responsibility means understanding what public life is about and how to do it right. The following pages carry dozens of success stories and a few failures. Each contributes insight into the job of governing. These lessons must be absorbed and understood by every new public official. Only then will pervasive cynicism decline and Americans get the government they deserve.

4

It's Not a Business

As we seek to improve the management of the federal government, we should keep in mind that the government is not a private corporation. What may make sense for a large corporation may not always make sense for the federal government.

—William S. Cohen,
U.S. senator and later
U.S. secretary of defense

Getting Down to Business

Idaho might seem like a strange place to plant the seed that was the second-biggest corporate merger ever, but this was not just any place or any event. The place was Sun Valley. The event was the 1995 Herbert Allen retreat, an annual affair for the (supremely) rich and powerful of the media elite. If it could be read, watched, or heard by millions, it showed up there. The top executives from Time-Warner, Viacom, Walt Disney, and Capital Cities/ABC attended, to name just a few.

The conference is a casual, bring-your-wife-and-kids affair, and the inspiring, snow-capped surroundings are as much a draw as the stirring business conversations. Even media moguls need time away from shop talk. So it was quite natural that Disney chairman Michael Eisner and Cap Cities/ABC chief executive officer Thomas Murphy decided—separately—to take a walk through town.

It had been a tough year for fifty-three-year-old Eisner: He had quadruple bypass heart surgery, his number two executive and close friend Frank Wells died in a helicopter crash, and his longtime colleague Jeffrey Katzenberg had become a significant rival after the pair's bitter split.

For Murphy, meanwhile, it had been an excellent year. His company's stock had risen more than 40 percent during the previous fiscal year; ABC was television's number one network; and Murphy, at seventy, was ready to announce his replacement and ease into comfortable retirement.

So when Eisner saw Murphy strolling in Sun Valley, it was a meeting of two men traveling in opposite directions. They stopped to chat. Eisner had an idea.

"I literally passed Tom Murphy on the street and said, 'Tom, I think the time is right now.' " So there on the sidewalk, Eisner and Murphy decided to merge their billion-dollar companies.

Two weeks later they were on *Good Morning America*, breaking the news that Disney would buy Capital Cities for $19 billion. To the surprise of journalists everywhere—especially those at ABC News—no word of the merger deliberations leaked. The biggest media story of the year had been completely missed by the network where more Americans got their news than any other news source.

The business world was as clueless as the journalists. Katzenberg thought something was up, having seen Eisner's corporate jet in New York just days before the deal was announced. But even with his Disney ties, Katzenberg didn't guess ABC. "Everything I speculated on was wrong," he said. "This one wasn't even on my radar screen."

The second-largest corporate merger in American history was a complete surprise. Eisner and Murphy already had the go-ahead from their respective boards of directors. As for shareholder approval, that was all but guaranteed. At a crowded press conference where they formally announced the decision, both company heads were flanked by their largest shareholders—Disney's Sid Bass and Cap Cities' Warren Buffett. In the one-share-one-vote system of approval, Bass and Buffett held some 50 million votes.

At their press conference, Eisner and Murphy insisted that the deal was good not only for shareholders—the stock prices of both companies shot up that day in frenzied trading—but for consumers, too. The new interactive media services customers were demanding would soon be available, and the synergies between the two companies would leave everyone better off.

In just two weeks, the deal was done.

*   *   *

TO THOSE involved in the merger, it was a bruising couple of weeks. Secret meetings were held. Teams of bankers reviewed dizzying financial statements, evaluated consolidation scenarios, and created complex spreadsheets to analyze the merger's impact on shareholders. Scores of lawyers researched arcane antitrust laws, negotiated intricate details, and drafted the final agreement.

It was hard work, but really nothing special for private-sector organizations. As corporate managers, Eisner and Murphy simply did on a grand scale what millions of businesses do every day. They made a strategic decision and implemented it. They determined what was best for their shareholders and their customers and got it done.

Many voters seek the same ability from their government. Frustrated with the inaction of political leaders in solving the country's most pressing public problems—from improving public schools to providing welfare benefits—making the government act more like the private sector has dominated public debate.

Once the exclusive domain of conservative Republicans, calls to "run government like a business" are now heard from all points along the political spectrum. Billionaire Ross Perot's third-party campaigns attracted millions who believed only a successful businessman could fix government's problems. Vice President Al Gore's pledge to reinvent government incorporated private-sector management techniques and compared citizens to customers. And House Speaker Newt Gingrich promised to turn over dozens of government functions to the private sector through an ambitious privatization campaign.

But each year more is promised, less is accomplished, and the voters grow angrier.

A Sure Thing

It's the dream of every newly elected president, governor, and mayor: Convince a millionaire business consultant to join your staff and assist in the takeover. His former clients include the CEOs of many of the world's largest corporations, from Volvo to General Electric. His ability to analyze a problem, recommend a solution, and implement it have earned him recognition—and a $600 hourly rate—throughout the business world. Now he wants to give something back through a stint in public service.

It seemed like a sure thing when President Bill Clinton hired Ira Magaziner.

Magaziner made millions advising corporations on business strategy for the Boston Consulting Group and later for his own firm. No one disputes his record. He increased the profitability of dozens of blue chip corporations by telling them which operations to sell, which to keep, and which to expand. No one disputes his intelligence. He graduated from Brown University as valedictorian and was a Rhodes Scholar with Clinton.

"I have a successful, twenty-year career in the private sector, which doesn't take too kindly to people with ideas that don't work," Magaziner said in an interview soon after taking his job. "And I had one of the most successful track records as a business strategy consultant—with firms that had pretty hard folks to please. So my ideas have had to be practical and to stand the test of time."

So when Magaziner was appointed assistant to the president in charge of designing a new national health care system, he approached the job like a consultant. He created a task force of experts to study the health care problem and spent long hours devising a proposal for delivery to the CEO—in this case President Clinton. His methodology had worked in the private sector; he had little reason to believe it wouldn't work in government.

But it didn't, and here's why.

ON JANUARY 28, 1993—just eight days after the Clinton takeover—Magaziner launched the health care reform effort. He said a twelve-member task force on national health care reform would work through "a highly structured process, a highly formalized process" and deliver a proposal to Congress within one hundred days.

But this deal would not be completed quickly like the Disney–Cap Cities merger. Government realities soon intruded. Congressmen and senators wanted their staff members on Magaziner's task force. Federal agencies pressured the White House to include their staffs as well. Trade associations, think tanks, and universities also used political pressure to put their representatives in the group. What started as a twelve-member task force quickly ballooned to more than five hundred people.

In his zeal to meet the looming deadline, Magaziner failed to adjust his business plan to government realities. Unable to recognize the developing disaster—or unable to do anything about it—he stuck to his original strategy.

For example, Magaziner held regular "tollgates," management-consultant-speak for meetings where progress reports are given and course corrections made. Because of the task force's unwieldy size, the tollgates became traffic jams. Some sessions dragged on sixteen hours; one lasted past 2 A.M. on a Sunday morning. The grueling process soon wore down staff members. One private-sector consultant called the meetings "a cross between Ph.D. orals and the Spanish Inquisition."

Meanwhile, problems developed outside the White House. Magaziner kept the meetings and names of the members private so his task force would not be influenced by industry lobbyists. It's not an outrageous thought. Government proposals are famous for being dirtied by the political sway of selfish forces. Magaziner vowed to avoid this trap.

But while paying mind to one difference between the business world and government—lobbyists—Magaziner forgot a second: Government can't operate in private. When conducting the people's business, every government action is a matter of public concern.

Like lions on the hunt, health care reform opponents saw their opening. Instead of attacking the plan on its merits, they attacked the process. Their first charge was that the Clinton administration had created a "secret task force" to devise a nationalized health care system—a system against the interests of most Americans. "The secrecy . . . angered consumer advocates, doctors and health care executives, and Administration officials now acknowledge that it was a political mistake," *The New York Times* later wrote. When Magaziner refused to turn over a list of the working group members to the media, the attacks and suspicions increased.

The Wall Street Journal, recalling that "in the days of the Soviet Union and Mao's China, to find out who was running things in those countries, Western experts would pore over photographs of government functions, checking out which officials were present," lamented that now "things aren't that easy." The White House hadn't released any photographs of task force meetings.

In its crusade, the *Journal* set up a dedicated fax line and asked readers to send in names of people who might be in the group. Only

after the paper printed a partial list of task force members did Magaziner finally release an official roster.

But it was too late. Three lobbying groups sued to force the meetings open to the public. A judge recommended that the government
prosecute Magaziner for giving deceptive testimony to a federal court
about the task force's makeup and called his statements "misleading,
at best." When Clinton and Magaziner later traveled the country for
public comment on the plan, the hearings were widely labeled by the
media as staged public-relations events. Instead of debating ideas, the
administration expended valuable energy defending the process.

Although Magaziner's strategy was very similar to Eisner's—he
wanted to develop the details of his plan privately—it caused a political battle and helped galvanize the opposition. This was not like
incubating a megamerger in Sun Valley, Idaho, and announcing it
two weeks later in New York. When Magaziner's proposal was finally
released in September, 1993—a 1,100-page bill nearly five months
after it was promised—few even read it. Worse, many had already
dismissed it.

Magaziner's next problem was with his board of directors, the
535 members of Congress. Like Eisner at Disney, Magaziner knew
the board's importance as a decision maker. Congress would ultimately vote to accept or reject his recommendations.

As a business consultant, Magaziner carefully tried to understand
each director's particular views and make sure to avoid strategies that
would pit someone against him. But he had never dealt with a board
of directors so large.

"I'm used to company environments, where if somebody dis-
agrees with you, they just say they disagree with you and you sort of
shout it out over a table," Magaziner said. "But here, you find a lot of
people smiling, patting you on the back, and so on and so forth. But
they don't really mean it. So it's less of a direct atmosphere. Those are
the kinds of things that make this more difficult."

And unlike the homogenous corporate boards of perhaps ten to
twelve white men, Congress was much more diverse. Members had
different levels of education and various backgrounds. They came
from separate political parties. Perhaps most important, each was the
elected representative of thousands of taxpayers and would need to
explain votes to constituents at home.

Magaziner met frequently with members of Congress to educate
them about his task force's findings. After hundreds of late nights,

few in the country knew more about health care than Magaziner. But in most cases, lawmakers were not interested in being taught about the intricacies of the health care industry. They wanted to tell Magaziner what they and their constituents desired in a reform proposal.

"They came over and saw us all the time, but ignored what we said," said Representative Pete Stark, a California Democrat who headed the Ways and Means subcommittee on health. Complained Louisiana Democratic senator John Breaux: "We don't speak the same language. He is a technician; we are politicians. It doesn't work."

Magaziner faced still another problem. As a consultant, he made recommendations he felt would maximize shareholder value. In business, all shareholders want the same thing: increased return on their investment. After an extensive analysis of the options has been performed, the numbers generally point to the right answer. And numbers don't lie.

The shareholders of government, however, are the taxpayers. They have widely divergent interests, which cannot always be measured in numbers. And unlike the Disney–Cap Cities merger, where large shareholders such as Warren Buffett or Sid Bass could guarantee a giant vote for management, each taxpayer has the same number of votes. Magaziner's analysis might point to the best solutions for taxpayers in general, but every public policy creates winners and losers. And when one seventh of the American economy is at stake, the losers—once they knew who they were—used their voice to reject his plan.

Most Americans wanted to know how the plan would affect them. The reclusive Magaziner never had shareholders so interested in his work. As a consultant he dealt solely with the senior management of a company. But in his new job, taxpayers read reports on his plan every day in the newspapers. Hourlong news specials on health care aired between evening sitcoms. Harry and Louise—the middle-America critics of Magaziner's plan—became pop icons and favorites of late-night comedians. Magaziner moved from a behind-the-scenes operator to someone quoted frequently in the nation's newspapers.

In the end, Magaziner's business consultant experience helped him little in government. As the *Economist* wrote: "Mr. Magaziner acted like a parody of a consultant, intent on plan and blind to the demands of democratic politics. He recruited hundreds of experts from around the country, set up enormous committees and subcommittees, generated lorry-loads of documents, produced a gigantic blueprint—and watched it torn to shreds on Capitol Hill."

Magaziner's methodology virtually ensured the plan's demise. Congress rejected his health care proposal by never bringing it up for a vote. The plan was basically dead on arrival. Now if President Clinton were to pass a health care plan—his centerpiece legislation—it likely would be done without Magaziner at the helm.

"The administration should search for a new leader of its health care reform effort," said Washington representative Jim McDermott, a Democrat. "Ira had a good shot, a full shot. He had two years. I have no doubt of his intellectual capacity. But he simply doesn't have what it takes to put this effort together and get it done."

Reviews of Magaziner—who came into the process with a sterling reputation—became so harsh that he was listed on a World Wide Web page of "Clinton Administration Losers" with former Justice Department official Webster Hubbell, who went to prison, and former Agriculture Secretary Mike Espy, who resigned under federal inquiry. Said one Stanford professor who advised the administration on health policy: "They ought to make Ira Magaziner the Ambassador to Kazakhstan."

Magaziner summed up his experience with Washington's political bureaucracy: "Working in the federal government is everything I thought it would be—and worse."

ALTHOUGH Magaziner's health care proposal might have failed anyway—there was natural opposition to many of his ideas—the process effectively killed the plan before Congress even had a printed copy. As he got deeper into the project, and deeper into trouble, Magaziner didn't adjust. He managed government the way he managed business, and failed.

It didn't have to be that way, especially since many management techniques from the private sector are useful to public managers. For example, task forces are common in companies. They work because they cut across the traditional organizational structure and can stimulate more creative solutions from a wide array of people. A pet food company CEO testing the market for a new dog food might create a task force that includes representatives from marketing, sales, manufacturing, and finance. While the task force members do not ordinarily work for each other, they break out of the regular organizational structure for a limited time to develop fresh recommendations for top management.

The key to effective governing is knowing when to use private-sector management techniques and knowing when to adjust to government realities. When political pressures cause a government task force to grow to more than five hundred members, many common management strategies become irrelevant. Tollgates are impossible with so many people. Competing visions for the group emerge. Communication with members and with people outside the group becomes extremely difficult. In the end, the task force's recommendations will be overly complex and hard to explain. If, as in Magaziner's case, the plan's audience becomes skeptical before the plan is even finished, it will be nearly impossible to convince them of its merits later.

Magaziner missed the most important difference between government and business. Every government action—from painting yellow lines down the middle of a road to ending welfare benefits—is a matter of public interest. When an official spends the public's money, citizens deserve and demand a voice in how it is spent. This is the essence of democracy. Government officials who ignore the public's concerns, regardless of their reasons, invite failure.

Instead of fighting government openness, successful public officials embrace it. They invite citizen input. They recognize that allowing public participation might slow the process, but without it they will probably never achieve their goals.

Elliot Richardson, who served as an elected and appointed official in state and federal government, knows this well. "Making decisions and issuing orders won't cut it. For every important initiative it is essential to seek and win support," he says. "Indeed, this conspicuous difference between the day-to-day roles of government managers and corporate executives may explain why success in business is no guarantee of success in government."

It seems Magaziner may have learned his lessons. Four years after the health care debacle, he headed a presidential task force on government's role in Internet commerce. This time Magaziner's effort was widely praised for its openness and clarity.

A Businessman's Metamorphosis

Inside the tinted glass skyscrapers on Wall Street, investment bankers taking a break from capitalism gaze across the Hudson River at Jersey City, New Jersey, a town long neglected by America's financiers. Abandoned factories, rusted water towers, and crumbling highways clutter the waterfront view. Beyond the riverbanks and less visible mount troubling signs of despair and poverty. Fewer than half of the city's residents finish high school; more than 14 percent are on welfare.

While most bankers go home to their swanky Manhattan apartments, Salomon Brothers bond salesman Bret Schundler always went home to Jersey City. Schundler, a Republican Harvard graduate, wanted to get into politics. And when longtime mayor Gerald McCann was sentenced to prison for fraud in the summer of 1992, Schundler saw his opening to bring a business background to the job of managing a city.

In a town where two-thirds of the population are black, Latino, or Asian, few gave Schundler, who is white, a chance. So when he won on November 3, 1992, with a stunning 68 percent of the vote, the national media took notice.

Schundler was among a group of politicians profiled by *Time* magazine as a new breed of big-city mayors with business backgrounds. "Wielding corporate-style tactics, the CEO mayors are taking on city hall," wrote *Time*. "Managers rather than politicians, they apply private-sector solutions to chronic urban woes and switch over to the technocratic jargon without pause."

In his first months in office, Schundler lived up to his fiduciary promise and brought ideas straight from the business world to run Jersey City. He talked of "securitizing tax liens," the process of packaging financial debt and selling it as securities for investors. For years, many homeowners had never bothered to pay property taxes. They knew that liens placed on their property by the city rarely led to foreclosure. In fact, fewer than 1 percent of homeowners with delinquent property taxes were ever challenged in court.

Schundler attacked the situation like a business deal. He bundled together almost $45 million in tax liens and sold them to investors on Wall Street, an action most other mayors wouldn't consider, much less understand. This first-of-its-kind move, taken from his Salomon

Brothers' experience, turned a liability into an asset, helped push the tax collection rate from 78 to 90 percent, and immediately raised $25 million. It also allowed the mayor to cut property taxes. The deal promised the city another $19 million by 1998—money that would otherwise take a decade or more to collect.

"We took dormant assets sitting on our balance sheet, realized value on them and provided tax relief," said Michael Cook, the mayor's chief of staff, likening the city's financial condition to that of a private business.

The move paid off and several other cities later copied the innovation. With a stable budget and a new source of funds, Schundler put an additional sixty police officers on foot patrol in crime-ridden areas of the city. He pledged to put another 240 officers on the streets within the year.

But after six months, the pace of change in Jersey City slowed, and Schundler faced obstacles they don't warn you about in business school. Civil service opposition derailed many of Schundler's more innovative community-policing initiatives. Hostile city council members, including several who were elected on the mayor's slate, blocked his legislative agenda. Even the newly elected Republican governor—an ally!—delayed approval of his school choice proposals.

Schundler had been successful in managing government like a business. In many areas he achieved his goals without needing approval. Now he was stuck. But recognizing the realities of managing in a public environment, he changed tack. "I spent my first year putting more police on the street and selling our tax liens, and those were both things I could pretty much do on my own," he said. "What I have to do next is going to take much broader support. It's going to attract organized opposition."

To accomplish his goals, Schundler began acting very unbusinesslike.

For starters, though the municipal bureaucracy was overstuffed when Schundler took office, the mayor did not initiate layoffs. In fact, Schundler boasted that he had not fired a single city worker, a move he admitted would be "politically counterproductive." Instead he planned to shrink the size of government through attrition. By not hiring replacements and reassigning others, Schundler reduced the city workforce by nearly 10 percent in his first five months.

Consider what would have happened if Schundler had treated government as a business. Shareholders would have insisted that management cut costs and people to remain competitive with other companies. In the banks where Schundler worked, people were laid off regularly. It was called "rightsizing." A bank CEO would conduct a management study and cut the organization accordingly.

Schundler needed to move more slowly than he did on Wall Street. Launching a wild crusade to reduce bureaucratic fat might be political suicide. In a city that was only 6 percent Republican, the mayor could not afford to lose public support for his priority initiatives of school choice and community policing. In addition, every city employee was also a voter and taxpayer, a shareholder of government. And each of these employees had friends and families who also voted. Schundler would still reduce staff, but it would be a slower and more deliberative process.

Schundler's metamorphosis didn't stop there. When he acted to literally clean up Jersey City by removing graffiti and trash, his proposal was innovative but nothing like what happens in the private sector. Rather than simply turn the task over to the low-price company that provided the best services, Schundler held a fair.

The mayor invited residents to the Jersey City Armory—complete with concession stands and colorful balloons for the kids—to meet the companies bidding for cleaning services. He divided the city into 133 "special improvement districts." At the fair, residents could buy a hot dog, learn about each company's strengths and weaknesses, and vote for one to be hired in their district. The firm with the most votes won the business.

"We want those directly affected by services to be in charge of hiring them," Schundler said. More important, the mayor wanted residents to share responsibility for choosing city services. Bringing city residents into the decision-making process anchored the mayor's approach to governing. A side political benefit: Any dissatisfaction would be harder to blame on him.

Schundler's approach to economic development also underscored his break from private-sector management techniques. He had little time and almost no budget for marketing, an important tool for any businessman. The mayor dismissed the idea that Jersey City could attract businesses by putting out glossy brochures and newspaper advertisements. He called politicians' claims that they can create jobs "the height of hubris." Instead, Schundler put his efforts into reforming the core functions of government—education, infrastructure, and public safety.

Asked to describe his philosophy, Schundler said: "I'm not a conservative; I'm a revolutionary."

Unlike so many public officials, who try to run government like a business and fail, Schundler succeeded in bringing a better life to Jersey City residents by treating government like government. He took innovations where he could but always recognized the difference between managing on Wall Street and managing at City Hall.

Takeover Tips

In campaigns, politicians score points with calls "to run government like a business." After the takeover, they find it's not always possible. While many modern management strategies work effectively in both sectors, the differences cannot be ignored. For public officials, the key is rejecting business techniques that run contrary to how government works.

Dall Forsythe, an investment banker who later served as New York State's budget director, says new public officials must know the difference from the start. "You really don't know what to expect when you come into government from the private sector. If you think you do, then you're going to be in trouble."

One study of three nations' governments—the United States, Canada, and the United Kingdom—interviewed dozens of public managers who were trying to reform bureaucracies. In virtually every case, the managers highlighted differences between government and the private sector:

> They stressed how the constantly changing political environment plays havoc with virtually every long-term planning exercise they ever engage in; how goals in government agencies are often vague; how past experience tells them it is more important to follow prescribed rules than dart off in an uncharted direction, even though it may hold considerable promise; how there are always many "bosses" in government; and how those at the top of the hierarchy are constantly managing crisis situations. All of this suggests that government managers are in the business of "coping," not managing in a private sector sense.

Of course, these differences don't mean that government leaders can't share business's entrepreneurial spirit. Any institution—public, private, or nonprofit—can be innovative. Any agency can provide incentives for improved employee output. And all successful organizations must strive for efficiency. Indeed, citizens can get rather surly when they put money out but see little in return. From the Boston Tea Party to the 1994 congressional elections that swept the Democrats out of power after forty years, citizens have always demanded high-quality service from their governments.

But when government fails, it cannot simply hang an "out of business" sign in the front window. For example, as Bridgeport, Connecticut, teetered on bankruptcy's edge in the early 1990s, city officials had no choice but to deal with its massive problems. The troubled government could not simply close its doors when its services—from repairing roads to preventing crime—were still needed.

"People say the city should be run like a business," Bridgeport city alderman Thomas White told *The New York Times*. "If it were a business, it would have moved out. It would have gone south."

These differences make the public official's job particularly difficult. The incentives that create efficient organizations in business do not always exist in government. Many obstacles government leaders must overcome don't exist in the private sector. Understanding these differences—and applying the similarities—is critical to being a successful public official.

Tip #1: UNDERSTAND YOUR BOTTOM LINE.

Business and government are driven by different bottom lines. Private-sector managers focus on profits, targeting their most promising customers and ignoring those unlikely to buy their product. In 1995, AT&T chairman Robert Allen voluntarily split his company into three independent firms. Only the telephone division would keep the AT&T name. Allen's reason: the company wanted to focus on its most profitable business. With no advance warning, the leasing and finance businesses were sold, the personal computer business was shut down, and some 8,500 workers expected to lose their jobs. Cutting costs meant more profits for the shareholders. The financial markets applauded Allen's strategic move, and AT&T stock jumped 11 percent.

Imagine, then, if a private enterprise ran the U.S. Postal Service. It might conclude that rural mail delivery was not profitable and eliminate the service. Government leaders, however, must satisfy the broad range of voters who elected them. Ignoring rural citizens would cripple a politician's ability to govern. Even if the postal service were privatized, the government would require that private carriers deliver mail to all citizens. In government, the bottom line is not profits but voter satisfaction.

When Ira Magaziner developed a new health care plan that helped the 15 percent of Americans who were uninsured, he ignored the 85 percent who had insurance. Magaziner argued that his plan would save folks money. But to cover those without insurance, his plan would necessarily alter the health insurance of people already covered. Magaziner's critics argued that most people would be worse off under his plan. In a democracy, one can rarely afford to alienate a majority and still win.

Tip #2: HEDGE YOUR RISKS.

Business leaders and public officials respond to risk differently. When the makers of Arizona Iced Tea decided in 1992 to market a line of flavored iced teas, they took on Snapple Beverage, a twenty-three-year player in the soft drink industry. With pinpoint distribution, wily store displays, and distinctive packaging, Arizona went from zero to some $400 million in sales in just four years. In 1995, the company then made its move to take on soft drink giants Coca-Cola and Pepsi-Cola with a line of flavored colas. It was a bold entrepreneurial move. If it succeeds, Arizona will have accomplished what many have tried and few have done.

When company CEOs are right, their firms gain tremendous advantages and quick profits. When they are wrong, their calculated business risks are often balanced by many others that succeed. If investors think the company takes unwise risks, they can always pull out their funds.

Government works differently. For years, as the elected treasurer of wealthy and conservative Orange County, California, Robert Citron received national attention for earning some of the highest returns of any municipal investor. To outpace other local government investment pools, Citron borrowed money and invested in risky derivative securities. But when his bets on interest rates soured during 1994, Citron lost millions and forced the county into bankruptcy. He lost his job and landed in jail.

In government, risk taking is rarely rewarded. If a risky venture fails, the government raises taxes to cover the loss. Failed initiatives are frequently plastered on the front page of the newspaper. Those responsible often testify in legislative oversight hearings. Calculated risks can become embarrassing scandals if they fail. Taxpayers pay considerable attention to government, and, unlike private investors, they cannot pull out their funds.

This doesn't mean that public officials should avoid taking risks. Public officials can make strategic bets and still survive if they fail. But while business leaders seek the large upside for bets that pay off, most public officials try to avoid the huge downside of those that fail.

Tip #3: TREAT CITIZENS AS OWNERS, NOT CUSTOMERS.

In business, customer satisfaction drives most decisions of top management. But in government, citizens are not simply customers—they are owners.

The differences start with how each sector raises revenues. Businesses earn money from customers who buy products and services of their own free will in competitive markets. As many failed businesspeople know, inferior products or poor service typically means lost customers. So the private-sector manager's incentive is clear: Keep the customer satisfied. Nearly everything the businessperson does serves that goal.

Governments, meanwhile, raise revenues by levying taxes to ensure that everyone pays part of the bill. If a citizen stops paying, he violates the law and faces jail time. Many of the products government provides—drivers' licenses, building permits, marriage certificates— may be necessary for society, but few people enjoy having to purchase them. For example, no matter how efficient the tax department is, citizens will always hate paying taxes. Reducing the time to receive a tax refund might be good management, but public officials will not receive much praise from their "customers."

In addition, government requires that people pay for many services they rarely use. Only a minority of citizens have contact with the police department during a typical year, but everyone shares the bill for public safety. The same is true for roads, bridges, and public schools. Specific individuals may not use specific services, but society as a whole benefits from them.

Since citizens cannot opt out of this social contract, treating them as mere customers is inappropriate. Instead, citizens should be treated as owners—shareholders—of their government. As owners, citizens will think more about the overall return on their investment than the individual services they might receive.

Tip #4: DON'T CLOSE THE BOARDROOM DOOR.

Business leaders, like Disney's Eisner and Cap Cities' Murphy, typically make decisions quietly behind closed doors. Virtually no one knew about their deal, despite its being, at the time, the second-largest corporate merger in American history. With competitors always looking to steal market share, secrecy in business transactions is essential. It allows companies to move swiftly and take advantage of changing markets.

Government, however, must be open. Public managers must typically allow for comment before decisions can be made. When solving a public problem, task forces are created with varied representation. Hearings are held, public comments solicited. If a law must be changed, the public's representatives debate the change in the legislature. Information in public offices is subject to Freedom of Information Act requests. In addition, many governments operate under "sunshine" laws that prevent public meetings from being held in private.

"In the corporate world, you can arrive at conclusions a lot faster," said former White House chief of staff Donald T. Regan, an investment banker before entering government. "You can stick to plans a lot better than you can in government."

A public official's challenge is to accomplish goals without needlessly slowing the process. Many new public officials, such as Ira Magaziner, fight the realities of working in a fishbowl. They ignore media requests for information. They try to keep meetings secret and confidential. Instead of working toward the final goal, effort is wasted in defending a private process that will never work in government.

Former secretary of state George Shultz told the story of appointing a friend to a top diplomatic position: "He was an extraordinarily successful businessman and very interested in the State Department. He worked very hard at it, but finally he just left. He said, 'Around here, when you decide something, that's just the beginning. Anybody who doesn't like it goes to Congress, goes to the press or something. It's a different process.' "

Secrecy is imperative in some government actions, such as national security. But even in these cases, effective public officials recognize that public participation can be harnessed to help get the job done. In 1990, President Bush asked Congress to vote on his proposal to send soldiers to the Middle East to evict Iraqi soldiers from Kuwait. Bret Schundler held fairs to select neighborhood cleaning services. Other public managers have spent long hours educating the public and then used the public's support to convince skeptical legislators. Although the lack of privacy seems an obstacle to many private-sector managers, successful government officials encourage public involvement to accomplish their goals.

5

Rethinking Government

When government tries to be everything to everybody, it becomes nothing to anybody.

—*Richard M. Daley,*
mayor of Chicago

Gaebler's Gamble

Ted Gaebler was the brain behind an eight-year experiment in "enterprising government" in Visalia, California. As city manager, Gaebler found ways to finance government services without increasing taxes.

Visalia was a fine place to live. Gaebler described it as "a leafy oasis of 75,000 people in California's hot, dry San Joaquin Valley. . . . It is an All-American city: the streets are clean, the lawns are mowed, the Rotary Clubs are full." And throughout much of the 1980s, local citizens believed they owed their town's success to their enterprising city manager.

For Gaebler, the need for new revenues came quickly. Just two months after his takeover, California voters passed Proposition 13, slashing city tax revenues by approximately 25 percent. Gaebler scrambled for new sources of funds and soon started charging for the use of city-owned recreation facilities such as baseball fields. But he had a twist: He priced them at a profit to make money for the city.

Gaebler was more CEO than city manager. When Visalia needed more portable toilets at the athletic fields, he encouraged the recreation department to invest in twelve new ones, paying for them by leasing out an adjacent concession stand and selling advertising. In less than three years, the toilets were paid for and the concession stand was earning an annual profit for the city.

With these successes Gaebler's plans grew, and he moved into an area where government does not usually bother to go. When the New York Mets minor league baseball team dropped an unprofitable franchise it owned in Visalia, Gaebler's enterprising government bought the team. It could not afford to lose the business the ball club brought the city. Six years later, the city sold the team for a profit. At one point Gaebler even tried to turn the city into an insurance company, selling its own fire protection coverage to local businesses.

"It was a real test-tube situation," recalled Greg Collins, a Visalia city council member from 1975 to 1992. "It was an exciting time. We were doing a lot of futuristic stuff."

But Visalia's boldest venture—the one that finally got people to ask: "Is this what government should be doing?"—was yet to hit. It came in the form of the Radisson Hotel, part of an economic development scheme to attract visitors to a new convention center next door. The project was undertaken by Don Duckworth, Gaebler's successor as city manager. The city bought a parcel of land and found a private hotel developer who persuaded the city to guarantee his loans. But when the developer went broke in 1991, the city was forced to purchase the hotel to protect its initial investment. In the end, Visalia was left with property appraised at $6 million after putting in more than $27 million. Approximately $21 million of taxpayer money was lost on the venture.

Over time, as it became clearer that the only deal worse than the Radisson would have involved Florida swampland, citizens soured on enterprising government. In 1989 Visalia residents had elected a mayor and city council majority opposed to a profit-seeking government. With the Radisson failure, they had a chance to act. They fired Duckworth.

"Government was competing with the private sector in being a developer with public money," said Visalia Mayor Basil Perch, "and I felt, and the public felt, that this was not right."

In 1985, Visalia boasted a healthy budget surplus. But ten years later, city officials were cleaning up the mess of their entrepreneurial predecessors. Visalia struggled with persistent budget deficits. By the 1990s, however, Gaebler was long gone, spreading his management gospel to other governments as coauthor of the book *Reinventing Government* and giving speeches for as much as $8,000 a day.

Meanwhile, Visalia moved back to basics and abandoned most of Gaebler's initiatives. The new city council even banned the "E-word"—*entrepreneur*—from city hall. "We've struck any reference to it," said the plain-spoken Perch.

The city that thought it could run like a business had gone bust.

FEW WOULD disagree that government should build roads and bridges, run the fire department, and provide police for public safety. In addition, most citizens believe that government should care for those who cannot care for themselves, ensure children's education, and protect the environment.

But new officials often find that government is not that simple. What about the print shop in the basement of the social services agency? A human services commissioner may be great at managing social workers but clueless when it comes to running an internal copy center. Had it not existed when she took the top job, she probably would have had the local Kinko's handle her duplication needs.

Government is not a business. But if a government agency or function can be run like a business, perhaps it should be one. Today, many new public officials head agencies where the day-to-day work goes far beyond what they signed up for.

A city manager may balance a budget brilliantly or negotiate competing political interests of a mayor and city council. But he may have no idea how to run a baseball stadium, an insurance company, or a hotel. That print shop in the agency basement should not be part of government. That's what the private sector does best.

Through enterprising government, Visalia's city managers dramatically increased their government's scope. They expanded the boundaries of what they were appointed to do. They sought profitable investments. In the private sector, investors understand that they might lose money. It disciplines the business world. But when a government venture flops, and public officials use tax money to cover the loss, as Visalia did, citizens rarely remain sympathetic.

Indianapolis mayor Stephen Goldsmith advised new public officials to take the "yellow pages test." He said if they can find a service provided in the telephone directory's yellow pages, government probably should not be doing it: "The private sector is better than the public sector in many ways in delivering goods. The public sector should only be involved when the private sector isn't working."

Reasonable people feel that government can play a role in schools and hospitals and other areas where public and private sectors mix. But when a major accounting firm told Goldsmith that his wastewater treatment plants were running efficiently, and that private management would save less than five percent, Goldsmith still took the yellow pages test. He invited five companies to bid for the job.

"The winner brought down our costs by 44 percent—about $11 million a year," Goldsmith said. "Not five percent, but 44 percent for one of the most efficient plants in the country."

When Goldsmith put Indianapolis's twelve golf courses to the yellow pages test, the city saw immediate benefits from private-sector competition.

"The golf courses were awful," Goldsmith said. "It was fairly easy to bring customer satisfaction. We now have lots of different things happening in our golf courses. Some are priced one way, others another. Some have bunkers. Some have carts, others have clubhouses where there was nothing before. There is a lot more variety out there."

Abraham Lincoln gave simple guidance more than a century ago: "The legitimate object of government is to do for the community of people whatever they cannot do at all, or cannot do as well for themselves in their separate or individual capacities. In all that people can individually do as well for themselves, government ought not to interfere."

Lincoln's words are even more urgent today. New public officials must rethink what their government does; extraneous activities only distract from what officials were hired to do. The questions are straightforward: Is this activity part of our main responsibility? Is this function still necessary? If we were not already doing this, would we start today?

New York mayor Rudolph Giuliani asked these questions before spinning off city-owned television and radio stations in 1995. Connecticut governor Lowell P. Weicker did it before selling the state's off-track betting operations in 1993. And Visalia's new city council asked these questions as it reined in the excesses of enterprising government.

Most of these programs were created through the give-and-take of the political process. Usually, some narrow constituency benefited from the projects. But in an age of limited resources, government officials need a new approach. Specific tasks exist that a government can and should do well. But many others are better left to the private or nonprofit sectors.

Rethinking government does not end, however, with weeding out government functions better left to the private sector. Sometimes government agencies compete with each other, needlessly duplicating efforts and wasting resources. And then there are the government programs that continue but are no longer relevant to citizens' needs.

These low-priority activities pull public officials from their primary duties. New public officials must make sense of what their agencies should and should not do. They must concentrate on fewer activities and on doing them better. In the private sector, market realities force companies to shed unrelated businesses and focus on what they do best. But in government, some agencies cling to functions because "that's the way we've always done it."

"We don't need another efficiency study," complained a *Philadelphia Inquirer* editorial about Al Gore's National Performance Review. "We need to rethink government, what it can do and cannot do."

Banking on Reform

After authoring landmark banking reform legislation in 1991, and losing much of it in a political fight with the Bush administration, Senator Donald W. Riegle Jr. saw a glimmer of hope when Bill Clinton was elected president. With new administration officials eager to take a fresh look at the sprawling federal bureaucracy, Riegle believed he finally had a chance to untangle what he saw as one of America's most dire bureaucratic messes—the bank regulatory system.

Riegle understood the problem better than anyone. As chairman of the Senate Banking Committee, he oversaw the absurd bank regulatory apparatus. The system needed changing. It consisted of four entirely separate federal banking agencies, each with its own squad of examiners, its own bureaucracy, its own regulations. But all four branches basically did the same thing.

"No one would ever design such a system from scratch," Riegle said in a speech on the Senate floor. "In fact, nobody planned our present bank regulatory system. It's a product of historical accident."

Like many government programs, America's bank regulatory system grew largely out of crisis. To coordinate Civil War financing efforts, Congress created the Office of the Comptroller of the Currency in 1863. To stabilize the industry after a series of banking panics, Congress established the Federal Reserve System in 1913. To introduce a system of federal deposit insurance and restore confidence in the financial system after hundreds of bank failures, Congress created the FDIC in 1933. And, finally, to deal with the 1980s savings and loan crisis, the Office of Thrift Supervision was transformed into its present regulatory form.

The result was a four-headed monster, with each head controlling a different body part. Worse, each head wanted supreme control over the whole body, but none would give up its own limb to complete the whole. A chart published by the Federal Reserve Bank of New York used twelve columns, seventeen rows, and thirty-one footnotes just to explain what each regulator did.

Riegle wasn't alone in his opinion. "We have the most bizarre, entangled regulatory system in the world," said Senator William Proxmire, Riegle's predecessor as Banking Committee chair. "It never ceases to amaze me that it lasted this long."

Indeed, the majority of Democrats and Republicans on Riegle's committee agreed.

Riegle knew that his best chance to see change become reality was through a change in administration. He was so optimistic that the new government would bring revived interest that he sent two committee aides to Little Rock during the transition to understand President-elect Clinton's banking policy views. And as the new administration came to town, Riegle put the finishing touches on legislation to merge the four bank regulators into one. The senator estimated the plan would save millions of dollars for taxpayers and the banking industry.

Riegle hoped the Clinton administration would incorporate his proposal as part of the vice president's much-publicized effort to "reinvent government," since the bank regulatory system symbolized government bureaucracy at its worst. Moreover, the system did not work, as the savings and loan industry bailout and hundreds of failed banks proved.

"If one wants to talk about 'reinventing government,' " said

William Seidman, who served as FDIC chairman from 1985 to 1991, "one doesn't have to be a Thomas Edison to recognize that this is an obvious place to start."

Riegle's plan would collapse the four regulatory agencies into a new superregulator, the Federal Banking Commission. He believed that the proposal not only would save money and increase efficiency but could boost the economy by providing more money for banks to lend to businesses.

The idea was not new or radical. The need to merge the federal bank regulatory agencies had been widely acknowledged for decades. But because of power struggles, nothing had ever changed.

"I seriously underestimated the depth of the entrenched opposition to regulatory consolidation," Proxmire said in 1991. "All [the] bank regulatory agencies vehemently opposed the legislation. Privately, however, each agency let it be known it would withdraw its objections if it could assume the powers of the [others]."

Warned former FDIC chairman Seidman: "Do not bother to ask regulators about it; their turf is their only message."

Riegle hoped to overcome turf battles. He knew that consolidation served many vital interests beyond those of the regulatory agencies. For the banking industry, consolidation would reduce examination fees, duplicative examinations, and conflicting regulatory guidance. For the general public, it meant a more accountable, more responsive bank regulatory system. And for the American economy, consolidation meant a more vital, more competitive banking industry.

But despite the proposal's wisdom, the Clinton administration excluded the reform from its initial reinventing government effort. Only after pressure from Riegle and House Banking Committee Chairman Henry Gonzalez did the administration finally agree even to put a proposal together. But it came two months after Al Gore's reinventing government train left the station. The vice president's office issued only a lukewarm statement saying that the proposal "was in keeping with both the substance and the spirit of reinventing government."

With the administration unwilling actively to fight the needless duplication, the bill faced increased levels of the same bickering between regulatory agencies that killed previous efforts. This time, the Federal Reserve openly fought the proposal and even convinced some of the banks it regulated to lobby Congress against it as well.

Without the new president's support, Riegle knew he could not push the proposal through the Senate, let alone the entire Congress. Once again, the regulatory agencies supported the concept of consolidation, but not if they lost their own turf. And Riegle could do nothing but sit, frustrated, because the Clinton administration had no interest in taking them on.

THE POWER of tradition—whether a blatant duplication of duties or a naked fight for turf—is one of the biggest barriers to getting things done in government. Sometimes only a takeover can break it down. To Senator Donald Riegle, the Clinton administration lost a once-in-a-term opportunity to make dramatic, tangible improvements in the way government worked.

The duplication Riegle tried to eliminate in the bank regulatory system is just one example from the federal government. A 1995 report by the nonpartisan General Accounting Office described a massive problem: "Generally, and not surprisingly, our analysis illustrates that duplication appears to be endemic. Our current environment is a product of an adaptive federal government's response over time to new needs and problems, each of which was reflected in new responsibilities and roles for departments and agencies."

For example, the GAO study found that 8 agencies performed functions relating to regulating natural resources and the environment. More than 80 programs in nine agencies dealt with teacher training. Federal food safety programs were administered by 12 different agencies. The Department of Education ran more than 200 different education programs while 30 other agencies managed an additional 308 education programs. At least 19 agencies were involved in trade promotion. And an astonishing 163 programs in 15 departments involved a job training or employment function.

Like the tangled bank regulatory system, other parts of the federal government evolved in a haphazard fashion. The GAO concluded: "Many departments and agencies were created in a different time and in response to problems very different from today's. Many have accumulated responsibilities beyond their original purposes. As new challenges arose or new needs were identified, new programs and responsibilities were added to departments with insufficient regard to their effects on the overall delivery of services to the public."

A new public official's first few months on the job are the most crucial for governing success. It may be their only chance to rethink the government they inherit. Riegle hoped the Clinton takeover provided such an opportunity for the banking industry. It didn't.

Surely, Clinton had reasons. Among them: not wanting to make an enemy of Federal Reserve Board Chairman Alan Greenspan, arguably the most powerful unelected man on earth. Clinton couldn't have known that the country would exit the recession so smoothly, and might not have wanted to aggravate financial markets. But not thinking about the overlap of banking oversight agencies didn't make the problem go away.

New public officials must seize the opportunity to rethink government early, because waiting only creates more headaches later. Imagine if, instead of four bank oversight agencies, there were one, and the saved resources helped solve the Medicare crisis, erase the budget deficit, or fix America's crumbling interstate highways. Anything would make more sense than having four organizations do basically the same thing.

The problem, though, goes far beyond just duplicated tasks. Some of what government does simply is no longer needed.

Out of Business

As the woman scraped the painted sign off her office door, flakes of white enamel speckled the sleeve of her stylish red business suit. The office was closing. Another enterprise had succumbed to the competitive marketplace.

But instead of appearing depressed at the lost enterprise, State Treasurer Martha Whitehead smiled broadly for the television cameras. Shortly after taking office in 1993, Whitehead did the extraordinary—she pledged to abolish her office. She argued that the State Treasury was a useless government agency that time had forgotten.

"The taxpayers of Texas are demanding 'fat free' government," Whitehead said. "This is a critical first step in reducing excess."

With Whitehead's energetic campaigning, Texans voted in 1995 to eliminate the agency, transfer some functions to the private sector, and merge others with those of the state comptroller. One memorable television advertisement showed Whitehead standing in front of the state capitol promising to eliminate her office as her image faded from the screen. The outcome wasn't even close: 70 percent of Texas voters agreed the office was no longer needed.

After 158 years in business, on September 1, 1996, the Treasury closed its doors for good.

Historically, the Texas Treasury served as the state's bank, investing and managing public funds. It also carried a smaller responsibility, the unclaimed property program, which collected abandoned cash and securities and, after attempting to return them to their rightful owners, turned the remainder over to the state.

At one time, having an elected treasurer and comptroller seemed important to Texas citizens. Two officials provided checks and balances on each other. In household terms, one state official held the checkbook, and the other wrote the checks. Money left the state coffers only when both officials agreed.

But by the time Whitehead entered the statewide political scene, the treasurer's office had long lost its relevancy. The need for additional checks and balances had disappeared. State auditors now existed, the state legislature was more sophisticated and more involved, and technology had eliminated the urgency for two separate offices.

"I came from a business background," Whitehead said. "And after a month or so in Austin, I asked the deputy treasurer, 'What am I supposed to be doing here?' And without batting an eyelash, he said, 'You've got an election to run in a year. You've got to be out there giving speeches to rotary clubs and getting your name in the press and raising $1 million.' That was the first glimmer that something was wrong. There has got to be more to the Texas Treasury than running your next election."

Whitehead argued that private firms could perform the Treasury's main tasks at least as efficiently, and for much less money. And if most of the work was done externally, Texas did not need an elected official whose only responsibility was to hire private firms to do her job.

"We had a budget office and human resource workers and travel aides and a communications staff, all apart from the three or four core duties of the Treasury office," Whitehead said. "If you merge these with the comptroller's office, you can get the same job done, because he has all those things, too."

The idea had been floated before. More than a decade earlier, then State Comptroller Robert Bullock suggested that the Treasury be closed. He claimed the Treasury had so few duties that all he would need to take over the state treasurer's tasks was "an extra desk, chair and telephone."

But most people felt that Bullock was merely trying to grab the Treasurer's powers. Whitehead did what few public officials have the guts to do. She knew her office was no longer needed and proposed to put herself out of work.

Specifically, under Whitehead's proposal, most of the Treasury's main functions would be submitted for competitive bid to the private sector; others would shift to the comptroller's office.

"This transition has been what pilots call a 'soft landing,' " State Comptroller John Sharp said afterward. "I hope it serves as a model for saving even more money and streamlining other areas of state government in the years ahead."

Sharp (who was not an unbiased figure; his stature increased when Whitehead stepped aside) estimated that closing the Treasury cut the employees performing the agency's functions by two-thirds, from a high of 253 when Whitehead took office to 83. Forty additional former employees of the Treasury's unclaimed properties division were spread among existing comptroller divisions to continue administering the program.

Sharp also noted that abolishing the State Treasury would allow him to return 38,000 square feet of unused office space to the state government. The unused office space in the downtown Austin business district had an annual lease value of more than $600,000. According to Whitehead, closing the Treasury saved $8 million a year.

"Today, Texans have agreed that they can get along just fine with one less state agency," Sharp said. "The fact is that another bureaucracy has gone out of business, and Texas taxpayers will get along just fine."

After Whitehead left office, she took a job at the University of Texas. But she remained popular.

"I give a lot of speeches around the state," she said. "And I always ask my audiences, 'Do you miss the Treasury? Did you ever know it was there?' And they say no, they don't. But they sure like having an extra $16 million every two years when the legislature meets."

*   *   *

WHEN NEW public officials come across programs that seem broken, the common response is to reinvent them. But some programs do not need reform. They need retirement. This reality is difficult for many public officials to recognize. No one wants to come into a new job and discover that significant parts of it—even one's own position—are unnecessary.

When a former official recommends such changes, many wonder why the proposal did not come earlier. People suspect ulterior motives. For example, when Lamar Alexander suggested to eliminate the Department of Education as a 1996 Republican presidential candidate, most analysts took it as a cynical election ploy. After all, Alexander had served as President Bush's education secretary for two years without ever recommending it be disbanded. Why should anyone believe him now?

But some officials, like Martha Whitehead, realize that their job is simply a dinosaur in government's evolutionary history. In Texas, the treasurer's office continued for many years primarily as a stepping stone for elected officials. For example, Whitehead's two immediate predecessors used the treasurer's post as a launching pad to higher office. Ann Richards became Texas governor in 1990 and Kay Bailey Hutchinson went to the U.S. Senate in 1992—a rather expensive way to ensure promotion.

Said Whitehead: "I could name a hundred agencies in our state that have tremendous duplication."

And Texas is not alone. Many states have elected comptrollers and treasurers. Scores of agencies, departments, and programs at all levels of government have outlived their usefulness. For example, the Connecticut legislature voted in 1995 to close the Second Injury Fund, a state-run insurance operation, since the national Americans with Disabilities Act of 1991 adequately prevented companies from discriminating against workers with injuries. The program, which dozens of other states still have, was started after World War II to provide insurance to injured veterans who would otherwise not be hired by private companies. But after fifty years and a new federal law to prevent discrimination, it served little purpose.

The challenge for public officials entering their new jobs is to rethink their responsibilities. And sometimes, the only appropriate action is to say good-bye when the job is done.

Takeover Tips

Many new public officials fail because they ignore a fundamental question: What should government do? When most new officials think of improving management, they usually try to reform the process of government. Instead, the first step after the takeover is to decide what the proper functions of government are.

Unfortunately, it's not hard to find a government agency engaged in needless or redundant activities. After years of sweeping top management in and out, government's right hand rarely coordinates with its left. A cursory review of most government agencies will uncover some central functions, others that are better done by someone else, and still others that could be eliminated entirely.

Said former defense secretary Donald Rumsfeld: "The first task is to decide what your core business is. Once this decision is made, then everything else in the enterprise is secondary. . . . Once one has determined the core functions to be performed by the federal government, all other activities should be scrutinized for elimination, cuts, reorganization, or movement to the state and local governments or to the private sector."

Rethinking government is imperative. But it should not simply be confused with attempts to cut bureaucrats. In fact, some public officials may find that significantly more resources are needed to be effective. By rethinking government, these public officials will create better-focused agencies. Reaching goals will become easier. In effect, rethinking government means developing a personal theory of what government should do.

"No major political thinker—at least not since Machiavelli, almost 500 years ago—has addressed this question," writes Peter Drucker. "All political theory, from Locke on through the *Federalist Papers* and down to the articles published by today's liberals and conservatives, deals with the process of government: with constitutions, with power and its limitations, with methods and organizations. None deals with the substance. None asks what the proper functions of government might be and could be. None asks what results government should be held accountable for."

Tip #1: TAKE ADVANTAGE OF YOUR HONEYMOON.

When Hawaii governor Benjamin J. Cayetano took office in January 1995, the Aloha State found itself saying hello to its worst financial crisis ever. "The highest priority of the Administration is to get its fiscal house in order," Cayetano said repeatedly.

Cayetano had an activist agenda that would not begin until the state regained control of its finances. "Like many of you," he told legislators during his State of the State address, "I support early childhood education and affordable long-term care as programs which are sorely needed by our people. I am determined that these needs will be met."

The new governor knew that his best chance for results was to act quickly. He entered office, after all, as the people's choice. The first months might be his only opportunity to act decisively on touchy political issues. Moreover, too many public managers waste these precious days, only to find that the chance for change has passed.

Surely, change creates enemies. But public officials get the most slack during the honeymoon period after the takeover. Cayetano wisely used his honeymoon period to build support and redirect resources toward his vision by cutting services duplicated by other agencies.

As a symbolic measure—and to show potential enemies that everyone faced cuts—the governor started with his own office, trimming his staff by more than 20 percent. He axed the governor's Agricultural Coordinating Committee, because its functions were already handled by the Department of Agriculture. He ended the governor's Office of International Relations, because its duties were duplicated by the Department of Business, Economic Development and Tourism. And he eliminated a governor's special office on affirmative action, because its services were replicated by every state agency's personnel department.

"We have taken the lead to eliminate duplication of government functions," Cayetano said.

Still in his honeymoon period, Cayetano next focused on other parts of state government. He proposed merging the Housing and Finance Development Corporation with the Hawaii Housing Authority, agencies both charged with providing affordable housing. He also suggested folding the Office of Collective Bargaining into the Department of Human Resources Development, since both dealt with personnel and labor issues. Finally, Cayetano urged the legislature to eliminate ten additional programs he felt were duplicated by other government agencies or had outlived their usefulness.

"After only 45 days in office, we were forced to take action and we did," the governor reflected a year later. "Today there are 2,750 fewer employees in the Executive Branch of State government." And he had more cuts in mind for the next year.

Cayetano was not giving up on government by making these cuts. He believed he was elected to fulfill a specific, limited purpose. Education was a major part of that purpose. But government had grown beyond its means and was wasting resources that could be used for his initiatives. Cayetano knew his vision would suffer without rethinking the rest of state government.

Tip #2: SEEK THE OBVIOUS TO REDUCE DUPLICATION.

Saving Florida taxpayers millions of dollars couldn't have been more elementary. In the early 1990s, truckers entering Florida were greeted not with a glass of fresh orange juice but by employees of two different state agencies. At the state's twenty-two inspection sites, Department of Agriculture employees inspected trucks for agriculture law violations, such as diseased plants or nonimmunized livestock. But before the truckers were sent on their way, Department of Revenue employees, wanting to collect sales taxes, verified that the seller had registered with the state.

By 1993, Revenue Department Director Larry Fuchs had seen enough. It was laughable—two agencies both inspecting trucks shipping goods into the state. Fuchs suggested merging the duties, with just one employee doing the work of two.

"One of government's faults is that we don't look across agency lines," Fuchs said. "You have to look at government as a whole if you want it to work better. By looking beyond an individual agency, it's easy to find ways to save money by cutting duplication."

Under the new system, agriculture inspectors were trained to identify invoices subject to sales taxes when they entered an inspection station. These invoices were photocopied and sent to the Revenue Department for review. If the seller was not on file to collect sales taxes, Fuchs's department sent the company a letter explaining that Florida required them to pay a 6 percent sales tax on all goods sold. The simple plan saved the state $14 million the first two years.

Fuchs measured his success by collecting more revenues without passing new laws for higher taxes. By combining inspectors' duties Fuchs increased efficiency, and the state collected tax money it previously missed.

"In today's political environment, the option of standing still doesn't exist," he said. "You must move forward, or you'll surely fall behind."

Tip #3: BEWARE OF ELECTION YEAR POLITICS.

By 1994, Washington's 500-bed DC Village nursing home had hit rock bottom. Patient care had fallen to abysmal levels. Officials found cockroaches, asbestos, and patient medication errors during their inspections. The federal government even threatened to stop payment to the home.

Despite little attention given to care, the cost of running the place had exceeded all estimates. And no one could offer a financially reasonable solution that kept the home in government's hands, because labor expenses ran too high. So it should have been no surprise— indeed, it should have been widely hailed—when the District's Department of Human Services tried to hire a private firm to run the home.

The DC Village privatization was a textbook example of how to spin off a government function to the private sector. The city solicited competitive bids in a mind-numbingly detailed process that ensured fairness and objectivity. A transition plan and ongoing monitoring process for the successful bidder was drafted even before the bidders were interviewed. Nonetheless, the plan failed as politicians got nervous.

Despite the skewed balance sheets and the numerous financial reports that seemed to show conclusively that the place should close, health department officials ignored one critical factor affecting their plan: campaign politics.

Privatizing the nursing home meant losing seven hundred public jobs. Those seven hundred people and their families also voted. In addition, the move would give the impression that the council didn't care about the poor. So despite potential savings of $6 million (20 percent of the nursing home's budget), the threat of job losses was too much for city council candidates in the 1994 municipal elections. The proposal died.

"Election year politics can unravel even the best of alliances," wrote two analysts involved in the initiative. "What killed privatization of DC Village? No single event to be sure, but one does not have to look much deeper than election year politics."

In fact, after the election a solution was quickly found. In 1995, once the federal government filed suit under the civil rights laws to close the facility, the D.C. city council ordered the nursing home closed and the residents transferred to private-sector care providers. With the elections behind them, council members took fast action.

"Closing that facility means no more crimes can be committed against residents, no one else's civil rights can be violated, because there are no more residents there," said Harriet A. Fields, who was appointed by the court to monitor the closing of the nursing home and ensure its residents' well-being.

This doesn't mean government is on hold during election years. But it does show that timing is as important a factor as an idea's merit. The right idea at the wrong time adds up to a bad plan.

Tip #4: USE PUBLIC-PRIVATE PARTNERSHIPS.

Connecticut's gold-domed state capitol sits atop a hill overlooking Bushnell Park, a graceful thirty-seven-acre, tree-lined public green in the center of Hartford, Connecticut. It's a stunning setting for the majestic building. But Bushnell Park wasn't always such a beauty to behold.

In the 1970s and early 1980s, it was a mess. Graffiti covered statues and monuments, benches were broken, and the dimly lit sidewalks attracted muggers and gang members after sundown. Few city residents, much less those from the suburbs, found much use for the park.

The City of Hartford, which owned and operated it, never seemed to keep up with the maintenance. With so many other functions tugging at city resources—from fixing schools to repairing potholes—officials simply let the park go.

"For the city, it was like a distress signal from a ship, a signal to the world that the city was in trouble," said Sandy Parisky, a local urban planner. "The park was just being ignored by government."

Privatization was out of the question; the land deed would not allow a sale of the historic city park to a private company. And even though hiring a private contractor to maintain it might be possible, the city had no money.

So municipal officials turned to Parisky, who pledged to create a public-private partnership to restore it. Parisky created the Bushnell Park Foundation, a nonprofit organization with board members from the public and private sectors. The organization would take over strategic planning functions from the city and would tap the private sector and foundations to raise funds for the restoration.

"A public-private partnership allowed access to resources that would otherwise be unavailable," Parisky said. "Some private funders will not give money directly to government because they think it will be wasted or spent on something else. We could tap those funds. Second, this mechanism allows you to tap the energy and spirit of the citizens. Everyone involved is focused on one project that they consider important, and it is great visibility in the community for local corporations. The third advantage is continuity. With governments changing leadership all the time, a public-private partnership can usually span the terms of office of elected and appointed officials."

The public-private partnership raised money to build a carousel, an amphitheater, an art gallery, and a man-made pond. In addition, the effort helped restore a Civil War memorial arch and numerous statues and monuments. Dozens of new trees were planted and fresh walkways laid.

Bushnell Park, once a symbol of civic neglect, is now Hartford's focal point. The park is packed with workers on their lunch hour and concerts play throughout the summer. City schoolchildren regularly visit with their teachers to take part in new educational programs, ride the carousel, and tour the historic monuments. The park is back.

6

The Vision Thing

For we must consider that we shall be as a city upon a hill. The eyes of all people are upon us.

—John Winthrop, first governor of
Massachusetts Bay Colony

Filling the Vacuum

It was a cold January evening in 1989, but inside the West Wing of the White House, the midnight fire burned. A government takeover had occurred and some of the Bush administration's best minds—including Deputy Assistant to the President for Policy Planning Jim Pinkerton—were seated around a polished maple conference table, trying to solve the country's enduring education problems. After all, their leader, George Bush, had anointed himself the Education President.

But as the meeting dragged on, Pinkerton grew concerned. The discussion was going nowhere. Everyone present spoke in buzzwords and sports metaphors about what was wrong with American education, but few had solutions. "Invest in our future," one person suggested. "Hit the ground running," offered another. The speech they were trying to write had a title, "Building a Better America," but no content. Suddenly, a higher awareness chilled Pinkerton: No one knew what the president wanted them to do.

Trapped in this surrealistic, bureaucratic setting, Pinkerton's

thoughts escaped to the 1946 filming of *The Big Sleep*. During shooting, director Howard Hawks realized he didn't understand the plot of
his own movie. The actors, too, had no clue. Neither did the
scriptwriter. In desperation, Hawks tracked down the author, Ray-
mond Chandler, in London to have him explain it. "That night, we
were acting out our own Washington version of *The Big Sleep*,"
Pinkerton said. "We had lost the plot to the story. We were more like
scriptwriters with no sense of the storyline."

Pinkerton, a thirty-something veteran of the Reagan years and
four presidential campaigns, joined the Bush administration with
high hopes as a midlevel domestic policy aide. While many of his
friends from the campaign accepted tangential jobs in tangential
agencies, Pinkerton had a White House post. From the center of
power, he could make an indisputable impact on public policy by
turning the president's campaign promises into action.

In the Old Executive Office Building, Pinkerton, whose rumpled
hair and Ichabod Crane physique suggested a mad genius at work,
toiled late drafting and redrafting position papers, fact sheets, and
speeches on issues ranging from educating children to housing the
homeless. He spent most days in his office or in meetings with other
officials. But occasionally he was asked to go to Room 450 to brief vis-
iting business leaders, interest groups, or students on the Bush
agenda. It became one of his regular responsibilities and one of his
few chances to hear the concerns of real citizens.

But as the months passed, he noticed that his audiences in Room
450 asked fewer and fewer questions. They—and Pinkerton—were
frustrated with a president who had broken his "Read My Lips, No
New Taxes" pledge, yet had no alternative agenda to offer. The visitors were not interested in hearing an aide they didn't know try to jus-
tify the president's inaction. "If Bush didn't care about his domestic
agenda," Pinkerton asked, "why should they?"

Later, he elaborated: "The federal government, and the White
House itself, is a holding company of a million different institution-
alized interests, from budget cutters at the Office of Management and
Budget to the big spenders at the departments and agencies. If the
cat—the president—isn't imposing his will on these things, then the
mice will play."

Sensing that higher-ups cared little about what he did, Pinkerton
began straying from the official White House line in his propaganda
sessions. Intellectually curious, he listened more and tried to respond

to what needed to be done. If Bush wasn't interested, he felt, perhaps some future president would be. As Pinkerton formulated his ideas, he started giving speeches outside the White House before small audiences.

In a talk to the New World Society in February 1990, Pinkerton's concepts took a loftier form. He described a major shift in American politics. After decades of partisan struggling with the growing bureaucracy of New Deal and Great Society programs, Pinkerton believed that Americans had finally arrived at a consensus about many grand issues: Democracy was better than socialism; markets worked better than government controls; tolerance and compassion in government were essential. Pinkerton called his vision of American politics the "New Paradigm."

If these were common American values shared by Republicans and Democrats, all that was left to argue about was implementation or how government should manage itself in this new environment. Pinkerton was ready. He had built a policy agenda that centered on choice, decentralized power, inclusiveness, and helping people solve their own problems. A New Paradigm agenda would ensure that Bush was reelected. It was a true vision in an administration that had none. Pinkerton hoped someone on Bush's team would listen.

Several months after his speech, the listening began. A debate over Pinkerton's agenda broke out among the nation's opinion leaders and talking heads. Opinion pieces appeared in *The New York Times*, *The Washington Post*, and *The New Republic*. His ideas were discussed on *The McLaughlin Group* and other political talk shows. As political theorist Norman Ornstein later wrote, Pinkerton was "an idea man—a standout in a roster of stupefying conformists." In an administration that seemed empty of new ideas, Pinkerton filled the vacuum.

Of course, the irony that developing a vision had dropped several floors below the penthouse to this midlevel operative was lost on no one. Richard Darman, the president's budget director and self-appointed policy czar, publicly attacked Pinkerton's ideas and ridiculed the notion of a New Paradigm agenda. He chided reporters interested in Pinkerton's plan for the disadvantaged by asking them, "Brother, can you paradigm?"

Although Pinkerton shared the same 456 telephone prefix as the President of the United States, that was about as close as he got to the Oval Office or the president's inner circle ever again. "I survived,"

Pinkerton later wrote, "but my clout inside the building, never great to begin with, was at an end."

Pinkerton's vision was rejected, and two years later, so was Bush.

WHEN A friend suggested to George Bush during the 1988 campaign that he spend some time thinking about what he would do as president, Bush blurted, "Oh, the vision thing." After eight years in Ronald Reagan's shadow, he didn't have a policy agenda of his own. "I'm following Mr. Reagan—blindly," the vice president once said. Driving home the idea that the president had no substance, Garry Trudeau's *Doonesbury* cartoon depicted him as invisible.

Bush's résumé for the presidency couldn't have been better. He had been vice president, a congressman, CIA director, ambassador to China and the United Nations, a war hero, Phi Beta Kappa Yale graduate and the son of a popular U.S. senator from Connecticut. On paper, he was one of the best-prepared men ever to run for the presidency. Bush felt he had worked his way up the political ladder and deserved the country's highest office.

In his inauguration speech, Bush offered his vision of a "kinder, gentler America" with "a thousand points of light." They were memorable lines, but few knew what they actually meant or how they might be implemented. It was clear to most Americans—and perhaps even to staffers like Pinkerton—that their new president was reading a speech he did not write and did not feel.

One might assume that the friendly takeover from President Reagan to Bush would be seamless. The two had worked together for eight years and many of the same people would serve both administrations. But as the Bush White House got to work, Pinkerton and others lacked direction in their efforts. The administration seemed paralyzed when a national recession hit in 1990. They stumbled when a string of bank failures threatened to bankrupt the federal deposit insurance system. The Los Angeles riots and Hurricane Andrew's aftermath in Florida further highlighted the administration's inability to meet the nation's needs.

"When I worked in the Reagan White House," a former staff member recalled, "I knew every day without being told what I was supposed to do: cut taxes, fight Russians, reduce government spending. It was just in the air." Another Reagan aide recalled, "If a congressional staff member called up and said 'My boss is thinking about this amendment or that amendment,' there wasn't a blank stare about what the Administration position would be."

Bush's 90 percent approval rating after the American victory in the Gulf War—the largest presidential approval rating in history—quickly faded. Just ten months later, it had been cut in half. While success in war inspired most Americans, few felt it indicated an overall Bush strategy for America.

Soon Bush's reelection was in jeopardy. Eight months before the vote, 58 percent of those questioned for a *Washington Post*–ABC News poll would not describe him as "inspiring." Fifty-two percent felt he did not have "a vision for the future of the country." Just six months before the election, Bush had slipped to third place in polls behind Bill Clinton and Ross Perot.

Jim Pinkerton, who had moved from the White House to the Bush reelection campaign staff, was sent to Harvard University's John F. Kennedy School of Government to give an afternoon speech on the prospects for a second Bush term. Pinkerton tried to weave in as many New Paradigm ideas as he could, suggesting that they made up the president's vision for the future. Referring to the aftermath of the racially charged Los Angeles riots, he even compared George Bush to Abraham Lincoln as a healer of the nation.

But the speech fell flat. Bush was no Abraham Lincoln.

Preserving the Union

Abraham Lincoln was one of the least experienced and most poorly prepared men ever to become president of the United States. In school, he went no further than the fourth grade. He held numerous odd jobs. Yet, although just fifty-one years old when sworn in, Lincoln became one of America's greatest leaders. He may have lacked George Bush's credentials, but his vision for the country—that the union would stay together—never wavered.

As Lincoln took office, the nation was on the verge of breaking up over slavery. There was no time for him to settle into his new job. On the morning after his takeover, he faced an emergency decision regarding dwindling provisions for federal troops at Fort Sumter off the South Carolina coast. Lincoln was told that he had to resupply the troops or surrender the fort to hostile South Carolinians. Losing the fort would likely mean the first step to losing the South.

But Lincoln, who had little military experience and had won the presidency with less than 40 percent of the vote, was unprepared to make a decision. He had only a handful of staff members. The Senate had not confirmed any of his cabinet officers. His secretary of state—designate had not yet even agreed to serve. Lincoln later admitted that when he became president "he was entirely ignorant not only of the duties, but in the manner of doing the business" of the presidency.

But Lincoln had a vision: He would not lose the union. He resupplied his troops. A month later, with navy supply ships offshore at Fort Sumter, Confederates began shelling it. The Civil War and America's greatest crisis began.

Despite his uneasiness as the country's top administrator, Lincoln's commitment to keeping the country together was absolute. While historians agree that Lincoln was not motivated by a visceral hatred for slavery, he understood that slavery would tear apart the young nation. That was unacceptable. "It is the duty of the President to execute the laws and maintain the existing government," he wrote. "He cannot entertain any proposition for dissolution or dismemberment." All of Lincoln's political beliefs were derived from the premise of preserving the union that was first stated in the Declaration of Independence.

As his cabinet began the task of managing the crisis, everyone knew what Lincoln wanted. While no one could predict the events of the next few years, the president had declared a course of action. He had communicated an unmistakable vision for his administration.

LACKING A vision in government is like picking up a phone with no one to call. Nevertheless, a shockingly high number of public officials enter office without one.

A clear and compelling vision tells people what can be accomplished and instills a sense of common purpose. It steers a department of transportation to build new infrastructure while limiting construction delays for travelers. It guides a budget office to produce accurate financial reports in half the time of any other agency. It pushes a motor vehicle department to become a model of efficient service for other state governments.

But articulating a vision is never enough. It must become a natural part of the workplace, a blueprint for action within the organization.

A public official must institutionalize the vision so that it becomes a common standard. For example, North Carolina governor James Hunt required that his appointees carry a card at all times with his administration's five goals. When new problems or obstacles arose, the state government could shift gears to meet the new demands without drifting off course, and achieve the governor's priorities.

Former labor secretary Robert Reich, who served three presidents and taught public management at Harvard, suggests that a clear vision provides the foundation upon which all future success is built. "There is ample evidence that the most accomplished government leaders—those who have achieved significant things while in office or at least set the direction of public action—have explicitly and purposely crafted public visions of what is desirable and possible for society to do," Reich writes. "These ideas have been essential to their leadership, serving both to focus public attention and to mobilize talent and resources within the government."

While a vision must be achievable, it cannot be too simple. It may take years to reach. It may require removing many obstacles. For example, Lincoln needed to fight and win a civil war to fulfill his vision of national unity. It took four years and more than 600,000 lives to reach. But Lincoln knew that a good vision stretches the limits of an agency, department, or even an entire country. Successes along the way inspire even greater effort.

Unfortunately, many public officials are more notable for their drift than their mastery in leading their governments. As President Bush found, spin doctors and political consultants cannot invent a vision for which there is no core belief. A worthy vision resonates with staff and the public at large because it proposes a course of action for their government. People understand it right away; it takes little explanation.

The Turnaround

When Chris Burnham took over as Connecticut treasurer, he knew to expect the worst. After all, many incoming public officials complain about the impending disasters left by their predecessors, and Burnham's had been a particularly hostile takeover.

In the single meeting that outgoing treasurer Joseph Suggs granted Burnham after the election, Suggs showed up late and left early. Little of substance was covered. After the meeting, Suggs told Burnham that he should only contact one of Suggs' staff members. Others at the Treasury were forbidden from talking to the Treasurer-elect.

Once in position, Burnham quickly learned why Suggs avoided him. The Treasurer's office fit the stereotype of government at its worst. The staff had ballooned more than 250 percent in just eight years, despite a state budget crisis and no new responsibilities. Few of the career staff found their jobs challenging. "Good enough for government work" could have been the slogan. Morale was low. Anyone standing near the exit at 4 P.M. might have been run down by the herd of bureaucrats racing to go home.

Then Burnham discovered what had gone wrong.

The $12 billion pension portfolio the Treasury was responsible for investing had become America's worst-performing fund over the previous ten years. Abuses ran rampant. Whether bailing out a local company facing bankruptcy or sinking millions of dollars into a downtown office building at the peak of the real estate boom, many investments were made for political and not financial reasons. Stock trades were directed to what Burnham called F.O.T.s, or "friends of the Treasurer"—a.k.a. big campaign contributors—who saw it as their right to make large commissions. Money managers were rarely fired if they had political connections, despite poor investment results year after year.

But the pension fund was just the beginning of the management challenges. As Burnham later recalled about his first few months in office, "Several times a week one of my senior staff would bolt into my office exclaiming, 'Guess what we found now!' It was just amazing how screwed up the Treasury was."

In the Cash Management Division—which oversaw an annual cash flow of $26 billion—the staff used pencils, ledger books, and old desktop calculators for much of their accounting work. The Second Injury Fund, a state-sponsored insurance program for injured workers administered by the Treasury, issued checks not only to dozens of people with fraudulent claims but to some who had been dead for several years.

The agency was a shambles.

Burnham gathered his top staff for a retreat to develop a clear strategy. The meeting was held at a local university, away from the office, where Burnham insisted that no one could take phone calls.

Before making comments himself, he asked each staff member what needed to be done. Burnham listened intently as each person spoke. He had heard much of it before, but the problems they described never ceased to amaze him.

When it was his turn, Burnham just shook his head and slammed his fist on the conference table. "I am just appalled at what we've found," he told his staff. "Connecticut does not deserve this. We can do much better." Then he challenged them with their task for the rest of their term. "Our vision," he said, "is to create the finest public investment bank in the nation."

ON THE WALL behind Burnham's desk hung a framed picture of Alexander Hamilton that his father gave him on inauguration day. To Connecticut's new treasurer, the sketch was an inspiring symbol of what he could achieve in public service. Although Hamilton is probably best known as one of the youngest delegates to the Constitutional Convention, he was also America's first treasury secretary. Hamilton settled the new nation's shaky finances after the American Revolution and established policies that helped the country prosper.

Like Hamilton, Burnham did not have the hands-on experience for such a massive job. Burnham was an investment banker and trader by training; he had limited managerial experience. He had never handled so much money before. He did have vision, but to attain it, Burnham needed a strategy. He outlined four first-year goals for his staff.

First, he turned the Treasury upside down. When visitors or staff questioned the need for a complete upheaval of the office, Burnham rattled off a list of the three government evils: waste, fraud, and abuse. Burnham ultimately trimmed staff by 25 percent and saved nearly $3 million annually.

Second, Burnham revamped the Treasury's investment operations, the largest public pension fund restructuring in Wall Street history. The fund was so mismanaged that had it simply been indexed to match the market's performance over the previous decade, it would have been $2.3 billion richer. Burnham fired forty-one investment managers, hired sixteen new ones, and paid them on a performance basis. "They only make money if we make money," said Burnham.

Third, Burnham created a treasurer's annual report to disclose the state's finances at a higher standard than any private-sector bank. When Burnham campaigned for treasurer, he tried to get a list of the pension fund investments but was told that no list existed. When he asked for one to be compiled, he got no response. Ultimately, Burnham took his case to the state Freedom of Information Commission, where former treasurer Suggs fought his request. Burnham never got the information. As treasurer, Burnham vowed that he would never let his public Treasury operate in secret. By the end of his first year in office, he had a new annual report, and a list of all the investments was available on the Internet for anyone who cared to look.

Burnham's fourth goal was to ensure that his changes would live long after he left office. He sponsored campaign finance reform legislation that would prevent politics from perverting the Treasury's investment functions. His bill would prohibit anyone who gave a campaign contribution to a treasurer's race from doing business with the office for four years. The "pay-to-play" policy at the Treasury would end.

In just over a year, Burnham had achieved all four of his goals. His vision was in place. Connecticut's Treasury was on its way to becoming the finest public investment bank in the nation. Ultimately, Burnham resigned before his term ended to return to the private sector. While some criticized him for leaving office early, he had accomplished everything he set out to do.

How DID Burnham achieve so much in his first year?

"I knew what I wanted to accomplish," Burnham said. "We could have done the job many different ways. We changed course many times, but we always kept our eye on the objectives we set at that first retreat."

To motivate his crew and prepare the public for far-reaching changes in his office, Burnham insisted that they move fast so the vision didn't get lost. He let people know that the Treasury's past mismanagement was a multi*billion* dollar problem for the state. He reminded his staff that a dollar squandered by the Treasury, unlike other state agencies, was worth more than a dollar. Every dollar spent or wasted was a dollar that could not be invested.

Burnham also focused on communicating his vision. Everywhere he went, the new treasurer spoke of creating the finest public investment bank in the nation. When he gave speeches to local groups or met individually with people in his office, he always made sure they heard what he was trying to accomplish.

Burnham regularly held brown bag lunches with low-level staffers to talk about how their jobs fit into his vision. Everyone from the mail delivery clerk to the computer technicians was necessary to transform the Treasury into a top-performing financial institution. On the masthead of the biweekly office newsletter, *The Exchange*, and on his Internet Web site, Burnham's vision statement ran in large letters for everyone to see.

Takeover Tips

For many new public officials, the takeover is about power. These rookies can command significant resources, often more than they had in their previous jobs. Newspapers write about them, and their decisions affect the fates of thousands, if not millions of people. It is only natural for new public officials to feel important when their mail is addressed using "The Honorable" instead of "Mr." or "Ms."

Other new officials take jobs in the public sector for future financial gain. While a public servant's salary may not make anyone rich, some figure it will enhance their future business by making valuable contacts for them. Burnham, for instance, left the Treasury to head an investment firm that has done business with the state. The revolving door between government and the private sector has rotated smoothly since the nation's birth.

But most successful public officials, including Burnham, are not motivated by achieving political power or financial wealth. Their service is part of their life's mission, not just a job. They want to build institutions that will survive them. They have a concrete set of goals they want to achieve. Political power and financial wealth are at most by-products of their public service.

In short, effective public officials are driven by a vision.

Tip #1. DEVELOP A CLEAR AND UNDERSTANDABLE VISION.

When Mark J. Green took office as New York City's first public advocate on January 1, 1994, he had a greater challenge than most public officials. Although the City Charter made the newly created post second in line to the mayor, few New Yorkers considered him the second most powerful official in the city. In fact, Green's office was widely perceived as ceremonial.

The public advocate position was created to replace the city council president but was weakened in the process. Green presided over city council meetings and served as a "go-between" or ombudsman for citizens and their government. But while the former city council president controlled a staff of 65 and an annual budget of $3.7 million, Green's staff and budget were cut by about one-third. Worse, under its new name, few citizens understood Green's job.

Green knew that an effective vision captures, in an attention-getting fashion, the dream of what an organization wishes to become. He needed something that not only would be understandable but would help him define the newly created post.

Green decided he would search out obstacles and deliver solutions to make New York's government more responsive to its citizens. As a proactive official, he would answer any complaints citizens had about their government, from trash collection to broken traffic lights. Green, who previously worked for Ralph Nader, pledged to be chief advocate for city residents.

To spread his vision, Green met with business groups, government officials, and local citizens. In his first year alone, he issued more than twenty reports on issues ranging from problems with the lifeguard training program to wheelchair accessibility of the city's mass transit system. He even launched a study to make certain city services available on the Internet.

A clear vision was Green's most important tool. "How do I implement anything?" Green asked. "Through the power of persuasion. The strength of my office is that it's exhortatory. The weakness of my office is that it's exhortatory. You mobilize public and political support around a good idea. And you hope you can have some impact."

Green did. He often changed the course of debate in the city council and even propelled national issues such as the lack of supervision of overworked medical residents in city hospitals. The platform was working, and by the end of his first term, Green was raising money for a possible bid for U.S. Senate.

Tip #2: PREACH FROM YOUR PULPIT.

When Larry Fuchs took over the Florida Department of Revenue in 1990, the previous director had resigned in disgrace, accused of ordering a tax investigation of her husband's political enemy. The agency was a model of government inefficiency—too many forms, too many regulations, and very few satisfied customers. About the only people pleased with the department's service were deadbeats who didn't pay their taxes.

"Contrary to popular belief, it's not impossible to change government even if limited to one four-year term," Fuchs reflected. "But many public officials fail because they have no idea of what they want to do and their employees sense this immediately."

Fuchs's vision sought to transform the 5,000-employee department into the most efficient revenue collection office in the nation. His challenge was to link that vision to individual departmental objectives and communicate it throughout the organization. For example, secretaries and tax return auditors had very different roles. But Fuchs needed each to understand how their jobs fit within his plan.

While a vision may begin with one person, it requires acceptance from many to move an organization; it must be preached regularly by everyone.

"We put together a damn good team," Fuchs said. "In order for a culture change to take hold you must seize every available opportunity to voice your vision. I recruited disciples to preach my reform message to workers throughout the department."

Every day these people would communicate Fuchs's vision to employees. They would show how changing a process here or eliminating a step there could save time and money.

It didn't happen overnight, but the Florida revenue department became known as a model of user-friendly government to be copied around the nation. In 1995, it was named the best-run tax department in the country by the national Federation of Tax Administrators. "It was a hands-down, no quibble decision," said an organization spokesperson. "All of the judges agreed almost immediately that Florida was the winner."

An efficient tax department may never make Larry Fuchs a popular public official, especially around April 15. But Fuchs did what many public officials have tried—he preached his vision, changed the attitudes of his staff, and harnessed their energy to achieve his goal.

Tip #3: CREATE A SENSE OF URGENCY.

To change an agency's direction, effective public officials must convince employees that achieving the vision is crucial to citizens and time is critical. For Labor Secretary Robert Reich, change was driven by a competitive global economy that had turned the American middle class into the "anxious class."

During the previous decade, Reich had written seven books and more than two hundred articles outlining the crisis facing America's workers in the global economy. Now it had become even more dire. To Reich, the American workforce was not adequately prepared for the challenge. It was the country's most urgent problem. "Americans are working harder for less and are more anxious about their jobs and their children's futures," he told his staff.

After twelve years in exile at Harvard University, Reich finally helped a Democrat win the presidency in 1992. In past elections he had advised Senator Gary Hart, former vice president Walter Mondale, and Governor Michael Dukakis in their bids for the White House. None came close to winning. Now his former schoolmate Bill Clinton had been elected president and named Reich as his secretary of labor.

"I've always been on Bill Clinton's short list," joked the four-foot, ten-inch professor.

The job was not a small one. As labor secretary, Reich was finally able to do more than write about the problem. His takeover would transform a low-profile cabinet department into a force to revive the American Dream. To verbalize his vision, he started calling himself the "secretary of the American workforce" and the "central banker of the nation's greatest resource."

"A generation ago, most Americans could expect to find decent work right out of high school, and many could hold the same job until retirement," Reich wrote. "That old economy is disappearing." Reich was particularly concerned about the less educated, those with only a high school diploma. "Their real wages have been sinking for years, with no end in sight."

"He is being heard," said Representative David Obey (D-WI). "It is the job of the Secretary of Labor to be out in the forefront, on the ramparts sounding the alarms."

Although as a university professor Reich managed just one employee and a few part-time research assistants, he now had a staff of more than eighteen thousand and an annual budget of $35 billion. To motivate the department's employees, Reich required not just his uncanny ability to communicate. He needed the staff to understand how important their work was to the American people.

To demonstrate the urgency, Reich embraced a clear vision that included First Jobs, New Jobs, Better Jobs. The agency would assist young people to move from school to work, help unemployed workers find the training they needed for new jobs, and foster an improved labor-management climate for better workplaces. If the department did these things, Reich believed, the American Dream might survive for his two young sons, Adam and Sam.

To stress further his vision's urgency, Reich signed a "performance agreement" with President Clinton promising that the department would make significant progress in these areas during the next four years. Each assistant secretary received a copy of the agreement, and a letter explaining the necessity of meeting the goals was distributed to all employees.

Reich's deputy, Thomas P. Glynn, used a similar strategy when he headed the Massachusetts Bay Transit Authority. "I've seen these work before," Glynn said. "You've got to get employees mobilized behind the mission." The problem with most government agencies, he added, is that "the leadership never tells them where they want to get to."

Reich's actions raised the department's profile. By creating a sense of urgency, his message was heard.

Tip #4: PUT 'EM ON A PEDESTAL.

Even with a clear idea of what a new top official wants, career government workers need role models. Highlighting individuals who work toward a public official's vision personalizes the crusade.

Connecticut Treasurer Chris Burnham used this tool well. As his first year in office came to an end, Burnham asked all employees to submit nominations for Employee of the Year. All civil service staff were eligible, but the winner would be the person who did the most to help achieve his vision.

The winner had helped move seventy-five Treasury employees into new office space at a savings of more than $250,000 in rent and overhead. When Burnham initially asked for the move, he was told that it would take at least six months. A career bureaucrat gave Burnham an impressive array of excuses: They needed to find architects, space planners, movers, time for the phone company to switch the phones and install a new computer network, and so on.

Burnham shook his head in disgust. This was not how the finest public investment bank should be run. He turned to Mike Last, a junior staffer who had impressed many Burnham senior aides. It was unusual to assign such an important task to a lower-level employee. Yet Last got the job done in just six weeks.

At the awards ceremony, the other employees cheered for their colleague. They knew how hard Last had worked to achieve the new boss's goal. He deserved the award. More important, his work ethic personified Burnham's vision. By putting Last on a pedestal, Burnham created a role model for others to follow.

Tip #5: STEP BACK AND REMEMBER THE BIG PICTURE.

The biggest vision "blinder" is the crush of day-to-day events. Managing in government—even more than the private sector—often means moving from one crisis to the next. In such a chaotic environment, public officials need to set aside time to remove themselves from the daily hustle and think only about the big picture and why they got into government in the first place.

Joseph Nye knows this lesson well, having served as a national security official in two administrations.

"What you have is the tyranny of the in-box," Nye said. "If you go into office and say, 'Boy, this is fascinating, and I'm just pleased to be here,' the staff will steer you in whatever direction they want. Your in-box will overwhelm you, and you'll be like a leaf in wind. Crises will come up, and you'll be driven by the in-box. So, getting your eyes above the in-box—and driving it and not letting it drive you—is difficult.

"Having a vision is the most important thing," Nye counsels. "Set priorities and stick to them. Check your progress regularly. You must make clear to your staff that these are priorities."

But even with a clear, well-thought-out vision, it's easy to lose track of the big picture in the day-to-day job of governing. To help new public officials keep focused, Nye offers several insights.

"You have to impress upon your closest staff how you want to handle your time on the margins, that you want to go to the meeting that's on your priority list, not necessarily the one that's a little sexier. You also have to keep yourself on course and remind yourself where you are on your priorities. You can be easily seduced by other things.

"Also, you have to build time into your regular calendar for some forward thinking time," Nye said. "Stepping back from everyday events helps you keep perspective. It's not easy to stay on track. It sounds easy when you're at a distance, but when you're in the middle of a crisis and drinking from a fire hose, it's very hard to keep your eye on the priorities."

7

Changing of the Guard

The best leader is the one who has the sense enough to pick good men
to do what he wants done, and the self-restraint to keep from med-
dling with them while they do it.
                                        —*Theodore Roosevelt,*
                                           U.S. president

Moving In, Moving Out

There could hardly exist quieter, more discreet employees than the
White House travel office personnel. They work in the same building
as the president but handle no state secrets, make no public policy.
They make travel reservations, mostly for the media. Their work
went largely unnoticed until the Clinton administration took over.
The new team cast attention on the shy little office in a way only a
plane crash could have. And the disaster that followed left almost as
much wreckage.

Seemingly, little could be less complicated than transitioning the
travel office between regimes. It had happened many times before
without so much as a fender bender. But whoever said takeovers were
simple has never traveled in the rarefied air of government.

David Watkins's first government job came with the Clinton
administration in January 1993. An advertising executive in Little
Rock, Watkins became assistant to the president for management and
administration; he ran White House operations. As Bush administra-

tion political appointees packed their boxes, Watkins and his aides unpacked theirs. A new government was coming to town.

By Inauguration Day, Watkins's group needed office space reconfigured, computer networks installed, and a new telephone system ordered. In addition, one of Watkins's chief duties was to help keep his boss's campaign promise to reduce White House staff by 25 percent. He had to find those cuts.

Watkins arrived at the job on the strength of managing Clinton's campaign operations, one of the most efficient and tightly run crusades in history. But that was campaigning. This was governing. Watkins couldn't wait. "I wanted," he said, "to be part of history."

Certainly not, however, in the way that developed.

Catherine Cornelius, an eager twenty-five-year-old aide Watkins hired from the campaign, urged him to look for staff reductions at the travel office. Cornelius, too, had no government experience, but she was related to someone who did—she was a distant cousin of the president. Notably, Cornelius also had done commendable work arranging travel during the campaign. She had expertise and wanted to make a contribution.

The seven-person travel operation was managed by Billy R. Dale, a career bureaucrat who had worked at the White House for nearly thirty-two years. Although the employees served at the pleasure of the president, the office was traditionally seen as nonpolitical and of little significance to the leader of the free world. Most new administrations, Democrat and Republican, kept the existing staff.

A few weeks after the takeover, Cornelius gave Watkins an eight-page report detailing travel office problems. She had conducted an undercover investigation, secretly copying files and eavesdropping on staff conversations. Cornelius documented an appallingly inept operation with heavy suspicion of wrongdoing. She found that no accounting system existed, despite the hundreds of thousands of dollars that might flow through the office in any given month. Incredibly, the money was kept in drawers, and, it was later found, even in Dale's personal checking account. (Dale was later acquitted of federal embezzlement charges.)

Cornelius proposed a solution: she could run the travel office. Watkins, however, felt Cornelius lacked experience and put off making a decision.

Soon, however, Watkins received a phone call from Harry Thomason, the president's friend and part owner of an air charter company. Thomason independently told Watkins that the travel office employees were incompetent, the office was mismanaged, and he should do something about it. Because of Thomason's closeness to the president, Watkins took notice. He ordered an outside audit and management review. The scathing thirteen-page report confirmed many of the management problems that Cornelius found. The travel office was in a tailspin.

After discussions with lawyers, Watkins dismissed travel office staff, citing the president's campaign goal to reinvent government. On May 19, 1993, the seven employees were asked to pack and leave by the end of the day.

What should have been the end of a transition, however, was just the beginning of a scandal that plagued the administration throughout Clinton's first term. Although Watkins had every right to dismiss the non–civil service workers, the next morning's papers told a different story: Watkins had irreverently fired seven career employees to benefit the president's cousin and close friend. The press obtained leaked copies of Cornelius's memo proposing to put her in charge of the travel office and another note pitching Thomason's company for White House travel business. Most journalists had dealt with the travel office personally for years and considered the employees among the most efficient at 1600 Pennsylvania Avenue.

Then the White House made a bad situation worse. Acting as if still in a campaign—and not in a takeover—the administration escalated the charges against the travel office staff to prove their incompetence. White House officials told stories of the dismissed workers' "lavish lifestyles, minimal work, kickbacks and missing money." White House press secretary Dee Dee Myers alleged serious wrongdoing on Dale's part and even commented that the Federal Bureau of Investigation was starting an inquiry. Not only did this portrayal conflict with the media's view of the travel workers, but the very mention of using the FBI—a supposedly independent law enforcement agency—in the investigation increased press scrutiny.

The travel office firings continued as front-page news for days. Republicans charged political cronyism and vowed to initiate congressional hearings. A week later, recognizing that it had gone too far in its public statements, the administration tried once more to calm the media, announcing that it would find government jobs for five of the nonmanagerial staff members and conduct an investigation of the dismissals.

The reaction nationwide was harsh. The takeover screw-up was replayed on Sunday morning political talk shows and newspaper editorial pages. Said one: "In a single week of political hari-kiri, the Clinton White House fired its travel office staff, dabbled in character assassination, then rehired most of the staff and vowed to investigate itself."

In the end, the savings Watkins originally hoped he would achieve by reinventing the travel office disappeared. The mess actually cost the taxpayers more money. Five of the seven fired employees received six months of paid leave and were given jobs elsewhere in the federal government. Congress approved $500,000 to help pay some of their legal fees. And at least three government investigations into the matter continued years after the original firings took place. "When you add this thing up, it's going to cost hundreds and hundreds of thousands of dollars," said Representative Frank Wolf (R-VA).

THE PUBLIC'S first view of a new official in action comes during the takeover. The change from one administration to the next can set the public's attitudes about their new government for the rest of a term. For Clinton, the travel office problems contributed significantly to the administration's difficulties in its early months. And the resulting fallout plagued the administration four years later during the reelection campaign.

Takeovers are never easy. Staffers entering government from the campaign war room must switch from electioneering to governing. Those coming from private-sector jobs must learn the business of government. Each changeover causes newcomers to be confused, career staff to scramble, and some former political appointees to try to bury themselves in the bureaucracy in an attempt to find permanent jobs.

But staff changes are crucial to taking control of a public office. Elected officials deserve to have their own people. As the top managers in government, they ensure that the voters' will is carried out and get the blame when they don't deliver. They must recruit the right people to successfully implement their vision. At the same time, new public officials must work to gain the trust of career staff. Skillfully merging the old with the new defines a smooth transition. Without it, progress on a public official's agenda will stall.

Problems such as those of the travel office are common during a takeover. David Watkins broke no laws in dismissing the seven employees. While the civil service system protects honest bureaucrats from the whims of politically appointed managers, the travel office staff served at the pleasure of the president. And since the office was severely mismanaged, which even the administration's critics recognized, few could blame Watkins for wanting his own staff.

"We need to get those people out," Hillary Clinton allegedly told Watkins. "We need our people in."

As Watkins learned, it's not always that elementary.

Cronyism frequently traps new public officials, and the media, always hungry for a juicy story, look for it. After a campaign, many who helped win an election feel they are owed something in return. The travel office review was crawling with self-interested campaign staffers. Cornelius wanted to run the office. Thomason wanted business for his company. Both had something to gain from the dismissals.

"One of the greatest but least utilized tests of a leader's wisdom and prudence is the quality of those with whom he chooses to surround himself," observed former senator Gary Hart. "The leader must know that those in whom he places his trust will wisely advise him, faithfully execute his wishes, and diligently carry out his policies."

Cleveland mayor Michael White agreed: "I can get 100 bureaucrats who can fill this position. I'm looking for leaders, people who are willing to challenge the status quo, people who can take risks, go in when there is a problem and rip it apart and put it back together and deliver a good service."

The takeover is difficult enough when a new government manager, like Watkins, has complete freedom to dismiss workers and replace them with his own. How can it be done when the system severely limits the ability of a public official to recruit his own staff?

Shifting Gears

When Emil H. Frankel was named commissioner of Connecticut's Department of Transportation in 1991, he took over an agency that knew how to build. The department had nearly completed a ten-year, $8 billion construction program—a record that left staffers feeling proud. The state's 5,000-plus-mile latticework of roads and 3,600 bridges were in their best shape ever.

But the 1990s would be different. Connecticut was in its worst economic condition in half a century. The state's fiscal crisis meant no more large-scale transportation programs. Frankel made sure his new workers understood that the department's vision would change with the times.

"The era of building is over," he recalled telling the staff in his first meeting. "In this new era we must manage the system effectively. I pounded at that message constantly."

Managing the system now meant making sure the trains ran properly, potholes were filled, and bridges were regularly inspected for wear and tear. It wasn't a glamorous vision, but it needed to be done. Frankel's challenge was to convince his department that he was right.

As if the loss of high-profile building projects wasn't bad enough for the department staff, Frankel didn't arrive exactly loaded with transportation experience. A lawyer by trade, he mainly developed real estate. His only prior government experience was as a young aide on Senator Jacob Javits's staff in Washington, D.C., where he handled few transportation issues.

"There was a lot of dismay when I was appointed," said Frankel, stroking his now-silver hair. The department staff had been very accustomed to former commissioner Bill Burns, who led the agency for a decade. "He was a good manager; people felt comfortable that he wouldn't disturb things too much. And now, oh my God, we've got this lawyer coming in who doesn't know that much about transportation."

To steer the department in his direction, Frankel needed his own people at the wheel. Then came the shock. In an agency of almost five thousand employees, he had the authority to replace only seven—six deputy commissioners and an executive assistant. These were the only appointed positions in the entire department; the rest were career civil service.

Although Frankel's new vision required that everyone from maintenance garage managers to accountants at DOT headquarters understand their new roles, he had little authority to bring in his own people. He needed a plan, and he knew he had little time to make it work.

Frankel dismissed one top staffer immediately, the first deputy commissioner who traditionally acted like a chief of staff. Frankel questioned whether this holdover, who had served as a gatekeeper for the previous boss, would be loyal to the new guy in town. On his first day as commissioner, Frankel "told him to start looking for new work."

Frankel's next step was basically to do nothing. He kept the other deputy commissioners in place, though everyone knew it was a probationary period. It was a calculated move to ensure a smooth takeover.

"I wasn't going to keep all of them," Frankel said. "But I wasn't quite ready to replace them. They do the job every day. They wanted to be assured that I wasn't going to get in the way—to interfere with their ability to get the job done. They had a whole set of procedures to make the roads clear and the trains run on time." Frankel used this transition period to understand how the department operated and learn valuable lessons from the old guard.

To gain their trust, Frankel made sure the entire staff understood that he valued their work and contributions over the years. Although he was part of a new administration—and had close ties to the new governor—he was not the enemy. He singled out his predecessor for special praise. "I went out of my way to compliment Bill Burns. He had been there ten years. A lot of the people were his people. I didn't do a public event that he wasn't invited to and that I didn't acknowledge his role in building the state's infrastructure.

"It was a very conscious way to create loyalties with people who viewed themselves as his people," Frankel said. "I wasn't going to badmouth the guy who promoted them."

Finally, ignoring the lessons of most management books he had read, Frankel used a strategy that can only be called micromanagement. "Everyone dealt with me directly. I wanted to be told everything. I saw every single piece of mail that came to the department. I saw and read it and decided who it should go to. It was a terrific way to get educated on every issue."

The unorthodox move also allowed Frankel to reduce the risk of employees acting contrary to his vision. "The civil service soon developed a view that they couldn't get anything past me."

As he assumed more control, Frankel began recruiting "his people" to the department and letting them do more of the work. He hired an executive assistant, a "big-picture thinker," who helped Frankel keep up on the latest trends in transportation policy. This aide was Frankel's "vision protector," the staffer who would always keep his eye on what the new team was trying to accomplish and never let them get sidetracked.

The deputy commissioners' probationary period proved valuable in another way. After studying their work habits and skills, Frankel reappointed three of them. Each brought different strengths. One of the deputies, Frankel felt, "was the best manager in the place." Another was the consummate bureaucrat, "a warhorse who knew how to get things through the bureaucracy." The third served as deputy for highways. "I knew I would have trouble keeping the highway construction going without him," Frankel said.

By taking time before making wholesale changes, Frankel gained loyalty that couldn't exist when he first took over. By keeping three deputies on board, Frankel sent a powerful message to the career staff. By looking inside the agency for some of his top aides, Frankel boosted morale.

But boosting morale is different from changing direction, and Frankel could not alter the department's course by just replacing a few people at the top. So he initiated a major restructuring, remodeling the functions of the agency's bureaus to meet the new mission. Instead of building more and bigger roads, under Frankel the department would manage the system better and encourage greater cooperation between the air, road, maritime, and rail modes of travel.

Frankel saw other hidden advantages to the restructuring as well. It allowed him to put better-qualified people in important positions. "In his first few months, he paid close attention to which career employees were the best workers," remembered Erik Bergman, a transportation staffer. "The star employees found themselves with greater authority after the restructuring. In many cases Frankel chose younger, more energetic employees."

Now Frankel was in position to move forward on the agency's new mission, from building to managing.

THE TAKEOVER of Connecticut's transportation department couldn't have been more different from the one at the White House travel office. Emil Frankel and David Watkins both had authority to replace seven employees, but for Frankel that meant just seven out of five thousand. Yet Frankel successfully managed the transition, took control of his agency, and changed its mission. In contrast, the travel office scandal derailed the president's early agenda, and fallout rained throughout President Clinton's term.

Every public official has his or her own approach to the takeover. And every transition is different. Richard N. Haass served as a national security aide to President Bush after stints at the departments of State and Defense. "Some moments call out for dramatic change—say after a major scandal or failure that precipitated your arrival, or after an election in which the winning side gained a mandate for change," Haass observes.

An official who takes over a troubled agency—a department racked by scandal or unable to carry out its basic mission—might require dramatic changes. And newly appointed managers with untainted reputations are perfect in such situations. "You can use the Western movie analogy," said Charlie Royer, the former mayor of Seattle. "If a town needs to be cleaned up, you get a gunslinger from somewhere else."

Frankel, however, took over an agency that functioned relatively well. He had a different vision for the department and needed a transition strategy to implement it. Frankel moved slowly, learned about his agency from those who worked there, and made his moves, however few, when he was ready. And he wouldn't have done it any differently. "In retrospect, the appointments fit my style," he said. "It was probably the right pace of change."

Notes Haass: "As is often the case, no single rule applies to all situations. The style and tenor of any transition must be tailored to the circumstances; your first order of business is to decide whether a message of continuity or change needs to be sent to those both inside and outside the organization."

But changing people is only part of a takeover. The impact of a new public official is sometimes not felt until the direction of government changes as well.

The Gamble

As Louisiana governor Mike Foster stood on the Baton Rouge Old Capitol grounds in January 1996, ready to lead the state into the twenty-first century, he reflected on his grandfather, who as governor from 1882 to 1900 led the Pelican State into the twentieth century.

"Governor Foster was a man of courage," Foster said. "He ran gambling from our state and rid Louisiana of the corrupt Louisiana Lottery Corporation. My grandfather was a man of vision. I come here today with a desire to make my grandfather proud."

In the previous few years, however, Foster's grandfather was likely turning in his grave. Gambling had returned to Louisiana, at the behest of outgoing governor Edwin Edwards, the four-term chief executive Foster beat the previous November. The flamboyant Edwards brought betting back to New Orleans.

"This day marks more than the orderly transition of government for our state and people," said Foster, whose plump figure and uninspiring demeanor made him an unlikely visionary. "It marks the end of an era."

Andy Kopplin wanted to believe Foster. Kopplin, a Democrat, had just taken the biggest risk of his young political career. A former aide to Senator Lloyd Bentsen (D-TX), he left his post with President Clinton's Americorps to become policy director to the Republican governor. Watching the inaugural speech, Kopplin wondered whether he was doing the right thing by working with a man in the other party.

"There are just two kinds of politicians in Louisiana: reformers and nonreformers," a friend assured Kopplin. "Foster is a reformer."

Kopplin wanted to be convinced. "Governing isn't about political parties," he told himself, "it's about doing the right thing for the citizens you serve."

Getting employees to come on board was not Foster's only challenge. A bigger job was to convince staffers like Kopplin that he would do the right thing, to keep them focused and motivated to implement his reforms. Anything short of their total commitment would leave Foster with his good family name soiled.

The reform started with the changing of personnel. But before the new governor took office, several of Edwards's political appointees hid themselves in civil service jobs. If Foster was going to implement real change, he had to "find the buried bodies and reverse the abuse of the civil service system," Kopplin recalled. Ending the use of government for personal gain sat at the core of Foster's reform agenda.

Foster focused only on the agencies most in need of change. For example, he asked the department heads of economic development and corrections to stay on the job. "They were doing a good job, and the governor saw no reason to replace them," Kopplin said. "He wasn't planning major changes to those agencies. And since they were from the previous administration, it was an olive branch to Democratic members of the legislature."

Foster wanted to move quickly on a reform agenda to give his staff direction and belief that their leader meant action. Unfortunately for Foster, Louisiana government is not built for speed. In even-numbered years, the legislative session would not start until late spring and the only issues that could be debated involved the state budget. Broader issues, including most of the reforms Foster wanted to introduce, only come up in alternate years.

To Foster, Kopplin, and the rest of the staff, this was unacceptable. The governor had just won the election with a decisive 63 percent of the vote. The people wanted change, yet the governor couldn't enact much of it without legislative action. And without legislative action, he jeopardized losing his support. Foster had to find a way to give voters the changes they wanted early in his term.

So Foster took a chance that made him look like a bigger gambler than the former governor. Not only did Foster risk infuriating the part-time legislators by calling them back to Baton Rouge for a twenty-seven-day special session, but he handed them 138 items for action, from banning riverboat casinos to lawsuit reform. Dealing with so many issues in a special session had never happened before. Foster put his entire reform agenda on red and spun Louisiana's political roulette wheel.

Kopplin thought it was a risk worth taking. "The voters were desperate for reform," he said. "The special session set the expectation and tone about what the new administration was about. The governor's actions in the session spoke clearly about the intent of his government and how he would govern."

And actions speak louder than words. On the morning the special session began, Kopplin read the newspaper headline: "Era of Reform Begins." He knew he had done the right thing.

In less than four weeks, Foster secured major lawsuit reform legislation, a new ethics law, campaign finance reform, new insurance laws, and higher-education reforms. About the only initiative Foster lost was his attempt to pass a constitutional amendment to ban gambling. He promised to bring the issue back to the legislature again.

"If they don't do it constitutionally, this thing is going to be here every year," he said. "And you show me a legislator who is going to be able to survive a vote on gambling every year for the next three years." The special session was a tremendous success.

The push told Foster's staff they were working toward reform. The new administration and the new philosophy were in place. The transition was over. "Strategically, we've done a terrific job," Kopplin said. "We set the stage for what this administration is about. Our people are in. Now we must begin some of the harder nuts-and-bolts issues of implementing the governor's reforms. We're right where we want to be."

RECRUITING new people is the first step toward fulfilling campaign promises. But government is more than just a random collection of new public officials. Mike Foster knew that the takeover would not be complete until his staff accepted his vision and his government started moving in the promised direction.

Foster's achievement can be measured through Andy Kopplin, a skeptic who came on board unsure what he had gotten himself into. Foster knew that staffers like Kopplin—not to mention voters— would measure his success greatly in the first one hundred days. While the number of days may be only an artificial time limit, a public official's successes and failures during this time set the tenure for the rest of the term.

"I think 100 days is a metaphor for making the system work," former Clinton aide George Stephanopoulos said. "And when you say you're going to get something done within 100 days, what you're saying is, watch me, test me, see if I'm keeping my promises."

Lyndon Johnson also knew the importance of the honeymoon period. "Every day that I'm in office . . . I'll be losing part of my ability to be influential," Johnson said to his congressional liaison officers after his inauguration in 1965. "So I want you guys to get off your asses and do everything possible to get my program passed as soon as possible, before the aura and halo that surround me disappear."

Calling the special legislative session was just the move for Foster to signal his reform intentions. It cemented people like Kopplin, who wanted action, firmly on his side. That helped finalize the changing of the guard. The victories, then, that came from the special session provided proof that Foster's government was on the move.

Takeover Tips

Staffing government is no easy task. Complicated hiring procedures, media scrutiny, and possible confirmation hearings make even the simplest personnel choices more difficult. In addition, new government officials must quickly learn to balance the expertise of career staff with their loyalty.

"Competence is achieved through experience and grows with time on the job. Loyalty attaches to a leader, a party, or a principle," Elliott Richardson writes. "When these are changed with a change in administration, a certain tension between competence and loyalty is inevitable. Just as a professional who stays on from one administration to the next cannot be expected to become a true believer in both, so the loyalist newly brought on board cannot be expected to possess the savvy of an old hand."

William Seidman agrees. He served as chairman of the Federal Deposit Insurance Corporation during the agency's greatest challenge: cleaning up the multibillion-dollar string of bank failures in the late 1980s. To get the job done, Seidman needed the right people to work for him. "No executive can succeed without good people," Seidman reflected. "Good staff cannot save a bad executive, but bad staff can pull down an otherwise competent one."

After a takeover, the permanent civil service staff may have trouble adjusting to the new direction voters chose. Likewise, the newly arrived management needs to learn how government functions. Only when they learn to work together can the new government begin to work.

Tip #1: CHOOSE EXPERIENCE BEFORE POLITICAL CONNECTIONS.

Fortunately for the newly arrived government official, there is typically no shortage of résumés of people looking for jobs. Unfortunately, many of the résumés have notes attached from legislators, agency heads, and other politically powerful people. Yet effective public officials try to ignore political pressure when choosing their staff.

William J. Bennett, the "drug czar" in the Bush administration, was vigilant in keeping political hacks out of his office. "We're a small office," he said on NBC's *Meet the Press*, "and I don't have any room for nice political people who don't know anything about drugs." The public official who succeeds in choosing experience before political connections is rare.

Remarkably, until 1993, the Federal Emergency Management Agency (FEMA) never had an experienced director. Instead, the government office that aids Americans in times of perhaps their greatest need—after hurricanes, floods, earthquakes, fires, and other natural disasters—served as a refugee camp for political hacks. It was a backwater agency where most presidents repaid political loyalists with cushy jobs. The temptation was great.

But during the 1992 presidential election, FEMA became the subject of national ridicule. A series of unusually harsh storms, the Los Angeles riots, and an especially clumsy response to Hurricane Andrew in Florida drew anger and disbelief. "Currently, FEMA is like a patient in triage," wrote the National Academy of Public Administration. "The President and Congress must decide whether to treat it or let it die."

President Clinton, who used FEMA mismanagement as a campaign issue, vowed not to make the same mistakes. The agency had 2,600 employees, an $800 million budget, and an important mission. He would appoint a disaster recovery chief who knew how to do the job.

Clinton's choice, James Lee Witt, was the first director of FEMA who actually had disaster recovery experience. Witt had served Clinton as head of the Arkansas Office of Emergency Services, but he got the job based on his effectiveness.

Because of his experience, Witt knew what changes the agency needed. On his first day, Witt waited outside the headquarters and greeted every staff member. He increased staff responsiveness to disaster victims. He met regularly with regional directors and solicited input from the lowest levels on how to ensure that the agency would live up to its new motto: "People helping people." He even distributed surveys to disaster victims to solicit feedback.

The improvements earned notice. In February 1996, President Clinton called Witt's work "a breathtaking turnaround" and bestowed cabinet rank on FEMA. "FEMA is now a model disaster relief agency," the president said. "In some corners, it is the most successful part of the federal government today."

Tip #2: WATCH YOUR BACK.

New York's governors have a simple rule for their lieutenant governors: Remember who's boss. It's an important principle. Whenever the governor leaves the state, the lieutenant governor takes command. Governor George E. Pataki thought he had a loyal deputy who shared his vision when he plucked Elizabeth McCaughey Ross from obscurity to be his number two. He could not have been more wrong.

Ross had worked as a researcher at the Manhattan Institute, a conservative New York think tank, where she wrote articles on health care reform. She was smart, glamorous, and, significantly, a woman. Pataki felt that balancing the ticket with a woman would help him beat incumbent Mario Cuomo. But rather than traveling the traditional route of choosing an elected local official who had worked her way up the party apparatus, Pataki chose Ross. She was not a politician and had not worked in government, a perceived asset given the negative climate toward public officials.

But a decision initially seen as bold and unconventional soon developed into a terrible mistake. The first signs of trouble came soon after taking office, when Ross took public positions opposing Pataki on two key issues, abortion and ballot access. Ross favored restricting abortion; the governor did not. Ross favored easing ballot access rules to allow more candidates in the primaries; the governor did not. Ross even traveled across the state giving speeches that made the difference clear. But the final straw was when Ross remained standing after introducing Pataki before his 1996 State of the State speech. Pataki aides felt that she guilelessly tried to steal the spotlight from their boss.

Had Ross made her opposition known to Pataki in private meetings, the relationship might have worked. All public officials need staff who will critically question their judgment and advise them on tough issues. No appointee who fawns over the boss serves him well. As a policy wonk, Ross probably had more to offer her boss than most previous New York lieutenant governors. But once Pataki made policy decisions, he rightfully expected Ross's support.

With the Pataki-Ross feud public, the intensity and embarrassment grew. Astonishingly, Ross arranged a series of media interviews, charging that Pataki aides were destroying her reputation, leaking unfavorable stories, even trying to humiliate her by delaying her arrival at major events. "This is the essence of McCarthyism," she said. "Go back and look at what Joe McCarthy did. It's exactly the same."

Ross was soon banished from the governor's inner circle of advisers. The state party chair even suggested barring the second-ranking party official as a delegate at the 1996 national Republican convention. Unwilling to take a hint, Ross remained firm. "I have no intention of quitting," she said.

The most critical quality for any appointee is loyalty. Disloyalty in a public official's staff corrodes the leader's authority more profoundly than opponents' political attacks. It shows a manager's inability to make important decisions. Pataki completely misjudged his deputy and paid for it in public embarrassment and management headaches.

Tip #3: VALUE CAREER EMPLOYEES.

Too often newly appointed officials thumb their noses at the career staff. Careerists are viewed as overly protective of the old way of doing things. In many cases, the criticism is accurate. But successful public officials realize that career employees provide the institutional memory and administrative expertise to help political appointees avoid repeating old mistakes. And they take advantage of the asset.

As a banker, Frank Newman knew something about managing money. He served as chief financial officer at Bank of America before President Clinton named him U.S. Treasury undersecretary for domestic finance in 1993. So when America's currency was redesigned to protect against counterfeiting, most expected Newman to tap a fellow banker to manage the process. Instead he chose career bureaucrat Dave Lybryk.

Although he was the third-ranking Treasury official, Newman had little authority to hire his own people. To accomplish his goals, he needed to identify and bring loyal civil servants into his inner circle by giving them important assignments. If Newman simply disregarded their value, as many officials do (though few admit it), he would get nothing done.

Few tasks could be more consequential than rolling out a new currency. Not only must American citizens have full faith in the new banknotes but Treasury officials would have to work through many countries' banking systems. The change would carry huge fiscal implications from Moscow, Idaho, to Moscow, Russia. And, Newman suspected, few could do a better job than Lybryk.

Lybryk entered government service in the last months of the Reagan administration. He saw two administrations come and go before Newman arrived. "My experience with most of the political appointees who come in is that they are not particularly good at managing," Lybryk says. "When it came time to make sure the place ran better or functioned better, we've had very few people who have kept that in mind."

Newman was different. He turned to career staff for important assignments. "He gave people responsibility and let them into the decision-making process," Lybryk recalled.

And Lybryk was different as well. He managed to roll out the new currency flawlessly. So flawlessly that Newman named Lybryk as his special assistant, a post that typically goes to a political appointee. And when Newman moved up to the number two position at Treasury, he brought Lybryk along.

Tip #4: RESIST THE TEMPTATION TO CRITICIZE PREDECESSORS.

While transitions from one political party to another sometimes get nasty, it rarely helps to criticize the previous administration. Slinging charges at former management can alienate holdover staff and the public.

When the Clinton administration resorted to attacking the character of travel office employees, the strategy backfired and kept the administration from making progress on its agenda. In Connecticut, Emil Frankel took the opposite route and found that praising his predecessor's contributions over the years helped gain the loyalty of career staff. The move helped him change his department's mission.

Tim McTaggart also believed criticism rarely pays. When McTaggart took over as Delaware's banking commissioner in 1994, he inherited an agency with no one truly in charge. An acting commissioner served temporarily for the previous six months, but little got done. The agency needed a jump-start.

"Most political appointees realize that there is a finite time to make changes once they take office," McTaggart said. "They want to get on with it."

But McTaggart's changes had to wait. First, he had to finish what his predecessor had never completed. Although state law required the agency to submit an annual report to the governor, it had not been done for two years. This, of course, made the previous management an easy target for McTaggart. Nonetheless, he cautions new public officials against taking aim.

"That is a losing strategy in the long run," he said. "In the career employees there is an institutional knowledge about mistakes that were made before. You'll need these people to help you avoid making the same mistakes again."

McTaggart entered during the middle of the governor's administration, so he had less reason to criticize the previous commissioner, an appointee of the same governor. No ideological shift or great change of direction was needed. But despite the friendly takeover, the temptation to badmouth the former guy still existed. Don't do it, McTaggart warns.

Tip #5: RESIGN IF NECESSARY.

Political appointees have the least job security of any public officials. Jobs last no longer than the elected officials who made the appointment. And since political appointees "serve at the pleasure" of elected officials, their stay often lasts much shorter than that. They must make the most of the time available.

With such constraints, some public officials quit rather than manage programs they don't believe in. Mary Jo Bane and Peter B. Edelman didn't wait for the end of President Clinton's first term to leave their jobs as assistant secretaries in the Department of Health and Human Services. They resigned to protest the president's signing of a welfare reform bill that they vigorously opposed and could not implement in good conscience. News of the resignations made the front page of most national newspapers.

"I had worked as hard as I could over the past thirty-plus years to reduce poverty," Edelman later wrote, and "in my opinion this bill moved in the opposite direction."

Bane and Edelman knew they could not effectively manage under those circumstances. By quitting, they burnished their reputations as managers who would lead only if they believed in their tasks. This not only gave them freedom to do what they felt was right, it also let underlings know they were not carrying out hollow policies no one believed in. Indeed, the opposite problem—officials staying in jobs everyone knows they don't support—erodes democracy and turns off the public.

Although not as common in America as in many European democracies, high-level resignations over principle have a long history. Attorney General Elliot Richardson quit rather than carry out President Nixon's order to fire the Watergate special prosecutor. Secretary of State Cyrus Vance resigned from the Carter administration after the president executed a military rescue attempt for the American hostages held in Iran. Vance disagreed with the policy and felt he had no choice but to resign.

Arnold Burns, U.S. deputy attorney general during the Reagan administration, also chose to leave over a policy dispute. "I could not permit my silence and my inaction to be construed as condonation. . . . With my tongue tied by the confidentiality demanded of me by law, there was only one way I could make a statement that something was wrong. I chose it. I resigned."

Sadly, many public officials dutifully carry out policies they know to be wrong. Memoirs of former public officials are filled with these disclosures. Defense Secretary Robert McNamara admits he disagreed with President Johnson over the escalation of the Vietnam War. Budget director David Stockman and his deputy Richard Darman write that they knew the Reagan tax cuts would balloon the deficit. Yet they proceeded with them and continued in their jobs. The public is not well served by such officials. They cannot possibly be effective managers of government.

The public deserves a government that believes in its own policies. Political appointees who find themselves at odds with elected leaders over serious issues and are unable to change their minds have an obligation to resign. Government can work only if public officials believe in the policies they are implementing.

8

Ending Bureaucracy as We Know It

The longer the title, the less important the job.
—*George McGovern, U.S. senator*

Runyon's Wreckage

Over time, the U.S. Postal Service has become one of the country's most bloated government bureaucracies. With some 750,000 employees, it ranks second in size only to the Pentagon. If it were a business, it would rank as twelfth largest in the nation and thirty-third largest in the world.

Cutting down such a behemoth and redirecting the workers would seem easy. After all, after years of curt window tellers, delayed deliveries, and enough embarrassing material to fill one hundred David Letterman monologues, things could hardly get worse.

Since the days of the Pony Express, the post office had become a place "where good performance is seldom recognized or rewarded, where reprimands for minor transgressions are issued at the drop of a hat and where poor performance is too often left unresolved," said Michigan senator Carl M. Levin. One government report ridiculed the postal service as caught in a "dysfunctional organizational culture." Worse, postal workers were literally killing each other. Since

1973, postal employees had turned guns on coworkers twenty-seven times, resulting in forty-eight deaths.

Things were bad, and this is the story of how they got worse.

In 1992, new postmaster general Marvin Runyon arrived as the streamlining business executive who raised the Tennessee Valley Authority from the dead by cutting the workforce by ten thousand. In the course of his career, Runyon had risen from automobile executive to "Carvin' Marvin" of Tennessee to, now, chief of the U.S. Postal Service. And one of the first things he did as mail boss was to cut thousands of employees.

Runyon's strategy was right. He hoped to remove stagnant workers, creating a more manageable bureaucracy that, rejuvenated by his structural changes, would attain his vision of an efficient postal service.

"We've got regions, divisions and headquarters. We've got redundancy," Runyon said. "When you fix that, you have people left over."

Runyon wanted to cut thirty thousand to forty thousand workers, most of them career managers who "don't touch the mail." These layers of management had ballooned dramatically over the years. Their job titles said it all: assistant postmaster general for philatelic and retail services and senior assistant postmaster general for human resources. The postal bureaucracy was stacked with bureau chiefs, deputy bureau chiefs, assistant bureau chiefs, and assistants to the deputy assistants.

With so many layers of career employees, the postmaster general had grown increasingly distant from the front lines of the mail service, and the front lines from him. Worse, Runyon was even more insulated from the citizens the post office served. To take control of his agency he needed to cut middle management positions. And few today argue against cutting paper-pushing bureaucrats.

So Runyon offered thousands of workers a lucrative buyout package: six months' pay for employees to hit the road and new jobs for selected people who stayed, with no pay cut.

Unfortunately for Runyon and anyone who enjoys on-time mail delivery, the wrong people took the deal. Nearly forty-eight thousand workers left. More than two thirds of these were carriers and clerks who do "touch" the mail. Thousands of lower-level postal workers who would rather quit than sort were given the chance to leave and did, putting the service in vital danger. One postal executive called the buyouts "institutional suicide." As the Christmas mail rush neared, disaster was delivered. To ensure that holiday cards and gifts arrived before Santa, the remaining carriers and clerks took on new duties and worked overtime. But few saw the problem coming, one senior postal official said, because many of the needed supervisors had left.

In Chicago, customers who had complained of late mail delivery for years stopped getting it altogether. Two hundred pounds of undelivered mail burned on a city street corner. One mailman stashed sacks of undelivered mail in his attic. More than twenty thousand pieces of undelivered mail were found hidden in a park.

"My magazines come months late, or they've been read already," complained one city resident. "I've had mail addressed to me that was stamped 'addressee unknown,' and my name is right there on the mailbox."

Postal inspectors conducted a test to determine the extent of the problem. They placed 119 first-class letters and priority parcels in mailboxes around Chicago. Although delivery within the city limits is expected in one day, just seventy-two pieces were delivered after three days. The remaining forty-seven pieces were later discovered in the dead letter office in St. Paul, Minnesota.

Runyon scrambled to correct the problem. But he had no solutions. Instead of increasing his command, Runyon's downsizing plan spun the postal service out of control. "This won't be fixed quickly," Runyon said in a town meeting with angry Chicago residents.

In fact, Runyon said it could take up to five years for Chicago mail delivery to be fixed. That infuriated Mayor Richard Daley.

"Welcome to the bureaucratic government," Daley said in a press conference. "I mean this guy must be living in never-never land. For him to say it's going to take five years to straighten out the post office problem in the city, we're talking about the year 2000. That's unbelievable. Why are we paying taxes?"

Daley then fired off a letter to President Clinton. But in case it never got delivered, he also gave copies to the press.

"It is unacceptable," Daley wrote. "You are part of an administration committed to reinventing government to better serve people. There is no justification for taking five years to fix a problem that should never have happened in the first place. In the real world, people go out of business when service declines like this."

One union boss compared the postal situation to a horror film: "We needed a surgeon, and we got Freddy Krueger."

An ineffective Freddy Krueger at that. Because of the growing volume of mail, Runyon needed not only to replace lost letter carriers but to add new ones. So by the end of 1994 the postal service employed more workers than when Runyon took the job. And instead of cutting bureaucracy to establish authority, Runyon lost control.

REMARKABLY, reformers actually created government bureaucracy as a solution to government's problems. Reformers wanted bureaucrats—career government professionals—to free the public sector from cronyism and favoritism and make it run smoothly. Instead of plum jobs or raises being given only to fat cat friends of the mayor or governor, specific criteria were established to level the playing field. The result, it was believed, would move government to a higher level of efficiency.

Perhaps the greatest believer in this system was Robert Moses, a New York City government reformer in the early 1900s. (Moses knew the system so well, he later perverted the very bureaucracies he built to give him, an unelected official, total control over dozens of city functions.) The man who was called the "power broker" by biographer Robert Caro proposed those early changes to save the city from the grips of Tammany Hall.

All government service, [Moses] said, could be divided into sixteen categories: executive, legislative, judicial, professional, subprofessional, educational, investigational, inspectional, clerical, custodial, street cleaning, fire, police, institutional, skilled trades and labor. Each category could be divided into specific jobs—custodial, for example, into caretakers, janitors, watchmen, storekeepers and bridge tenders. Each job could be scientifically analyzed to show its "functions" and "responsibilities." Each function and responsibility—and there were dozens of them for most jobs—could be given a precise mathematical weight corresponding to its importance in the over-all job. And the success of the employee in each function would, added together according to weight and combined in service records for each employee, "furnish conclusions expressed in arithmetical . . . terms" and these conclusions and these alone should be "used as a basis for salary increase and promotion."

Since Moses's days, bureaucracy has become, for the American psyche, an obscenity. It represents all that is disillusioning about government—the calcified layers of unneeded management slowing progress or, at the least, impeding one's attempt to secure a driver's license.

"It's as if we said 'Let's create a system of management and take out every incentive for management,'" Philadelphia mayor Ed Rendell said.

Bureaucracies fail mainly because they are set up in conflict with the public officials who take over government after an election. Layers of career middle managers stand between the elected or appointed officials and their front-line employees—not to mention between them and the people who elected them.

"In 60 years, we've gone from a nation with too little centralized power to a nation with way too much," said Minnesota governor Arne Carlson. "And instead of making intelligent choices in the 1950s, 60s, 70s and 80s, we allowed more layers of government to be created. In the process we built up a wall between the citizens and their government."

Politics and lack of trust also play a significant role. Like prizefighters, many political appointees bring their own cadre of handlers and hangers-on into an agency to watch over career managers. Likewise, scandals or publicized problems often cause legislators to increase the number of career managers to ensure that political appointees do not make mistakes. The vicious circle leads to bureaucratic bloat.

"We now hire managers to manage managers, watchers to watch watchers, and checkers to check checkers," said former Connecticut state senator Steve Casey. "Government bureaucracy is filled with people who do little else than make sure the process continues forever. Nothing gets done."

The art of energizing employees—imperative in any business—is especially complex in government. A successful public official must learn how to motivate workers within the rigid constraints of the arcane civil service personnel system. While these constraints originally were designed to prevent political managers from abusing their power, they now often stand in the way of getting the job done—sometimes to bizarre extremes.

Especially for private-sector managers entering government positions, the personnel system makes little sense. Employees get raises on a regular timetable, rather than for merit. Salaries are set by schedule, and bonuses for a job well done rarely exist. And because of regulations on firing people, it can be next to impossible to cut the deadwood employee who spends his career waiting for his pension to kick in.

Iowa governor Terry E. Branstad faced the problem in 1991 when the state legislature passed a law forcing him to cut costs and take on the bureaucratic monster of Iowa's government. Although he reduced the ratio of managers to front-line employees by 50 percent in just a year, he learned how hard it can be to fire somebody. "You have to stay with it until staff figures out that you're dead serious about it," Branstad said. "Eventually they either get with the program or decide to look for another job."

But these so-called plans to "flatten bureaucracy"—which represent a move in the right direction—fall short of where the focus should be: on the appointed and elected officials at the top of government's pyramid. These officials are directly elected or appointed to represent "we the people." They should have the power and responsibility to succeed or fail, because they remain directly accountable to the citizens—not some midlevel bureaucrat with five hyphens in his title.

As an executive at Ford and Nissan, Marvin Runyon always had a decent relationship with his employees. He began as a line assembly worker after graduating from college. He knew the culture of line workers and thought he knew something about motivating them.

Runyon's was like the story about the general and the corporal walking past an army barracks. Each time a private passed by and saluted them, the general barked back, "Oh yeah, same to you!" After several times repeating this, the corporal asked the general, "Why do you do that?"

"I was a private once," the general said. "I know what they're thinking."

Postmaster General Runyon's goal was not wrong. Many new public officials feel powerless over the bureaucracies they are supposed to manage. At the postal service, multiple management layers meant Runyon was not in control. He could not directly tap the wisdom and energy of front-line employees. Worse, with so many layers of insulation, no one was accountable for what went wrong. Management could blame the bureaucracy. The bureaucracy could blame management.

And they both would be right, leaving frustrated citizens poorly served.

Runyon failed in his attempt to flatten the bureaucracy by encouraging the wrong employees to leave. Employees with real skills were first to take him up on his offer of six months' pay because they knew they could get other jobs. Employees who were unemployable elsewhere, including many middle managers, stayed behind.

Like any good public official, Runyon simply wanted to take control of his agency. But instead of blindly cutting the bloated bureaucracy, Runyon should have focused on how to use the bureaucracy to strengthen himself, on how to motivate people he didn't hire and couldn't fire to reach his goals.

It's Psychology

Steve Soboroff's moment of bureaucratic clairvoyance came in 1986 while climbing into a model spaceship with his three-year-old son at a Los Angeles park playground. Soboroff cut his head on a sharp piece of metal.

"I went into the office to get a Band-Aid," Soboroff said, "and when the guy opened the cabinet, it looked like a medical center. I couldn't believe it."

"What is this?" Steve asked.

"Oh, people get hurt on this stuff all the time," the attendant said.

"Um, why don't you get new equipment?" Steve replied.

"Well, we just can't get it," the attendant snapped back.

Soboroff is a real estate consultant, a *macher*—a doer. Words speed off his tongue without resting. He wakes every day at 5 A.M., heads a zillion different task forces (including one to bring an NFL team back to Los Angeles), and still managed to be California's 1995 father of the year. A fiery, inspiring man, Soboroff had seen parks all over L.A. He knew many of them had new equipment. Why not his? He called city hall.

"The city," he recalled, "said they wouldn't have the money to fix my park for eleven years."

Soboroff took this as a challenge. With it, he got his first inside look at government bureaucracy.

He had recently read a book by another real estate man who

thought he could do anything—Donald Trump's *The Art of the Deal*. In it, Trump describes how he built in seven months an ice skating rink that New York City couldn't build in the previous decade.

"I said, if Donald Trump can do that in seven months, I'm going to do this in three months," Soboroff recalled. "I'm going to build a new playground in Los Angeles."

Money, he figured, could be obtained. It could be raised from private charities, foundations, or neighborhood groups. But he had never faced a government bureaucracy before and needed to decide whom to approach.

"I said to myself: 'If you want to get into movies for free, either you've got to know the guy who owns the chain or the guy who takes the tickets.' It's easier to know the guy who takes the tickets. That's what I did," Soboroff said. He took his plan directly to the local park director. "Later I went to the commissioner and luckily, I hit a commissioner who said, 'Go for it.' "

Soboroff raised $80,000 and hired the same architect, engineer, and equipment company that the city used. By working directly with employees who were excited to see parks rebuilt, Soboroff made the Los Angeles Park District do in three months what it said it couldn't in eleven years—fix his park. Ninety-one days later, children were swinging on new swings and climbing on safe equipment.

The parks commissioner who signed on to Soboroff's project was a fellow named Richard Riordan. So in 1993, when *Mayor* Richard Riordan needed to fill his old parks position, he knew where to look.

"I seek out commissioners who will bring a wealth of knowledge to the job," said Riordan, "as well as the ability to look at the problems from a new perspective. Soboroff is a leader, a thinker, a doer, and a visionary."

Now he became an insider. And suddenly, Soboroff needed a way to motivate 12,000 employees, none of whom he hired. He had to figure it out quickly; Riordan expected the same swift results he saw Soboroff deliver seven years earlier.

To get the job done, Soboroff knew he had to avoid the middle management trap of government—the layers that slow progress and halt projects. He had to understand what motivated the front-line people who actually did the work. Soboroff had an idea of what made them happy.

"It's psychology," Soboroff said excitedly. "I believe people want to go home thinking they enjoyed their day, did something good.

They don't want to go home and say, 'That was great. I just sat around doing nothing all day. You know, I've only got thirteen more years until retirement.' I don't believe it. I think there are people like that, but I think the masses like to succeed. They like to feel good about themselves and their work. And I think that if they don't, in many cases, that's the fault of upper management.

"The essence of the whole question to me is, how do you reinforce people, positively reinforce them, so they feel good about what they're doing and do what you need them to do, without giving them money and without giving them help and without giving them assistants? That's psychology. That's building teamwork, building structures that work."

Psychology was where Soboroff started. But results were only possible if he gave his employees the tools and flexibility to do their jobs. The department was such a mess that some projects that had been funded in 1974 had no work done on them. Using no extra budget funds, Soboroff got to work.

As parks commissioner, Soboroff oversaw 370 public grounds, and he couldn't single-handedly watch each one. But he was boss, ultimately responsible to Riordan and L.A. residents. So to get results, he selectively—and conditionally—gave employees the needed authority to get the job done. First, he divided the parks among eight project managers, none of whom was hired from outside the department. Soboroff gave each manager control over a predetermined number of projects, while maintaining close oversight.

"I'm the kind of guy, if I have a toy train set, I put the trains on the track and let them go. And if the trains fall off, then I put them back on," Soboroff said. "So I put teams on little projects, and then if they fell off, I put them back on the track. And that basically is a downhill track. You let it glide and if comes off, be there to put it back on."

Soboroff also used prestige to get things done.

"I hold the meetings in the mayor's conference room," Soboroff said. "These are people who had never even been across the hall from the mayor's conference room. Then I had Mayor Riordan stop by, and I introduced them to him. A mayor's conference room should never be empty."

Armed with influence, Soboroff next helped the project managers fix the parks—without increasing budgets. First, he greatly expanded the lists of preapproved architects and engineers. Next, he allowed each manager to choose freely from those expanded lists. Finally, he held each project manager responsible for results, but he didn't just turn his back and tell his deputies to give him updates next year.

He held meetings each month, where the managers were required to check off goals that they had set the previous month and accomplished. Too many unmet goals and Soboroff swept in, refocused the managers' objectives, and put the train back on track.

Results came quickly. Midway through his term, Soboroff had more than two hundred projects either completed or under way, more work than had been done in the previous fifteen years combined.

"It's a matter of relating to people and making them feel good about doing something—for them—that also helps me and helps the city," he said. "I don't classify them as bureaucrats. I think that the real bureaucrats are the ones that want to ride the system through to retirement. I think that beneath the bureaucrats are people who may not have the peace of mind that they get from working for the city, but still want to go home and look their kids in the eyes and say, 'I built a park today.'"

STEVE SOBOROFF took control of his department. Unlike many public officials frustrated with government bureaucracy, Soboroff didn't bash bureaucrats. Instead, he tried to understand what would make them perform. He helped his employees feel pride in knowing they performed a valuable public service. As a manager, pride can sometimes motivate better than money.

Many managers assume people dislike work. To motivate them, these managers feel they have to cajole workers or offer financial rewards in compensation for their discomfort. Soboroff realized that what also motivates people is responsibility, achievement, and the work itself. He proved this by selectively giving his employees the tools and authority to do their jobs well. He enticed his employees to help meet his goals.

Soboroff couldn't change the city's antique personnel system overnight, so he had to be creative. He gave out certificates of honor signed by the mayor. He bought hats inscribed "Team Rec and Parks: We Make LA a Better Place," and handed them out to selected workers. He also started an employee of the month program.

Soboroff faced the same obstacles that most new public officials confront. But not all problems can be solved with trinkets or by one person alone. Meanwhile, the hourglass that measures a four-year term marks time passing. So many new public officials simply must manage around a screwed-up system.

"Any change is resisted because bureaucrats have a vested interest in the chaos in which they exist," President Richard Nixon said.

Daniel P. Beard served as commissioner of the federal Bureau of Reclamation, a quintessentially bureaucratic department that manages rivers in the western United States. "The personnel and procurement laws and regulations under which you must operate are silly, asinine, and degrading," he said. "Even worse, there is little hope anyone will ever totally change them, or at least make them more humane.

"You can hope, or dream, that they will be changed. But it's more than likely that you can't change them, so accept them as reality—accept them as constraints within which you have to operate."

Many such constraints exist.

One is that government leadership is transient, bureaucrats are permanent. City employees knew if Soboroff couldn't get the job done (and he couldn't without their help), he would be gone soon enough. They had seen scores like him come and go. Many government workers take the same attitude toward political appointees that New Englanders take toward the weather: If you don't like it, wait a minute—it'll change. The new public official doesn't have much time to convince employees to follow.

James B. Lewis, who served as chief of staff to New Mexico governor Bruce King, sums up the view of many appointed officials: "It's a rude awakening when someone in a bureaucracy says to you, 'Hey, you're a short timer. We're going to wait you out.' "

Another constraint is that bureaucracies naturally discourage risk taking. They were designed to guard against corruption, scandal, and mismanagement of public funds. As a result, many line employees will never take bold approaches for fear of being accused of wrongdoing. Rather than do something that might be criticized, they move very slowly or not at all. The public official who wants to encourage risk taking must also be willing to shoulder the blame if something goes wrong.

Effective public officials must bridge this gap between their agenda and the bureaucratic system's realities.

"If you sit with people, and they think you're the smartest guy in the world, and you're the sharpest dresser, and the best looking and this or that, they go away resenting you," said Soboroff. "You've got to be able to relate to people. You've got to bring them in. You've got to be able to connect."

Connecting often becomes hardest in the initial stages of a takeover. Many officials get elected by campaigning "against government," a disturbing trend that only magnifies the debilitating rift between bureaucrats and the top officials. While this may acquire votes, campaigning is not governing. And the very people against whom the public official ran—the bureaucrats—are the ones she will need to fulfill campaign promises.

Portland mayor Vera Katz experienced how that conflict can cause trouble. After winning office in 1992 by condemning city hall during the campaign, Katz's ability to motivate the bureaucracy was still being publicly questioned nearly two years later.

"[The] bureaucracy is loaded with worker bees who felt the queen's sting when she ran against city hall in her 1992 campaign," read one Portland *Oregonian* article. Many felt Katz had undermined her ability to get things done.

"Vera is not utilizing her talents," said one official.

Although it took time, Katz offered an olive branch to city workers.

"I told them they were doing a good job, but that we can do better," Katz said. "I talked about having higher expectations in serving the community. I challenged them. I involved them seriously. I also told them if they have better ways of managing, I'd love to hear about them."

The skill to bridge that division between a public official's agenda and bureaucracy's rigidity is often elusive. Many don't figure out the system until their term ends. Understanding the psychology of a bureaucracy is the first step. Soboroff tried to work with and around the bureaucracy. But some people must flat out change it.

Without Merit

After a term as governor, Zell Miller could not tolerate Georgia's personnel system any longer. Many of his first-term goals were stalled in bureaucratic purgatory, because endless rules and complicated procedures made it difficult to hire, promote, or fire state employees. And with little to show voters, the governor nearly lost his job in a close 1994 bid for reelection.

So during his second term, he did something about it. He scrapped the personnel system entirely.

In his 1996 State of the State address, Miller announced an initiative to end the State Merit System, a fifty-plus-year experiment that sought to create a professional workforce free of political cronyism. In Miller's view, the experiment had failed.

"Too often in government we pass laws to fix particular problems of the moment," the Governor explained, "and then we allow half a century to roll by without ever following up to see what the long-term consequences have been.

"Folks, the truth of the matter is that a solution in 1943 is a problem in 1996. The problem is governmental paralysis, because despite its name, our Merit System is not about merit. It offers no reward to good workers. It only provides cover for bad workers."

Georgia's personnel system represented bureaucracy at its worst. No longer did it matter whether a worker was productive or lazy, skilled or incompetent. Once someone got a state job, it basically became a job for life. For many of Miller's agency heads, the system became so bad that they simply refused to recruit for vacant positions for fear that if they made a mistake, it would haunt them for years.

"It can take six to eight weeks to fill a critical position in state government," Miller explained. "It takes a year to a year and a half to fire a bad worker, because of a mountain of endless paperwork, hearings, and appeals. Productivity is the name of the game, and we lose it when positions go unfilled."

Miller wanted to eliminate the meaningless "competitive" tests designed to measure competence. No standardized test could effectively find an employee to develop solutions to Georgia's complicated public problems. Gone were the pages of standardized job qualifications, pay ranges, and hiring procedures. And perhaps most important, the new system gave managers greater flexibility to dismiss unproductive workers.

Miller explained his rationale: "We also encourage resentment among the many good state employees when they see a few bad workers kept on and given the same pay raises, because managers are discouraged and intimidated by the endless and complicated process of firing or even disciplining them."

But the move was about more than just blindly tearing down the bureaucracy. Postmaster General Runyon proved that's not always fruitful. Miller's action was about developing a system that would give public officials some control in a bureaucracy and give employees incentive to perform their jobs well.

All new state employees hired after July 1, 1996, were "unclassified employees," or workers not protected by traditional civil service rules. The new law also decentralized the personnel process, allowing individual agencies to hire their own workers. Like many in government, Miller never understood a system that forced candidates seeking jobs as disparate as medical lab technicians and budget analysts through the same central office. No central office could adequately gauge the qualifications of such radically different professions.

Just as the reformers who originally created the civil service system were considered radical, so was Miller. To appease critics, Miller built a better set of checks and balances to prevent abuses. The centralized personnel office became a watchdog rather than a coordinator. It set general guidelines for hiring and firing, helped agencies develop their own incentive compensation programs, and offered employee training. While giving more control to the public officials, Miller also increased protection against misuse of that power.

"As an additional safeguard," Miller explained, "regular and comprehensive audits will be conducted to ensure that the new state personnel system is not abused."

The new personnel system was only a first step. For example, giving bureaucrats incentives to work harder, but not giving them the tools—computers, political support, a budget—would only lead to greater frustration. This required shifting priorities and help from legislators to give him the flexibility state agencies needed to do their jobs:

"This government is not yours; it is certainly not mine. It belongs to the people of Georgia, who foot the bill and pay its costs. And the only reason, the only reason you and I are here, is to make it do what they want it to do."

MANAGING government bureaucrats has never been easy. In ancient Athens and Rome, public workers were slaves. The reason was simple: Slaves could be disciplined easily. Several hundred years later, the Chinese developed the first civil service system where jobs were awarded based on scores received in a series of exams. Raises or promotions were granted if the workers passed higher exams. Nearly every government in America employs a similar system today.

While most private-sector personnel systems are designed to attract the most talented people, most government systems are designed to promote fairness. The civil service system replaced the "spoils system," where jobs were assigned through political patronage. A system where someone with political or family connections gets a job over someone with better qualifications is certainly not fair. That's why so many rules exist.

But rules do not guarantee fairness either. As author Philip Howard notes, "Universal requirements that leave no room for judgment are almost never fair, even when the sole point is to assure fairness." Rules cannot replace people's judgment. At some point, public officials must be allowed to make decisions and be held accountable for their choices.

In most governments today, public officials are held accountable for doing—and are trusted to do—their jobs. Part of that accountability comes in the form of bureaucrats, hired to keep watch years earlier in response to political machines and corruption. But today, the pendulum has swung too far in the watchdog's direction.

Layers of rules overly restrain public officials because they are not trusted. Bound by bureaucracy, officials find it hard to accomplish their goals. Oversight, of course, is imperative. But how much oversight is too much? Sadly, corruption will continue to exist in government, and much should be done to fight it. But layers of bureaucracy have created the self-fulfilling prophecy of a bungling government. They cause more harm than good and breed much of today's cynicism.

Takeover Tips

Most new public officials get the same advice during takeover: "Empowering" employees is the key to making an organization work better. Management books overflow with buzzwords on how to motivate workers by giving them power, by saying, in effect, the buck stops with them. Most new public officials, however, enter government and learn they are not even "empowered" themselves. They find that the bureaucracy stands in their way.

Bureaucracy breeds an almost religious adherence to organizational charts. Most employees like them, because the charts help them understand where they fit. But organizational charts have an extremely negative side effect—they promote fatter, not flatter organizations. Ask employees to improve upon an agency's structure and they will try to add layers to elevate their own position and improve their own status. And over the decades that bureaucracies have been in place, layers have been layered on top of layers. The whole mess has left many elected and appointed officials virtually helpless.

Effectively taking control is about getting back to basics. It's about returning power to the officials closest to the people—those directly elected and appointed to carry out the people's work. They, after all, are the ones most accountable for government's successes and failures. The question, of course, is how does a new public official gain control?

Tip #1: BREAK OLD HABITS.

Jerry Abramson became a popular and effective Louisville mayor by changing the way decisions were made. Abramson knew that his government moved slowly. The bureaucracy was so thick, workers on lower levels would sit idly, doing nothing, waiting for decisions. Like Steve Soboroff, Abramson knew the negative effect powerlessness can have on the bureaucracy. He knew the difficulty of accomplishing anything if the bureaucracy mobilized against him. Also like Soboroff, he did something about it.

Abramson created a program called CityWork to make Louisville's traditional bureaucracy more thoughtful. He relied on city workers to solve long-standing problems. CityWork replaced the traditional management structure that dominates most governments with nimble work teams.

"We're trying to change the culture and mindset of the day-to-day business of city government," Abramson said.

Abramson created problem-solving groups with as few as five members and gave them authority to fix troubled situations. The sessions lasted one to three days. Each CityWork team recommended changes to the mayor or relevant agency head, who was required to quickly approve or reject the suggestions. The teams then tried to introduce changes within ninety days.

One group found new uses for vacant property. Other groups reorganized the city's law department (saving some $100,000), rearranged the parks department's maintenance operations to better utilize workers and equipment, and redesigned the city garage to reduce vehicle maintenance costs. In the program's first three years, some 22 percent of Abramson's employees took part.

By breaking the old decision-making structure, Abramson enhanced his power. For one, what he gave he could also take away. CityWork was not about creating new bands of permanent bureaucracy even further removed from the people. It was about creating temporary teams and giving them temporary authority.

Finally, by changing the way decisions were made, Abramson ultimately increased his standing not just with employees but also with voters. He even included citizens on some of his teams. It worked, and voters responded. In 1994 Abrahmson became the first Louisville mayor to win a third consecutive term.

Tip #2: REACH OUT AND TOUCH SOMEONE.

As deputy secretary of education, Madeleine Kunin was the chief operating officer of a 4,900-person federal agency. It was her responsibility to ensure that the department functioned properly and programs ran efficiently. But to make the department function and the programs run, Kunin first had to bridge the deep divide of one of the most jaded bureaucracies in federal government.

The level of trust couldn't have been lower than at the Education Department. The agency had been under attack, largely from within, for the previous twelve years. Both the Reagan and Bush administrations sought to shrink the department. And regardless of where one sits on that debate, the layoff threats left many of the 4,900 workers that Kunin had to motivate unwilling to communicate with their new bosses.

"When we came here, the relationship was dreadful," Kunin said. "In fact, we were greeted with kind of a scurrilous sheet that listed whom you should trust and whom you shouldn't, put out by the union. It was kind of sobering, like, what am I walking into?"

Kunin created new avenues of communication to break through the barrier that had grown between career employees and politically appointed managers.

"Nobody ever does quite enough communication," she said. "But we revitalized a newsletter that had gone out of existence. I would hold sessions where people could come and ask any questions they wanted. We would try to inform people about what was happening and be open about it."

But the biggest step came later. Kunin realized that only 40 percent of the workers had personal computers, and of those, only a handful had e-mail. In addition, no good voice-mail system existed. In this technologically advanced age, the Education Department was stuck in the era of a one-room schoolhouse with no electricity.

"Things like e-mail and technology, you can really communicate through that," Kunin said. "It sounds like basic common sense, but it didn't exist."

E-mail allowed Kunin to keep in touch with employees she might never see during her term. Front-line employees gave her suggestions and even commented on broader policy issues, bypassing the normal hierarchy. It also gave career employees the feeling that their ideas would be heard and helped reverse the negative mood that threatened to keep the Education Department from making the grade.

Tip #3: YOU DON'T NEED MONEY TO MOTIVATE
(OR, MONEY CAN'T BUY YOU LOVE).

About the only action harder than firing a government employee, it seems, is finding a way to reward one. Put those two factors together, and it's easy to see why many bureaucrats are viewed (sometimes wrongly) as unmotivated. After all, if nothing bad comes from a bad job and nothing good from a good job, taking the easy road makes sense.

As one California report states: "In too many cases, the incentives within government discourage excellence, innovation and incentive—and, thereby, discourage employees." To make progress, a public official must find creative ways to reward employees.

Only occasionally are material incentives possible. In North Carolina, Governor Jim Hunt gave eleven state employees $1,000 each after they came up with ideas that saved $1.7 million. In Portland, Mayor Vera Katz gives employees gold stars—made of 14 karat gold.

But because of budget constraints and public pressure, monetary incentives such as bonuses are rare. So some innovative public officials get creative.

In Louisville, Mayor Abramson uses authority as incentive. He lets small teams of employees find solutions to persistent problems. Good jobs are rewarded with positions on future teams and the chance to do good again.

In Seattle, employees at metropolitan water-treatment facilities who earn the right for greater decision-making abilities get to "run their own part of the business" with less interference.

"Tap the masses," Steve Soboroff advises. "Once you build enough momentum where you can bring in the upper management, bring the [higher-level] bureaucrats into the momentum. I try to do that publicly, because privately, it's too hard. Turn on the TV camera, put them in front, or say something good about them. But remember: I'm trying to get something done for the community, not for myself."

Tip #4: KEEP IT SIMPLE, STUPID.

Steve Kelman—an eccentric dynamo trapped in a policy wonk's world—had a crazy idea. As head of the White House Office of Federal Procurement Policy, it was Kelman's job to oversee how Washington buys what it needs, which is like keeping tabs on Imelda Marcos in a shoe store. Imelda did a lot of buying; the feds do a lot of procuring.

Kelman believed that bureaucratic rules frequently worsened the favoritism and corruption they were supposed to solve. With so many regulations intended to make purchasing fair (like requirements to take the lowest bid regardless of quality, and having to buy purchases under $2,500 from specially defined "small businesses"), government rules often hurt more than they helped.

After years of thinking about the dry topic of government procurement, Kelman came across a brilliant concept to make the system run better: Let others come up with ideas.

For example, Michellee Craddock, a career civil servant, made a little suggestion to Kelman that saved taxpayers big money—an estimated $25 million a year.

"I told him frequently we get requests to purchase from CompUSA, who has great pricing and is right across the street," said Craddock. "But we can't buy from them because they are a large business, unless we call several other sources and spend a lot of time satisfying the requirements."

Craddock's elementary suggestion—if CompUSA sells it, and we want it, then let's buy it.

It's not rocket science and hardly worthy of the press releases many public officials like to send out. But Kelman loved the idea. He also loved that the concept had come from deep within the system, that he found a way to motivate creative thought and energize the bureaucracy to work at a higher level. And many of the changes could be made without legislative approval.

"Michellee brought up . . . problems that were more important than any of the problems we had thought about," Kelman said.

But Kelman didn't stop there in freeing bureaucrats from the procurement chains that former Senator Sam Nunn had called "a bureaucratic nightmare." Kelman implemented another wild idea.

For years, government buyers were forced to hire only the lowest bidder. Kelman figured that a contractor's past performance should influence whether that contractor gets hired again. He knew that letting the buyers make decisions—using the same logic as if they were buying for themselves—would make buying more productive and cheaper. In other words, one can buy a bushel a bad apples for cheap, but have to throw half out and buy new ones. Buy good apples the first time—even if they're slightly more expensive—and nothing gets wasted.

"The commonsense view of this would be, 'You mean they never looked at past performance in contracts before. What is this?' or 'Hey, what took the government so long?' " said then Office of Management and Budget Deputy Director Alice M. Rivlin. "And that was the reaction of some of us."

Kelman understood common sense. In the baffling world of government bureaucracy, where raises come through preordained mandates and firing a corrupt employee can be nearly impossible, common sense often gets lost. Acting on it would help Kelman give bureaucrats the authority they would need to get the job done.

"All of these things," said Ohio senator John Glenn, "require people to exercise judgment."

Tip #5: SEND 'EM TO SIBERIA.

In the fossilized world of government bureaucracy, firing an employee is easier said than done. Unbelievable examples prove the point. One legal secretary at the U.S. Labor Department had her jaw broken in 1993 when a part-time employee clocked her with a right cross during an argument. Never would a firing seem more justified and easy to attain. But after hearings and intervention by the labor union, the part-timer was transferred to a permanent job that carried a $3,890 raise.

And the problem is not just in Washington, D.C. It happens in state and local governments as well. "There was an employee who physically attacked someone, physically assaulted them. I think it was the second time," recalled San Diego mayor Susan Golding. "The supervisor told the employee he was fired. . . . The civil service commission reinstated the employee because there was no written policy that said you couldn't assault someone."

Every government—federal, state, and local—has dozens of truth-is-stranger-than-fiction examples about no-show public employees or the ones who show up but do nothing. Few stories give government a worse reputation in the eyes of the public.

And still, firing a government worker can be almost impossible and ridiculously time-consuming. Laws established to stop elected and appointed officials from abusing their power with indiscriminate firings present an initial block. Strong public-sector labor unions are another obstacle. Many bureaucrats today must feel that the only sure things in life are death, taxes, and a lifetime government job. So what is a government official to do?

"It's an extremely tedious process, but if you stick to your guns you can get rid of nonperformers," said former Connecticut treasurer Chris Burnham. "It simply takes vigilance."

But few managers have time for vigilance. For many public officials, the answer is simply to separate out employees who are nothing but impediments. They are handled like bad weeds that won't go away but at least can be stopped from spreading and sucking life from the rest of the garden.

When three groundskeepers at a Los Angeles public golf course came up to Parks Commissioner Steve Soboroff and said they couldn't make needed improvements because one of their bosses got in the way, Soboroff wrote a "to do" list he knew the bad manager would have trouble completing. It cleared the way for that employee to be transferred.

"Sometimes it takes too much energy to fire for cause. You have to document everything. It's not worth the time," Soboroff said. "With transfers, you can get around the firing. You can move [undesirable workers] to other places."

Dall Forsythe, the former New York State budget director, warns that wasting too much time on disruptive employees may distract an official from larger goals. "For someone you're trying to fire, they can usually wait you out. They can usually figure out some way to stay on the payroll. Your only option may be to exile them to some Siberian location far away."

Adds Soboroff: "There are some places in our city government that are worse than Siberia."

Sometimes deadwood employees are simply a sunk cost—they can't be fired and will collect a salary regardless. One shouldn't lose more by wasting time or energy. Sometimes the only option is to partition off disruptive workers or nonperformers so they don't bring down the entire organization.

9

Juggling Many Balls at Once

There can't be a crisis next week. My schedule is already full.
—*Henry Kissinger,*
national security adviser
and later U.S. secretary of state

Freak of Nature

Even as far back as 1960, Michael Bilandic was being groomed to succeed Chicago's mayor-for-life Richard J. Daley. After all, the Machine—Chicago's political structure—was well oiled, and the City That Works could not break down during the inevitable takeover.

Bilandic all but solidified his fate as successor to the Boss on a chilly March day when the Beatles were just starting and Elvis's hips had only recently swiveled in prime time. In a skillful political maneuver that caught Mayor Daley's eye, Bilandic persuaded the South Side Irish to give up their traditional St. Patrick's Day parade and join the West Side Irish in theirs. In Chicago, this passed for high-level diplomatic negotiations.

In 1976, when Daley died, Bilandic took over. In fact, for the next three years—until just one month before Bilandic's first reelection day—it seemed Bilandic had succeeded in the political equivalent of playing first base after Lou Gehrig left the Yankees.

Then the snow began to fall. And fall. And fall. When it was all through on January 12, 1979, more than twenty inches of the white stuff had shut down Chicago, turning the City That Works into the City That Waits. Public transportation stopped. Schools closed. People sat at home.

Bilandic found himself in the middle of a major crisis. Worse, he didn't realize it.

"[Bilandic] thought the snow had been gotten rid of and complained that Chicagoans who wanted a place to park should be using the school playgrounds . . . plowed by the city," wrote one reporter. "Crack journalists, however, showed in story and song and photo that the playgrounds had not been plowed, the streets had not been plowed, the city had not been plowed."

Chicagoans were furious. The city government had not fulfilled one of its most basic responsibilities. While his exceptional political skills had helped him replace Daley, they couldn't remove snow from Chicago streets. The foul-up cost the city an estimated $75 million. It also cost Bilandic his job.

"We expected to win," Bilandic said, recalling his defeat to Jane Byrne in 1979 and lamenting the snow. "But there'd been a darn lot of snow, the weather stayed cold, and the snow wouldn't go away.

"A little bit of snow is fun, but after a while, it isn't. Where do you park your car? We tried dumping it everywhere, in the river, any place we could think. But there was no place left."

The mayor's handling of the blizzard defined his entire term. "Bilandic was never very fast on his feet; a laid-back guy who got hit with a once-in-a-hundred-years snowstorm," recalled Adlai E. Stevenson, U.S. senator from Illinois at the time. "He just couldn't handle it."

The stigma of failing to respond in the time of crisis stuck not only to Bilandic, but also to staffers around him. Staffers like Francis J. Degnan.

Degnan served the city of Chicago for forty-nine years. Just five of those years were spent as commissioner of streets and sanitation. But if Bilandic thinks the blizzard blemish will be forgotten, he should consider Degnan's obituary, written seventeen years after the snowstorm:

"Other than former Mayor Michael Bilandic, Mr. Degnan, who died Thursday of a heart attack, was considered the highest ranking political casualty of the great snow of 1979 that swept Jane Byrne into office."

Bilandic's fate is sealed.

*   *   *

LOOKING for a crisis in government is a bit like being one of those tornado chasers in the movie *Twister*. It's never so much a question of whether one will hit, but when and where. Success in government means not only handling the crisis du jour but maintaining steady progress on all the plans already in place.

"There always is another crisis around the corner," President Harry Truman said of government service.

Mayor Michael Bilandic's crisis came in the form of a blizzard. It could just as easily have been an office scandal or a bomb threat as a natural disaster. And not every government crisis arrives suddenly. Some develop slowly, like a growing illegal immigration problem in California or a housing shortage in New York City. And not every crisis concerns an external event; an impending budget shortfall or a crumbling educational system could present just as dire circumstances as the unforeseen snowstorm or scandal.

All crises, however, require the same special skill of being able to get many things done at once—in shorthand, juggling. A juggler trying to control ten balls at once can never hold them all at the same time. Inevitably, some of the balls will spill out of his hands. To control all ten balls, the juggler must juggle—holding only two at any given time and precisely tossing the other eight so he knows where they will soar and where they will land. This is the public official's task. And if that's not difficult enough, the official who ignores all other duties while concentrating solely on a crisis will soon find brand new crises (more balls) popping up.

"You can set almost any agenda or schedule for the day, but you better be damn well ready to deal with crises," Clinton White House chief of staff Leon Panetta reflected upon leaving his post. "I've always said this is not so much a management job as a battlefield job, because you essentially set what you want to do that day in terms of how you'd like the battle to go, but you also wind up having land mines and mortars coming in and exploding around you."

This is not to say that crises don't arise in the private sector. As America Online discovered during a string of service outages and the makers of Tylenol found during a wave of poisonings, they do. But just as government is different from business, so are the types of crises and how they get handled.

"In business you can handle crises by virtue of dictatorship," said

Steve Soboroff. "You can't do that in politics. In politics, you have to work through a system. When crises come up, you can't just make a decision. You have to go to a board, which goes to the ad hoc committee, which then goes to another committee, and they all have to vote. In business, you can usually predict what the crisis is about. And usually, it goes back to money. In government, crises hit on all sorts of things beyond money. And usually, it goes to political relationships, and that's more difficult.

"Big business, places like CBS or Circuit City, runs almost like a government, but it's still more predictable. In politics, you've got to determine your relationships with people more and everything comes down to a vote. And the vote is not predictable, because it never comes down to one single issue. In government, there's more consensus building. Dictatorship is much less exhausting."

From the snowstorm that cripples a city to a terrorist bombing, citizens look first to government for a solution—and they expect fast results. While a consumer can always subscribe to a different on-line service or use another pain reliever, citizens have only one government to turn to.

In addition, public officials are limited in how they can respond to crises. The constraints government officials face every day—from complicated procurement procedures to working with other independent branches of government—make each crisis more difficult to solve. Need to rebuild a bridge after an earthquake? A competitive bidding process for a contractor will take weeks. Need more money? The legislature must approve the request. While waivers to these rules are usually possible in an emergency, not all crises can claim that status. So even if businesspeople face the same crises as their public-sector counterparts, a businessperson has many more options in how to handle them.

It doesn't even always take a major crisis or turnaround situation to convince most public officials of this need to tackle many problems at once. Whether it is a phone call from an angry legislator or an unexpected recession that causes tax revenues to fall short, surprise situations that cause public officials to drop everything are inevitable. Effective public officials realize they cannot let a crisis derail progress toward other goals.

Crises, however, do not necessarily have to lead to disaster. Indeed, crises present opportunities to rethink old plans and create new ones. For many mayors, Bilandic's fiasco meant the chance to create new snowstorm procedures. (His successor, Jane Byrne, spent millions on new snow removal equipment.) The lesson for Byrne and many others around the country was not to be afraid to spend money on what's important.

Crises also can present the chance to stand out from predecessors or simply redefine oneself. Connecticut governor Ella Grasso could have taught Bilandic how to deal with a snowstorm. During a 1978 blizzard that dumped more than two feet of snow on the Nutmeg State, Grasso took full advantage of the crisis to ensure her reelection. She projected an image of control as she shut down highways, cleared away vehicles, and dispatched teams of workers from the state armory to remove the snow quickly. The television footage is now legendary in state politics. Later that year, Grasso was reelected with 60 percent of the vote.

Governing should not, then, mean stepping meekly from day to day, hoping to avoid the land mine whose explosion will bring reporters and television cameras racing to the office. So many land mines exist, one can't avoid stepping on them. And as at any gruesome accident, people will stop and stare.

Sometimes, as in Bilandic's case, the land mine explodes in the middle of the term. Other times, it's exactly what a public official gets elected to fix. Instead of dealing with a onetime freak of nature, as Bilandic did, these public officials are in full-time crisis management mode from their first day in office.

Cleaning Up a Municipal Mess

Despite the soapy scrub brush in one hand and sweatshirt sleeves pushed tight up his forearms, the man scrubbing the grimy city hall bathroom floor looks out of place. Even in the City of Brotherly Love, this public employee seems too happy. Perhaps it's the extra vigor with which he scours, an intensity unnatural for such an ordinary task. Perhaps it's the fact that a newspaper photographer would bother to shoot such a mundane activity.

But once it's learned that the man on all fours is Philadelphia mayor Edward Rendell, the scene makes more sense. Rendell wants people to know he is serious about cleaning up city hall. And unlike others who would do this solely as a publicity stunt, Rendell backed it up with action.

When Rendell was inaugurated as the city's twenty-seventh mayor in January 1992, he inherited a municipal nightmare. Just over one year earlier, Moody's Investor Service gave Philadelphia the lowest bond rating of any major city, only one step short of default. In addition, the city had accumulated more than $230 million in annual deficits—projected to rise to $1.4 billion in five years. If that weren't enough, the tax base—and with it the money needed to erase that deficit—was declining as the middle class sought refuge in the suburbs. Philadelphia was in a crisis.

"It was like I was elected doctor to a sick patient who had serious cancer," Rendell said. "But secondly, he had a bullet wound to the chest. The bullet wound was our financial situation in the city. Unless we cured the fiscal problems, we would be in a hole that it would take a quarter-century to dig out of. We knew what we had to do—get the bullet out of the patient."

Rendell had to remove the bullet without aggravating the cancer—the troubled schools, worsening city services, and a tax burden that had grown too high. He couldn't pick and choose what he would do first. He couldn't move slowly from one limited goal to the next. The patient was dying.

"We don't have time to pussyfoot around," Rendell said the day after his election.

Rendell understood a basic fact of political life: He must govern like a one-termer. Many new public officials ignore that fact and spend their time, in Rendell's words, pussyfooting around. Rendell knew that taking office in the middle of a full-blown crisis required different action than under normal circumstances. He felt he had to take risks that others wouldn't. Otherwise, he'd face the same fate as Chicago's Mayor Bilandic.

But Rendell had limited remedies. Raising taxes to balance the budget was not an option; that would only drive more people and businesses out of the city. Handouts from Washington, D.C., or Harrisburg, the state capital, were not available. And layoffs of city workers could increase social service costs like welfare and unemployment, only worsening the budget deficit. Better management across all city departments at once was his only option.

Rendell began with a gutsy move, especially for a Democrat: He stared down city labor unions during weeks of tough negotiations. Rapid expansion of wages and benefits over the past decade helped cause the city's budget problems, Rendell believed. So he froze employees' wages for two years, cut health insurance spending by more than 20 percent, and cut paid holidays from fourteen days a year to ten. He also negotiated union work law changes to allow greater efficiency. The new mayor needed every municipal employee to do more.

"We have to break the rules," Rendell declared in his inaugural address, a call to arms to the city's 25,000 workers. "Not only may you have to make eight widgets a day. You may have to make 10 or 15 or 20—do anything that's necessary to turn this city around."

Meanwhile, Rendell worked to bring the private sector back to the Philadelphia picture. Government could not solve the city's problems alone. So Rendell asked corporate CEOs to work with city officials to identify more than two hundred cost-saving initiatives—saving approximately $150 million in fifteen months.

Moving simultaneously on yet another front, Rendell privatized many city services that could be run more efficiently outside of city government. Now, private workers guard the city art museum, cut grass in the parks, and cook in the city prisons. Rendell even hired a private firm to clean the same city hall bathrooms that he scrubbed in the famous photo.

Citizens elected Rendell to resuscitate their dying city, and his quick-fire management moved Philadelphia out of intensive care.

To show voters the patient's recovery, Rendell regularly published annual performance statistics: Garbage collection improved dramatically, with 94 percent of all trash picked up on time, up from 64 percent; repair time for the city's 6,000-vehicle fleet got cut in half; and public libraries opened six days a week, thanks to an increase in volunteers made possible under union work rule concessions. These performance statistics made Rendell—or his successor—more accountable to the people.

The Philadelphia turnaround made Rendell a celebrity mayor. *The New York Times* wrote that Philadelphia "has made one of the most stunning turnabouts in recent urban history." Within weeks of their elections, New York Mayor Rudy Giuliani and Los Angeles mayor Richard Riordan—both Republicans—set up meetings with Rendell to learn how he had tackled Philadelphia's problems. *The Los Angeles Times* commented that if Riordan could match Rendell's record, "Los Angeles just might get another multi-term leader."

Rendell remained more modest. He compared his rescue of Philadelphia to how John F. Kennedy became a war hero: "Simple,"

Kennedy always said, "they sank my boat." Said Rendell: "Well, I came in and this boat—four-fifths of it—was underwater, so I had to try everything at once."

In Philadelphia, Ed Rendell turned crisis into opportunity. At the same time in Los Angeles, Steve Soboroff served as parks commissioner for Mayor Richard Riordan, a Rendell fan. Soboroff found getting something done in government much like the job of a telephone operator: "This whole business is a switchboard with twenty-five phones and all the lights are going at once. You have to be able to make small progress on all the lights all the time. You have to be able to turn one off and turn one on and turn one off and turn one on. You just have to be organized and keep track of a lot of things. You have to move a lot of things along slowly."

Like Rendell, Soboroff dealt with many political crises that developed outside his control. Again, each crisis represented an opportunity. For Soboroff, this meant new or better parks. For Rendell, it meant saving Philadelphia. Both realized that getting something accomplished in government requires a juggler's skills.

"It's different in business, where it's pretty predictable," said Soboroff, who has an extensive private-sector career. "In government you've got to keep a lot of balls in the air, so things eventually happen."

Not only is this true because of government's unpredictability but also because a public official's tenure is very short.

Ed Rendell had just four years before he faced the voters again. An agency director may hold her position only for half of the governor's four-year term. Some small city mayors may have just two years. That's why many new public officials tend to focus on changing policy, such as banning panhandlers on city streets or allowing gays to serve in the military. These moves get people's attention and, because they normally require no legislative approval, are relatively easy to accomplish.

But policy changes can be reversed quickly. Real management takes what a public manager often lacks—time. Instituting fundamental change, such as turning around a troubled department, changing management practices, or altering the way an agency does business, requires swift and certain action, often simultaneously. The approach of focusing on just one issue at a time won't get the job done. Otherwise, by the time two of the five steps needed to implement a vision are completed, so is the term in office.

For appointed officials who must implement their elected boss's vision in what can be a truncated period of time, the sense of urgency—the need to juggle—is even more intense.

Preparing for the Inevitable

No one ever said working for Mario Cuomo would be easy. The New York governor believed in an activist government and needed an active staff. Dall Forsythe expected to work hard.

"Mario Cuomo had a vision for what the state government should do for its people, which in many ways was the classic liberal vision: There were folks in need and government had an obligation to help them," says Forsythe, who served as Cuomo's budget director from 1988 to 1991. "Those were important functions of government, and they needed to be done."

Said Cuomo: "I did not come into government to win an award as the great accountant in the sky and balance budgets."

"But that's exactly what I came into government to do," the professorial Forsythe said. "I would cringe every time he said that."

Forsythe's job was to serve as a check on his boss. As budget director, he had to help the visionary governor keep his multiple promises in a real world that included limited time and tight finances. He was responsible for planning, negotiating, and executing a $52 billion state budget—the nation's second largest.

"Most elected officials do not believe that they will serve just one term. They often ignore details, like the budget, that might get in the way of their long-term plans. So in many ways it is up to their political appointees to serve as a check on them," Forsythe said. "I think it is very important as a public official that you have the understanding that you may have to leave at any time."

Forsythe believed deeply in Cuomo's vision. But as a former finance professor and investment banker, he knew fiscal goals existed as well—such as maintaining a stable budget.

"It's very hard to do any of the other things a government is supposed to do if its finances are not stable," he said. "The budget in many ways for Mario Cuomo was a force to be overcome. Fiscal stability on its own was not one of his goals. He was very respectful of my role. He understood the role of the budget office. But he also believed that the things government spent money on were valuable."

To Forsythe, working for Cuomo meant keeping himself and a staff of 240 focused on the governor's multiple priorities—even when Cuomo insisted they were all top priorities. And Forsythe had to do this all within tight budget constraints.

And then, even before his first day in office, crisis struck.

"Ten days before I was supposed to start my new job, the outgoing director called and said I needed to come to his office immediately for a conference call to solve a short-term cash crisis," Forsythe recalled. Just four weeks into the fiscal year, Forsythe learned that the state was $900 million short on its budget. By the end of the fiscal year, New York sat more than $2 billion in the red.

"Those types of crises can be massively disruptive toward trying to achieve your goals," Forsythe said in typically understated fashion. "It threatens to change everything you've planned for."

Forsythe recovered from that initial shock with creative financial management and a reshuffling of priorities. It meant weeks of meetings and long nights. But after that early lesson, he made sure to be ready for anything that might arise. To prepare his staff for the inevitable crises, he insisted they take time off when able.

"If you are already working eighty hours a week and a crisis comes up, you won't have any more to give to it," he said. "So I used to try to get the people in the budget office to go home at reasonable hours when nothing was going wrong, with the expectation that they would have to be there all the time when things were going wrong."

Next, Forsythe regularly gave his staff the bureaucratic equivalent of fire drills.

"During down times we learned to anticipate times of crises and try to test various scenarios," Forsythe explained. "What if there is a recession in six months even if our forecasts do not predict it? If the legislature doesn't pass a budget, what should we do? If legislative leadership comes back with their own ideas about a budget, how should we react?"

Forsythe would work out the answers with staff. And though most of the invented scenarios never took shape, Forsythe believed it made his office more able to deal with the unexpected.

"Most seasoned public officials know that preparing for the unexpected is the key to success in government," he said. "But it's a very tough lesson to follow because people are usually too busy all day with current work to worry about problems that have not yet occurred or might not occur."

Takeover Tips

Although they had very different jobs, and faced different takeovers, Dall Forsythe and Ed Rendell never faced a shortage of crises. With no time to spare, Rendell had to turn around a city that was nearly bankrupt. And Forsythe, who served a very popular governor during times of relative prosperity, faced the task of implementing multiple, sometimes conflicting goals with the inevitable crisis that challenged even the best-laid-out plans.

It's no different at the federal level.

In his book *Madhouse: The Private Turmoil of Working for the President,* reporter Jeffrey H. Birnbaum suggests that President Clinton created unachievable expectations as the federal government's chief executive. At a White House dinner party early in his first term, Clinton rose from his seat and declared that his administration would refuse to move from one limited goal to the next as many suggested. Instead, he would work on all the tough issues at once to try and fulfill his campaign promises.

After several years reporting on the Clinton administration, Birnbaum thought this was impossible. "Too much goes on too fast for the president and his staff to deal with," he writes. "Deeply considered decisions are rare luxuries at 1600 Pennsylvania Avenue. Just as the tide of one scandal, say Whitewater, subsides, another vexing trouble spot, like the war in Bosnia, explodes. Controversies, problems, and outright mistakes never stop. Not for an instant. Not for anyone. Certainly not for the people who work at the White House."

After following the ups and downs of six senior White House aides in his book, Birnbaum concludes that the federal government is unmanageable and that "an illusion of control" is all that is realistically possible.

Many crises cannot be controlled. But that doesn't mean a public official loses total control just because crises pop up. They will. Effective public officials learn to juggle many issues at once. It means acting quickly on the ball in the hand before it's time to toss it again. But instead of juggling it's called governing.

Tip #1: GOVERN LIKE A ONE-TERMER.

Ed Rendell claimed that he never worried about reelection. His mission was to pull Philadelphia back from the edge of bankruptcy and make the city government work again. The voters had given him only four years, and he could not expect another term if he did not make progress.

When Rendell spoke before a group of forty-four newly elected mayors at the John F. Kennedy School of Government after two years on the job, he counseled that a new mayor had limited time and needed to forget the next election. "Govern like you're going to be a one-term mayor," Rendell advised.

It's a powerful lesson. After President Clinton suffered devastating losses in the 1994 midterm elections, many felt Clinton should focus less on his place in history and more on finishing his term successfully. Former Carter administration speechwriter James Fallows suggested that Clinton would be a much better president if he assumed he would only serve one term. Fallows used an analogy that public officials at all levels can learn from:

> Movies and TV shows often feature a character who learns he has a year to go before a tumor overtakes him, so he suddenly starts doing everything he always meant to do. The implied question of these shows is, Why don't we live this way all the time? The same question applies in politics. The prospect of losing the race for re-election and being judged a pathetic "one-termer" has become so burdensome to presidents that even the normally buoyant Bill Clinton seems to be trudging through his first term in dread of the verdict ahead. . . . If, as in the movies, the president knew that a tumor would remove him from office in two years, he would gratefully make use of every moment he had. Ironically, if he started governing as if he didn't care about the next election, the president would increase his chance of surviving it.

Perhaps Clinton took Fallows' advice. Public officials who govern as if they will serve only one term will be more likely to make tough decisions. Without worrying about the next election, these public officials serve the public's interest before their own. And the public tends to reward public officials who get the job done; Rendell was reelected in a landslide.

Tip #2: TAKE A LONG-TERM VIEW.

At first glance, this might seem to contradict Rendell's "one-term" rule. It shouldn't. By not worrying only about reelection, public officials can plunge into long-term issues. These issues may not produce tangible results now, but will best serve the public in the long run. The challenge is to make the long run relevant to the public official now.

Clearly, finding public officials who focus on what happens to the public after their terms end is rare. Most seem to care only about what will play in their next poll. This so-called fact of political life has contributed as much as anything to the cynicism toward and distrust of public officials. Building huge deficits and postponing debate on issues like the bankrupting of Social Security and Medicare have left Americans convinced that public officials care only about holding on to office.

David Stockman, President Reagan's budget director, once said, "I'm just not going to spend a lot of political capital solving some other guy's problem in 2010." Five years later, after leaving the administration, Stockman wrote a book on how the policies he pushed had failed and left a huge mess for future administrations.

Dall Forsythe also warns aspiring public officials against short-term thinking. As New York's budget director, he insisted that Mario Cuomo make decisions on the budget as if he would always be governor. "It's important that politicians feel they have to live under the choices they make. They can't view the budget process as a candy store," Forsythe said. "Otherwise if they are fighting a tough reelection campaign they might give away the store in a last-ditch gamble to get votes."

The task, then, is to create incentives for public officials to take the long-term view. For example, investing in new computer systems may make sense for a tax collection agency, but the short-term costs in training and disruption of work may put off productivity gains for several years. In other words, money will be spent today on benefits that some future agency director will reap.

So in Philadelphia, Ed Rendell got creative. To help his political appointees take a long-term view, Rendell established a $20 million "productivity bank." City agencies could get money to invest in improvements that might not be felt until many years into the future. To qualify, an agency had to show that, over five years, the loan would increase future revenues or decrease future expenditures significantly more than the loan amount. For example, a $350,000 one-time loan to purchase energy-efficient light bulbs for municipal buildings now saves the city that much each year in lower electricity bills.

Rendell's productivity bank helped ensure that decisions were right for Philadelphia's citizens and not just the political careers of his appointees. It was an innovative way to encourage his managers to view the impact of their jobs long after they were gone.

Tip #3: RUN FIRE DRILLS.

Richard Nixon knew something about crises. As one of America's dominant political figures of the twentieth century, he managed his way successfully through a few, but got swallowed up by one for which he was completely unprepared. Watergate, after all, brought Nixon down not because of the original idiotic crime but because of the bumbling, dishonest handling of the emerging crisis. Nixon learned a lesson too late: "The ability to be cool, confident, and decisive in crisis is not an inherited characteristic but is the direct result of how well the individual has prepared himself for the battle," he wrote in his memoirs.

It's the reason Dall Forsythe forced his staff to deal with hypothetical crises during slow times: So they would have contingency plans for dealing with problems as they arose. He ran fire drills. There was no substitute for practice.

Ed Rendell also knew the importance of practice. Prior to election day Rendell had probably done everything but measure the windows in the mayor's office for new curtains.

Throughout his election campaign, Rendell held roundtable meetings on crime, housing, and, of course, the serious city budget problems. He invited experts, activists, and business leaders to talk about the problems and propose solutions. These forums also allowed Rendell to test reaction to his own ideas.

"He's really putting together what looks to be a fairly comprehensive blueprint for the first year of his mayoralty," city council staffer Kevin Vaughan said a month before election day. "It's not like Day One arrives and he has to figure out what to do."

In the end, Rendell was convinced that many of the city's problems were caused by gross mismanagement. He spent nearly three years before the election studying the solutions of other public-sector chief executives—governors and mayors of large cities.

"We studied literally every cost-saving initiative, every study, every task force we could get our hands on at the state or local level," says Rendell.

In short, he ran fire drills.

Tip #4: TAKE QUICK ACTION TO DEFUSE A CRISIS.

Emil Frankel, Connecticut's former transportation chief, learned from watching the news how quickly unexpected small problems can become big ones.

Frankel had cut a deal to put a decorative stone facing on an otherwise plain concrete bridge. Local residents wanted the beautification done as their condition for allowing the bridge to be built in the town. Without it, a bridge that could help many local businesses and commuters might never be constructed and the state could lose millions of dollars in matching federal transportation funds.

Yet the project was threatened when an evening newscast highlighted the bridge as part of its government "waste patrol" series. The compromise with town residents was portrayed as unnecessary and extravagant.

Erik Bergman, a Frankel aide, remembered the situation: "We immediately went into damage control mode. We had to make sure the public knew the full facts of the story. Ultimately, we were successful, but it was a real surprise to all of us."

"It can swallow things up," Frankel said. "You can spend so much time dealing with something that has nothing to do with what you are trying to do. No issue is too small to not become a big problem. What we tried to do is nip things in the bud."

Frankel survived this and other crises by staying focused on his agenda. "The one thing I can do is keep a lot of things going at the same time," Frankel says. "I know enough to ask the right questions and keep projects moving. But all those balls in the air at the same time were connected to an overall strategic plan—an overall change of mission of the department."

An emergency is much less likely to sidetrack a public official if it is dealt with immediately. "Decisive action relieves the tension which builds up in a crisis," Richard Nixon wrote after serving two terms as vice president. "When the situation requires that an individual restrain himself from acting decisively over a long period, this can be one of the most wearing of all crises."

Nixon, of course, later became more sidetracked and more weary than any previous president. Had he followed his own advice from a decade earlier and dealt decisively and properly with the Watergate break-in, the resulting cover-up and scandal might not have occurred.

"It is axiomatic in politics that the earlier one addresses a problem, the more the alternatives and the easier the solutions," Colorado governor Richard Lamm said.

Tip #5: TURN CRISIS INTO OPPORTUNITY.

In September 1995, the U.S. Armed Forces faced its biggest Japanese crisis since World War II. Instead of Hiroshima, this time the little-known town was Okinawa. And while no atom bomb hit, the damage was extensive—so extensive that it was felt all the way back in Washington, D.C., in the Pentagon, in the office of then Assistant Secretary of Defense Joseph Nye.

The crisis was the revelation that three U.S. Navy officers had kidnapped and brutally raped a young Japanese girl. Okinawa residents had long wanted the U.S. base closed. Now came a disaster that ruined this young girl's life and brought renewed attention to the American presence there. In the face of all this, Nye had been working on a new, bold plan to strengthen military relations between the two countries. It was sensitive work and the crisis jeopardized his plans.

"It threatened to destroy the initiative of strengthening the Japanese security alliance," Nye recalled. "It looked like it would drive the whole thing off track. We had to deal with it immediately."

Nye had been looking at ways to lower Japanese dependence on the Okinawa base. In the post–cold war era, the governments had focused most strongly on trade issues. The crisis changed everything.

"No one was looking at security," Nye said. "Then that initiative looked to be driven off course by the rape. The first goal, frankly, was trying to survive."

But Nye did more than just survive. He used the current crisis to create faster action on the U.S.–Japanese alliance. He sat down with

Defense Secretary William Perry and made it clear that once this crisis passed, "like a trolley, another will come soon." They had to act immediately.

The result was a brand-new Special Action Committee on Okinawa. It was staffed at the highest levels—Nye and U.S. Ambassador to Japan Walter Mondale on one side and the Japanese foreign and defense ministers on the other. The committee would report in one year on major steps to reduce pressure on Okinawans. By December 1996, the work was done and a treaty with concrete steps to make changes in U.S.–Japanese relations was signed by President Clinton.

Rather than leave his post with little accomplished, Nye achieved his original goal. For his work, Nye received a Defense Department medal from Secretary Perry and letters of thanks from citizens of Okinawa.

"We made some major changes that would have been very difficult to push through without the crisis," Nye said.

10

Managing the Message

Even though we never like it, and even though we wish they didn't write it, and even though we disapprove, there isn't any doubt that we could not do the job at all in a free society without a very, very active press.

—*John F. Kennedy, U.S. president*

Front-Page News

E. J. Knittel couldn't believe what he saw. Thumbing through *Governing* magazine at his desk, he got to a back-of-the-book article titled "Evaluate Managers—on Page One." As borough manager of Camp Hill, Pennsylvania, Knittel dealt frequently with the media. And while he says that some of his best friends are journalists, in the next breath he says the best way to deal with them "would be to shoot them." Knittel read on:

> What about the public managers who come and go as administrations change? Who is assessing the departing heads of the division of water resources, the agency for child protection or the department of transportation? When these top-level public managers leave office, journalists ought to evaluate their work as well. The public deserves an accounting of their successes and failures.

Knittel was steamed. The media aren't interested in public policy; they're interested in public spectacle. Shining the bright light on every move a public official makes is no way to encourage risk taking and bold public moves or make government work better. Put public managers on page one? How about with the obituaries? Knittel fired off a letter to the editor.

First he asked what planet the author was from. Then he really got going.

"As a public manager who has been evaluated on the front page, I can tell you it's not pleasant. Most reporters know nothing about local government and are only assigned to cover it as a last resort. Reporters look for headlines and dirt, not truth or good boring news. Even when the reporter gets the facts correct, the editor will write the headline to sell the news—in essence, to hell with the facts."

Knittel had a solution: "I challenge [the author] to obtain a real job as a public manager and to face the real issues that we confront every day. In fact, I invite [him] to come to work for me for a couple of weeks, and when he's done we'll publish his performance evaluation on the front page of our local paper."

Knittel later called his letter a "watered-down" version of how he really felt. "I was thinking, this guy doesn't understand what we do at all. We're evaluated every day. Every council meeting. Every budget."

Thin-skinned? Perhaps. But in twenty years of public service— most of it around Harrisburg, Pennsylvania—Knittel often felt burned by the media.

His worst experience came when he took the Camp Hill job. After three successful years as manager of nearby Newbury township, Knittel heard the position was open in Camp Hill, a town of nearly eight thousand residents. The combination of plentiful public services and a dependable tax base made the work attractive. Given Knittel's impressive background, he got the job.

But in what surely qualifies as the shortest honeymoon on record, Knittel awoke the next day to read the headline: "Fired Swartara Township Manager Gets Job on Opposite Shore."

It turns out, before Knittel managed Newbury, he managed neighboring Swartara for nine years. He lost the job, he says, when a new political party came to power. The paper reported he was "insubordinate." Regardless, instead of headlines celebrating his recent success in Newbury, on his first day in a new job the paper dredged up his failures in Swartara.

"I was never so angry," Knittel said. "It was a slap in the face. This is what my son has to see? This is what my wife has to see?"

The paper softened the headline for its afternoon edition, but for Knittel, the damage was done.

"Nine times out of ten, I believe reporters are good at heart," he said. "But they don't know bond issues or tax issues or construction issues. Generally, you're looking at reporters who maybe went to journalism school, maybe took one course on government, and have no idea what they're dealing with."

For Knittel, dealing with the press is a major obstacle to doing his job. The longer he talks about reporters, the more frustrated he gets.

"It becomes difficult to make policy," he said. "It becomes harder to get things done."

KNITTEL'S bewilderment is common among public officials. The late Washington governor Dixie Ray Lee so disliked the press, she named a litter of eleven pigs after local journalists. President Lyndon Johnson complained, "If one morning I walked on top of the water across the Potomac River, the headline that afternoon would read: PRESIDENT CAN'T SWIM." But Knittel, Lee, and Johnson faced nothing new. Negotiating this conflict between the public's right to know and a public official's ability to get the job done is democracy itself.

On the one hand, public officials should be completely open. They conduct the people's business. They spend the people's money. To withhold information undermines trust and creates cynicism. Indeed, much of today's disgust with government—from Watergate to Whitewater—comes from the belief that government officials are hiding something. And it becomes impossible to accomplish anything without the public's trust.

Elliot Richardson puts it this way: "Openness allows us to know what our governments are doing and thus decide whether or not they are meeting our standards and serving our purposes. By allowing us to stay in touch with and have a voice in the formulation and execution of our government policies, openness is vital to the ultimate aim of the democratic process."

On the other hand, the official who throws open her files to the public also risks disaster. Special-interest groups might use information selectively to stir negative publicity to support their cause. The public official could easily become paralyzed, unable to move in any direction for fear of offending someone. Again, nothing would get done.

Democracy requires openness, but where is the line between the public's need to know and the public official's need to get things done?

To govern in this gray area of our democracy, many legislatures have passed a Freedom of Information Act (FOIA). Citizens or reporters who feel stonewalled by a government agency can file a "FOIA request" to obtain information that public officials will not release. But even this legal mechanism has its problems.

For example: Connecticut Treasurer Chris Burnham took office with a policy of full and complete disclosure. He set a new standard for government financial reporting and regularly posted the state's investments on the Internet for the world to see. To Burnham, a FOIA request represented a major political blunder. Like Elliot Richardson, he believed citizens have a right to know what their government is doing.

However, even for Burnham, there was a case where he would not give out information—during an investment deal. Burnham would never publicly disclose the value of an asset while in negotiation to sell it. That would weaken the state's bargaining position. It also would violate a competing public trust—managing money to maximize investment returns.

Many other examples exist. From Pentagon troop movements to an individual's Social Security number, sometimes the public is better served when their government keeps some information under wraps.

The battles over this gray area keep the relationship between the public official and the media tense.

But in truth, public officials should love the media. After all, journalists are one of the few lowly groups that rate near them in opinion polls. But nearly every public official complains that journalists are interested only when something bad happens. Do something good, and the story gets buried, if it's published at all.

Camp Hill's E. J. Knittel complains, "There's never anything positive, like 'The town planted trees,' or 'The city cut the grass in the park.' Instead, it's 'The trees fell down' or 'The grass in the park didn't get cut.' It's very frustrating."

Complaints by public officials about press coverage are always suspect. No one enjoys criticism. But public officials take jobs knowing that microscopic inspection comes with the position along with their parking space at city hall. In addition, it is hardly news when officials do their jobs (whether that's planting trees or making payroll deadlines). After years as a public official, someone like Knittel should understand—even invite—public scrutiny.

Still, some journalists complain about much of today's coverage of government. James Fallows writes: "Mainstream journalism has fallen into the habit of portraying public life in America as a race to the bottom, in which one group of conniving, insincere politicians ceaselessly tries to outmaneuver another."

Marvin Kalb, a former television correspondent, agrees. "Officials and reporters, representing two sides of modern-day governance, are heading into what George Bush once called 'deep doodoo.' Neither seems to understand the basic ground rules of civilized communication, and in their apparent ignorance, they may soon blunder into a series of easily avoidable misunderstandings and political . . . embarrassment."

Despite the potential headaches, public officials need the media. Not only do they need the meddlesome scribes and prying reporters, they crave them. Nothing can boost an official's plan faster—or sink it quicker—than press coverage. And without the manager's input, the journalists will write what they want.

In short, public officials must manage their own message, or others will manage it for them.

The public official's challenge is to manage the message without spinning. It is a critical skill. But in this age of increasing voter cynicism, it pays to learn the difference. For sometimes, what starts as a simple spin can turn into a full-blown twister.

Missing the Mark

The experiments were of the most gruesome nature. Over forty years, brutal radiation tests were conducted in the name of science—not on animals but on people. In Massachusetts, hundreds of mentally retarded children were given radioactive iodine. In Washington and Oregon, more than 130 prisoners had their testes irradiated. In Rochester, New York, and elsewhere, nearly twenty people were injected with radioactive plutonium without their knowledge.

The tests were all sponsored by the federal government. In most of them, victims had no idea what was happening.

What public agency would expose such atrocities? Who would

have the courage—the public accountability and the public-relations acumen—to make such information known?

The U.S. Department of Energy.

In 1993, under new Energy Secretary Hazel O'Leary, an era of openness exposed some of the most secretive exploits in government history. The department published a 200-page book detailing the experiments, established an 800 number for victims to obtain information, and helped form a presidential commission to investigate the tests.

"We ought to go forward and explain to the Congress what has happened," O'Leary said, "and let the Congress of the United States and the American public determine what would be appropriate compensation."

While people were upset about the experiments, O'Leary received nearly universal praise for her honesty.

"O'Leary has shown she can do it," exclaimed a *Los Angeles Times* editorial. "If she can do it again and again, the Cold War may finally be over."

Said a former Reagan Energy Department spokesman: "Far more than her predecessors, [O'Leary] came to the realization that if you don't have the public on your side, or the media on your side, for that matter, you're going to have a very difficult time getting the cleanup going."

O'Leary, a former utility company executive, seemed to have mastered immediately a skill some public officials never understand: how to control a message. By taking the lead on radiation tests—and expressing outrage and openness—O'Leary's credibility soared. By choosing the proper time to be open, she put herself in charge of managing her message. O'Leary seemed to grasp the principles of controlling a message in an uncontrollable environment. And she got great press to prove it.

Then something went wrong. As if to demonstrate just how shifty the line is between controlling the message and appearing overbearing, O'Leary got tripped up. Just two years after receiving high marks from the press for her response to the radiation tests, O'Leary was caught giving marks to the press. She confused managing a message with spinning.

In a front-page story, *The Wall Street Journal* exposed that O'Leary had hired a public-relations firm to follow the reports of some two dozen journalists who covered the Energy Department, in addition to hundreds of newspapers, magazines, and newscasts. The firm then ranked thousands of stories from favorable to unfavorable and gave the lists to department officials, including O'Leary.

The program was designed to improve the secretary's and department's image and "build communication and trust," according to an agency spokesperson. She added that a reporter's negative rating "meant we weren't getting our message across." In other words, they had to spin better. The program ran some nine months and cost $46,500.

The backlash was immediate. Television networks picked up the story that evening, and the major newspapers replayed it for days.

A White House spokesman called the plan "clearly unacceptable." White House Chief of Staff Leon Panetta commanded O'Leary to cut her budget by $46,500. On Capitol Hill, Congress held hearings to investigate the abuses. Said one congressman: "The money involved may not sound much by Washington standards, but it represents the entire tax obligations of 21 average American households." Even *The Los Angeles Times*—the same paper that had praised O'Leary two years earlier—concluded that the stunt "threatened to overshadow her substantial achievements."

O'Leary rebutted that she had only seen a couple of reports, and that no negative action was taken against reporters who got bad marks.

But like a bad (spin) doctor, O'Leary had violated a basic medical principle: First, do no harm. The attempt to control her message and better her department's position backfired. It came at a terrible time. The Energy Department had been eyed voraciously by congressional cost cutters for years. Calls were now out for O'Leary's—and the agency's—surrender.

Senate Majority Leader Bob Dole said the deal was "just another reason to turn out the lights at the Energy Department." More than 70 House Republicans signed a petition calling for O'Leary to step down.

Even some mainstream media agreed. The local CBS television affiliate in Hartford, Connecticut, charged that O'Leary's press agent "was paid forty thousand taxpayer dollars to compile an enemies list of journalists for the secretary's use, and presumably, her abuse, if she saw fit." Comparing her to Richard Nixon, *The New York Times* wrote: "The Secretary could most effectively improve her department's coverage by resigning."

Though the White House eventually let O'Leary keep her job, the department's effectiveness was greatly hampered after her attempt to manage her message erupted into an uncontrollable media scandal.

THE TEMPTATION to manage one's message is immense. Getting policy right represents only part of the battle for a public official. Should that policy's aim be perverted by the opposition—or by an uninformed press—it might as well never have been initiated.

Hazel O'Leary controlled her message by releasing the information on radiation testing and explaining it to reporters. Had she simply let them find it on their own by opening sensitive files, journalists could have interpreted the testing—and O'Leary's silence—any way they chose. O'Leary could have been seen as part of the decades-long government cover-up. Instead, she created an image of being an open, honest public official. But the skill is delicate. Public officials must control without really controlling.

As O'Leary later learned the hard way, the media don't like to be spun. A public official finds trouble when process gains more attention than policy, especially when the process goes awry. By grading the reporters, the process went haywire. Instead of focusing on the guts of what she did—most simply, making energy policy—O'Leary focused on how it played in the news. That's spinning.

Much of the public's cynicism comes from an overdose of spin, from handlers saying their bosses meant "black" when they said "white." Public officials, out of fear that reporters will not print their stories, often resort to half-truths (or flat-out lies) in the wrong-headed attempt to influence a piece.

On the other hand, individual members of the media have minds of their own. Though they often follow each other on a story—and frequently won't acknowledge a story's importance until they've seen it elsewhere—they fight hard to maintain their independence. If public officials do not try to control the message, these authors of the first draft of history will set the agenda unfettered.

With officials actively managing their message, reporters (for fear of appearing not just biased but irresponsible) will be obliged to include what they say. Sometimes journalists will accept the "official" portrayal of events without much question. With tight deadlines, complicated issues, and human laziness, this latter scenario occurs more often than reporters or editors care to admit.

When she got caught spinning, O'Leary lost credibility. She appeared insincere and manipulative. Those qualities—and public officials who display them—help create the negative view of government that many voters hold. Those guilty public managers stand like road blocks directly in the way of making democracy work.

Telling His Story

If Ed Koch made his name as New York City's mayor by asking people "How'm I doin'?" then Rudy Giuliani did it by telling people. After all, if Giuliani gave locals the correct answer, he never risked getting a wrong response.

It would be hard to imagine a mayor having more immediate negatives when dealing with the media than Giuliani. He's a Republican mayor in a Democratic city, the first in a generation. He lost his previous run for the office and took over the mayoral post with a vocal and visceral opposition. Many see him as combative and cavalier toward civil rights and care of the poor. Many journalists openly dislike and distrust him.

In addition, he looks horrible on TV. His sparse hair hungrily hugs his forehead, requiring him to convince people it's no toupee. Furthermore, Giuliani rarely smiles. When he does, it resembles more a grimace from indigestion. This is the face of New York City?

Perhaps it is. Because no New York mayor—Koch included—ever has been better at managing his message.

"I absolutely love, and maybe I overdo this a little, to suggest something new and then watch the reaction to it," he said. "Sometimes I'm not even sure we should do it, but I love to watch the reaction from the so-called intellectuals."

Giuliani's hunt for reaction started almost immediately after his takeover. With many staff salaries still undetermined, with many of his plans still unformed, the new mayor took to the airwaves. From morning television to daytime radio to *Late Night with David Letterman*, New York media had virtually become "All Rudy, all the time." Of course, the mayor gave interviews despite telling his deputy mayors and commissioners to wait several months before speaking at length publicly in order to "concentrate on substance."

The New York Times described Giuliani's gift as "his ability to make people think the politically unthinkable." That means two things: managing what people think, and getting rid of underlings who don't think like you. Giuliani does both.

The easiest way to manage what people think is to own the presses. Giuliani and his staff do second best. They cajole, influence, and lobby those that do. Examples have become part of city lore.

One tale began after the 1995 Japan subway bombing, when the New York *Daily News* early edition ran a screaming four-word head-line questioning whether Gotham would be prepared for a similar incident. "We Have No Plan," was the paper's answer, and the mayor wasn't happy. So at 1 A.M., Giuliani placed a wake-up call to the *Daily News*'s sleeping managing editor with some suggestions. Not only did that lead article subsequently get demoted for the late edition, but it had a kinder, gentler headline: "Could It Happen Here?"

Of course, the calls don't always work. One night Giuliani's press secretary called a *New York Times* editor (this time at the office) at 11:45 P.M. regarding a story in the early edition about a young girl's shooting. The piece failed to mention that the mayor went to see the girl's mother at the hospital. The editor didn't feel the visit was news. The mayor disagreed and lost. But like a basketball coach baiting the referee in hope of getting that one favorable call late in the game, the mayor—or his staff—is always trying.

Giuliani and his press secretary have taken other steps to manage their message. Among the most controversial is granting interviews to media who write more favorably about the mayor than others (which risks, of course, encouraging nasty stories from jilted journalists). Reporters call it censorship; the mayor's office calls it smart business.

"Some of the criticism of my press and communications opera-tion," said Giuliani, "is that it is the press and communications oper-ation of my administration, and not the press and communications operation of the administration they would like to have."

Nowhere is Giuliani's effort to control the message seen more clearly than in police news. In fact, the mayor has, at times, crossed the elusive line of openness and held back pertinent information that the public should know. Specifically, when a woman was beaten and killed in Central Park in 1996, Giuliani—apparently worried about creating a panic—withheld details linking the murder to other recent attacks.

But New Yorkers care about crime the way Los Angelenos care about sunshine. And to be the bearer of good crime news in NYC is to be as popular as the L.A. weatherman who forecasts nothing but blue skies.

For Giuliani, crime news is where the goal of "managing what people think" and the harshness of "firing underlings who don't think like you" meet.

A year into office, with crime rates dropping, Giuliani ordered the reorganization of NYPD's public-relations staff. He told John Miller, head of police PR, to cut his staff by two-thirds and replace the remaining third with new people.

Many city hall watchers felt that Giuliani was tired of seeing the police chief get much of the credit for reducing crime. After all, as a former prosecutor and U.S. attorney, Giuliani had campaigned hard on the promise to control crime. Now he wanted to control that message.

If a battle was on, Giuliani won in a first-round knockout. Miller resigned. The police press office was reorganized. And eventually, Giuliani's competitor for the spotlight, Police Commissioner William Bratton, left office.

It wasn't the first time Giuliani had sacked officials over public statements or events. The same month that Miller resigned, three other department spokespeople left their jobs, not all voluntarily. One fellow allegedly got fired from a job he didn't even have yet. When the official—who had been offered a job in the Housing Authority—wrote an op-ed piece pushing Giuliani to reinstate money cut from housing organizations, his job offer was withdrawn the day the piece appeared. That's controlling a message.

Editorial writers warned periodically of Giuliani's impending doom. One *New York Times* piece titled "The Mayor's Censorship Office" cautioned Giuliani to "study the sad list of officeholders who became more obsessed with managing the news than with managing their duties." Public Advocate Mark Green called the strategy part of Giuliani's "government-by-enemies approach."

But Giuliani enjoyed great popularity throughout his term. And even among those who dislike him, one senses the grudging acknowledgment that Giuliani got his message out.

ANY PUBLIC official, from E. J. Knittel to Rudolph Giuliani, knows the importance of getting favorable press. Even officials who cannot speak to the press get into the game. Members of Giuliani's housing department have as much (if not more) interest in how housing stories are portrayed as Giuliani does. And while the Mayor would argue that these officials work for him, if housing plans get bad press, those staffers are on the front line. Often, they just leak facts to friendly reporters.

The question becomes, Does government information belong to the public or the public official? Not surprisingly, journalists and many others say the public. The official simply acts as caretaker for information that rightly belongs to the people who pay their salaries. Wrote *The New York Times:* "The press also has a professional obligation to remind readers and viewers of the fundamental error . . . based on the view that information belongs to the government. It belongs, of course, to the public."

While public officials profess profound agreement (at least on the record) with the concept that information belongs to the public, they don't always act like it. Press secretaries exist mainly to manage information favorably for their bosses. "The press always thinks the press secretary belongs to them, but she's not their water carrier," said former New York City mayor Ed Koch, speaking about the Giuliani situation. "The press secretary represents the mayor."

Both parties are right. The information does belong to the public, and officials who forget this usually end up in scandals with the suffix "-gate" attached to them. But it is unrealistic to expect humans with reputations at stake to avoid trying to manage that information. Even when public managers don't want to discuss an issue publicly, they often manage their message through leaks.

Surely an official who spends all day dealing with public debates loses effectiveness. The challenge for the public official is to control how the information is presented, while never violating the public's right to know.

Takeover Tips

Many people who enter public office have never dealt with the press before. The closest they've likely come to being quoted on the record was under their senior portrait in their high school yearbook. Yet after a takeover, every word a public official utters can appear the next morning in black and white—and that's if they get quoted accurately.

Joe Edmiston knows the feeling well. He is executive director of the Santa Monica Mountains Conservancy, the sole organization responsible for acquiring, improving, and making accessible and safe virtually all the remaining public spaces in southern California. He works in a media-saturated area with voters who care deeply about what he does. Says Edmiston: "If *The Los Angeles Times* is against you in this city, fold up your tent, go home, sell your house, buy a Winnebago, and travel around the country, because you're dead.

"You have this iron triangle between the legislators, the agencies, and the outside forces, essentially represented by the press. When we have the support of the press, we can't be stopped. When the press is indifferent or hostile, we never win. So cultivation of the press is probably the most important thing that I do."

Edmiston's been successful. In a job where, as he says "if four board members wake up and decide they don't like my haircut, I'm gone," Edmiston has survived since 1980. One of the ways he has done this is by talking to reporters at least once a day. These discussions don't always lead to a story, but it allows Edmiston to stay in touch.

Tip #1: MAKE THE STORY EASY TO REPORT.

When an ABC News reporter called to say he was doing a story on Ritalin, the Drug Enforcement Agency's Howard McClain knew what he had to do.

Ritalin is a common drug that helps children and adults with attention deficit disorder pay attention better. Properly prescribed, it has been called a wonder drug. But in its popularity, Ritalin became overprescribed. In addition, reports surfaced that the drug—which acts like speed by heightening one's focus—was being trafficked illegally and snorted and had resulted in at least one teen's death.

McClain knew that reporters move from story to story like young singles hopping from bar to bar. He had also seen enough stories on Ritalin reported improperly, including some several years earlier that declared a Ritalin shortage had occurred because of a DEA mistake. The result was a run on the drug, thousands of phone calls from panicked parents, congressional investigations, and a huge public-relations disaster for the DEA. The fact that there was really no shortage (the stories were wrong) went largely ignored.

McClain would not let a similar mistake happen again. He knew that most journalists prefer to attend a press conference or receive an easy-to-read press release rather than investigate a problem, understand possible solutions, and report critically on whether the public official's approach will work. Even for investigative reporters, who dig deeper than journalists with daily deadlines, time is short. Making a story easy to report greatly helps the public official manage his message.

McClain wanted the reporter "to get out the fact that, first of all, we weren't trying to stop anybody from getting the drug. Second, the drug is not an innocuous substance that can just be handed out to anybody. And the third thing is that there are two sides to all these stories. People were saying that we were deliberately withholding drug quota approval from a particular drug company. Well, we never do that."

What he couldn't do, however, was go on the record. McClain had to influence the story while remaining in the background. Most public officials face this challenge. Instead of just opening a file drawer and handing over documents, it means taking time with the reporter to explain what the information means. (Consider the disaster if Energy Secretary Hazel O'Leary had simply handed over documents about the radiation testing without explaining them.)

McClain made the potentially complex story as easy to report as possible. Any documents McClain could give, he gave. He was always available for analysis. He suggested other people for the reporter to consult. McClain helped advance the story.

The result was a nationally broadcast story that embodied the DEA's message.

Tip #2: MAKE THE STORY EASY TO UNDERSTAND.

It was the most costly government mistake in history. Billions of dollars were lost through neglect and fraud. It had policy implications that touched every branch of government and every citizen. Yet the savings and loan crisis was missed by most journalists.

Many public officials, academics, and bankers saw the disaster developing, and some were out front talking about it. Congressional hearings were held. But no major stories were written. No TV newsmagazine investigations were produced.

Several reasons contributed to the lack of reporting, including how newspaper staffs are divided between business desks and political desks, and the lack of pictures for television. But overwhelmingly, the story got lost because it was too hard to understand, and few public officials took the time to explain it.

Just because a story is important doesn't mean journalists are going to "get it."

"A lot of reporters don't know anything about economics," said Jerry Knight, a *Washington Post* reporter. "None of the political reporters understood the S&L story. Political reporters specialize in process, not substance. They would go out and write these mood-of-America pieces. Banks and S&Ls never hit the charts."

Public officials must keep their stories simple. Most journalists are unwilling to take the time to dissect a complicated event. They prefer stories that are easy to grasp. Not only do reporters not have the time but they must reexplain the issues to their editors and readers. Many public officials, including members of the House and Senate banking committees and bank regulators, had reason and responsibility to get this story out. Some tried. But it never happened until taxpayers were out several hundred billion dollars.

David Ellwood, an assistant secretary in the Department of Health and Human Services during the Clinton administration, believes many public officials make the mistake of complicating their communications with campaign rhetoric. "Recognizing that the public will hear and comprehend only a limited set of messages, keep your ideas and message simple and clear. Political language often obscures more than it clarifies; rarely does it have any real policy content."

Complicated stories can and do receive media attention. But public officials carry a greater burden to explain the concept fully. It may take several go-rounds. But it holds advantages: Many journalists feel that officials who take time to explain issues in depth must be telling the truth. Surely they wouldn't carefully explain something they were doing wrong. So a greater chance exists that the official's message will be accepted wholesale.

Tip #3: MAKE THE STORY PERSONAL.

In the movie *Postcards from the Edge,* Meryl Streep plays an impulsive character whose temperament is captured when she says, "The problem with immediate gratification is that it takes too long." Many Americans agree. And competition for citizens' attention span is enormous.

With hundreds of television channels, dozens of magazines and newspapers, and the Internet, the chance for a citizen to read and understand an individual reporter's story is slim. People have their own problems. How can journalists make them care about someone else's? How can public officials get journalists to care about theirs?

Journalists try to grab readers, listeners, or viewers with interesting characters. For the public official with a message to get out, framing a story around a citizen's personal struggle or one person's victory gets a reporter's attention.

Few issues are as emotional as abortion. And few abortion issues were as emotional as the debate over so-called partial-birth abortions, which Congress voted to ban in early 1996.

The procedure involves a partially delivered fetus that is killed before complete delivery. Supporters of the ban said the procedure violently destroys living fetuses. Opponents claimed that the procedure was occasionally necessary to protect mothers in potentially fatal deliveries and was central to the pro-choice concept.

President Bill Clinton vetoed Congress's bill, stating that, as written, it did not adequately protect the health of the mother. With such an emotional and moral-based issue, one would think that sincere presidential comments would suffice for the most powerful man on earth to get his message across. They didn't.

Onstage with the president were five women and their families, breathing testament to women's lives that would have been lost had they not been allowed to have partial-birth abortions.

Without much sense of irony, Clinton said: "These people have no business being made into political pawns."

Then came a rebuttal press conference by House Speaker Newt Gingrich. He stated that, despite not having the votes to override Clinton's veto, he would try anyhow. The issue was that important. One might think that sincere comments from the man third in line to the presidency would be enough to get his message across. Again, they weren't.

Onstage with the speaker was a group of children, breathing testament to children's lives that would have been lost had their mothers chosen to have partial-birth abortions. And while the debate didn't end with these incidents, the story became personal.

Tip #4: MAKE THE STORY SYMBOLIC.

Anyone who heard the story about Lenny Sutnik jumping into the freezing Potomac river to rescue passengers from a 1982 Washington, D.C., plane crash considered him a hero. But most Americans didn't hear about Sutnik until Ronald Reagan put him in the balcony during a State of the Union address to emphasize the president's point about community values. They called it "heroes in the balcony" at the Reagan White House.

Although some aides thought the stunt gimmicky, the president and first lady loved it. Reagan communications guru Michael Deaver loved it. Most importantly, the media loved it.

Journalists know that readers like to read about people. They like stories that reflect enduring American themes and archetypes. For example, reporters rarely tire of stories that expose government incompetence or highlight the pursuit of the American Dream.

When Reagan wanted to focus America's attention on the importance of traditional values during his 1985 State of the Union speech—and silence critics who said his policies were hurting young people—he pointed to a woman in the balcony and said:

Ten years ago a young girl left Vietnam with her family, part of the exodus that followed the fall of Saigon. They came to the United States with no possessions, and not knowing a word of English. The young girl studied hard, learned English and finished high school in the top of her class. This May is a big date on her calendar. Just 10 years from the time she left Vietnam, she'll graduate from the United States Military Academy at West Point. I thought you might want to meet an American hero named Jean Nguyen."

The young woman stood and smiled. Her picture and story—and the clear symbolism of someone with nothing making a life in America and then offering her life to protect others—appeared in dozens of newspapers across the country. While criticism of Reagan's policies continued almost immediately with the Democratic response to his speech, that criticism got lost. It was Morning in America. Reagan had gained the upper hand in the effort to control the message.

Tip #5: TELL THE TRUTH.

"I often tell my colleagues, give me good policy, and I'll give you good press," said Calvin Mitchell, when he was deputy assistant secretary for public affairs at the U.S. Treasury Department. "Part of the thing you do before talking to the press is learn the issue and try to figure out the holes that exist in a policy. When I say tell the truth, don't try to gloss over those difficult things. Attack them directly."

Mitchell developed his philosophy not just as a career spokesperson but after having spent several years on the policymaking side as a foreign service officer.

"I often think people make mistakes by making a decision and then calling their press people in and saying this is what we're going to do. Corporations make that mistake. They get out on the record a certain position, and then it's hard to move from that position once you've sustained it. I think that's really hard in government, too."

About the time Mitchell was saying those words, Transportation Secretary Federico F. Pena should have been listening. When ValuJet Flight 592 crashed nose-first into the murky, alligator-filled Florida Everglades, Americans were horrified. Not only did many viewers pray for the victims, but knowing the old adage "you get what you pay for," they wondered whether the government was letting an unsafe airline fly, all in the name of a cheap ticket to Miami.

Quickly and confidently, Pena moved to put such notions to rest. In newspapers, on television—seemingly everywhere—the handsome Pena went on the record in support of the airline: "Whenever we have found any issues, ValuJet has been responsive, they have been cooperative, they have in some cases even exceeded the safety standards that we have."

Pena made similar comments so many times—including stating that he had flown ValuJet before and would fly it again—that, as Mitchell warned in a different context, it was hard for Pena to move from that position.

It became even more difficult when statistics from the Federal Aviation Administration, an office overseen by Pena, showed that ValuJet had a higher accident rate than all major airlines and even most low-cost airlines. Pena was stuck.

Like many stuck politicians, Pena went on *Nightline* to defend his comments, an uncomfortable task. But it was too late. Pena's credibility had been greatly diminished. Just three days later, Senator Trent Lott said on *Meet the Press* what many people felt: that Pena had "gone too far" in his remarks.

"When I say be honest, you try to develop your core policy of what you honestly believe is your decision on something and then you build from there," said Mitchell, who later became spokesman for U.N. Ambassador Bill Richardson. "With the public affairs people who work with me, I stress that as well. We don't tolerate shadings when we deal with the press. I perfectly believe in people not answering questions that haven't been asked, and make journalists work for what they get. But at the same time, you never lie. You never tell a falsehood."

Mike McCurry, the Clinton administration spokesman, took this point seriously: "Precisely because press secretaries have lied in the name of presidents past, there is no greater sin at the White House press podium than to utter anything but words that are 100 percent truthful and reliable. To do otherwise is rightly considered career-jeopardizing."

Tip #6: FIND NEW WAYS TO GET THE MESSAGE OUT.

Andy McLeod had an odd problem. Because adversarial groups were successfully brought to the bargaining table over one of California's most volatile issues—water rights—the state's media stopped paying attention to the still-active problem.

"If you're not lobbing grenades, it's not news," said McLeod, deputy secretary of California's resource agency. "Because groups are trying to work together, people think the problems have gone away. They haven't. The politicians, including us, should not be lulled into a false sense of security by a decrease in volume."

McLeod has employed the traditional methods to broadcast news, including press conferences, speeches, opinion pieces, and meetings with editorial boards. But to ensure that the public would still learn about the debate surrounding use of California's limited water supply, McLeod had to find new ways to get the message out. His first job was to circumvent the Sacramento press corps.

"Obviously," said McLeod, "a story written by a paper's capitol correspondent is different from the one written by the environmental writer in Bakersfield or San Diego."

So when McLeod's department wanted to publicize the bureaucratic milestone of creating an agreement with the federal government on water management, they went outside the capitol. Specifically, they hosted a rare press conference at the delta where the Sacramento and San Joaquin rivers form the San Francisco Bay. There they stood a better chance of getting San Francisco and Sacramento news crews interested in the story.

McLeod takes the idea of circumventing the traditional media even further. He frequently turns to the alternative media, whether weekly newspapers or small, local radio stations, to plant a story. The key is to know one's audience.

"If it's not local, it may not be news," he said. "That's not rocket science, but a lot of it is not just pushing announcements out the door that are not tailored for local audiences."

Of course, McLeod has also made use of the Internet, bringing news directly to citizens. His department helped spearhead Internet public access in all of California's fifty-eight counties. And besides having one of the state's most sophisticated Web sites, McLeod always adds new information and finds new ways to get that information out.

11

Remember Who Sent You

> With public sentiment, nothing can fail; without it, nothing can succeed. Consequently he who molds public sentiment goes deeper than he who enacts statutes or pronounces decisions.
>
> —*Abraham Lincoln, U.S. president*

Love, Honor, and Obey

If nothing else, the old days were simple. Local politics ran like a machine, headed by a boss. In Chicago, that's what they were called. The Machine. The Boss.

The Boss, of course, was Mayor Richard J. Daley, and if it was legislated, appropriated, or adjudicated, it went through him. Not only did all issues touch Daley, but everyone was accountable to him. Not just accountable in the sense that Daley was elected by the people, so whoever worked in his name answered to him. Every public servant is accountable in that way. With Daley, a deeper accountability existed. Workers owed him more than their service; they owed him their jobs.

"Like the marriage vows," wrote Mike Royko in his landmark Daley biography, *Boss,* "the pact between jobholder and party ends only in either's death, so long as the jobholder loves, honors, and obeys the party."

Under Daley, the concept of accountability became a simple, if not weird, science of reverse gravity: the stabilizing force came from above. Employees were not first accountable to citizens but to whoever secured their job.

One of those employees held an official title that isn't found in many governments today: the director of patronage. "He brings a list of all new city employees for the day. The list isn't limited to the key employees, the professional people. All new employees are there—down to the window washer, the ditch digger, the garbage collector. After each person's name will be an extract of his background, the job, and most important, his political sponsor. Nobody goes to work for the city, and that includes governmental bodies that are not directly under the mayor, without Daley's knowing about it. He must see every name because the person becomes more than an employee: he joins the political Machine, part of the army numbering in the thousands who will help win elections. They damn well better, or they won't keep their jobs."

For citizens, the system meant the mayor could guarantee certain services—potholes got filled, and if cousin Johnny needed a job, all he had to do was ask. Favors were currency. It also created, however, an entrenched bureaucracy that had little responsibility to the people. After all, why be accountable to citizens when they have little influence over your standing?

THE DECLARATION of Independence states clearly that government derives its power from the "consent of the governed." Few would argue that public officials shouldn't be accountable to the people. It's the most basic principle of our democracy. Yet, too often, top government officials forget that rule.

"The best evidence of American perspective toward government is that nothing makes us angrier than public officials who seem to have forgotten that they work for us," Elliot Richardson wrote.

Richardson should know. As attorney general, he resigned rather than carry out President Richard Nixon's order to fire the special Watergate prosecutor. Richardson believed that hindering the investigation seriously violated the public's trust.

"The root of the problem is not so much that our people have lost confidence in government," said Jimmy Carter, "but that government has demonstrated time and again its lack of confidence in the people."

In Chicago, accountability has changed since Mayor Daley's time. It is no longer enough for government workers to be accountable only to the party hack who secured their jobs. Whether elected or appointed, individual responsibility matters, and public officials are judged by how answerable they are to the people. Instead of top down, accountability must run bottom up.

Weakened political parties caused part of the change. Though the Democratic party still reigns in the Windy City, the Machine no longer exists the way it did under Daley. Gone are the days when a single man would serve as head of the party and head of the government. Individual voters hold much more power than they did in the past.

In Chicago, Richard Daley is once again mayor. Only this time, it's Richard *M.* Daley, the Boss's son. Among the headaches he inherited upon taking office was the Chicago Park District, a city department historically so overrun with patronage it was said to house "park-barrel politics." Daley's first appointment to the top position didn't work out. In late 1993, he made his second.

Nobody's Fault

Chicago Parks General Superintendent Forrest Claypool speaks in revolutionary terms about his job. He refers frequently to the American and French revolutions. And he compares what he's done at the park district with the fall of the Soviet Union.

"The system was built originally as a patronage empire," he said. "The old bureaucracy was run like the Kremlin. And it was equally ineffective."

Indeed, the horror stories sound like they come directly out of Moscow's Gorky—not Chicago's Lincoln—Park.

For example, a career official basked in praise from a longtime coworker at his retirement party: "Twenty years ago when I was a young clerk in the system," the coworker said, "I used to roll out of bed when I rolled out of bed. Go to work when I felt like it. Usually arrive about 11 o'clock. Make a couple of personal phone calls, go out to lunch, come back, make a few more personal phone calls, and go home. He covered for me for all those years."

Claypool also tells of a city resident "who called her local park to see if a recreational program was still being offered and was told that the information was confidential."

Claypool took over a government department that was out of

touch with the people. Young enough to believe in the impossible (he was thirty-six when he arrived) and politically connected enough to make it happen (he took the job after serving as Daley's chief of staff), Claypool was ready to make major changes. And he knew where to start.

"This year marks our sixtieth anniversary," he said soon after taking office. "It will also mark the year of revolution. The Chicago Park District . . . failed to protect the civic jewels entrusted to its care. It has failed because layers of bureaucracy have replaced individual accountability. It's nobody's fault, because nobody can be held accountable."

When Claypool took office, a local watchdog group called Friends of the Park released its periodic report card on park services. The district had improved since the previous one. It got a D-plus.

"There are a lot of people at the Park District who work hard, but there are an awful lot of them who were not held accountable," recalled Erma Tranter, executive director of the watchdog group. "They didn't care. They were there for political reasons. They were protected. And they knew that."

To investigate the complaints, Claypool sent staffers anonymously into the field. Unbelievably, they found park employees who would not let them use the facilities. Randy Mehrberg, the district's general attorney, arrived at one park to catch a man lounging in the supervisor's office, feet up on the desk, watching a football game on the tube.

"Randy learned from a volunteer in the building that week after week, this park employee sits in the office watching football games, refusing to assist patrons," Claypool said. "Randy returned to the man watching TV in his office. By this time he'd been in the park for about a half hour. He asked the man to clean up garbage outside. The man responded it was not his job. [It was.] Randy asked this man what his job was. The man said his job was—and I quote—'To sit here and collect a paycheck.' This employee then asked Randy to leave the office, claiming it was for employees only."

The old system of accountability was still in place, and citizens remained forgotten. In addition, with the elder Mayor Daley gone, city employees seemed to feel little accountability to anyone.

One of Claypool's first actions was to bust the central bureaucracy. Previously, nearly every Park District decision labored through the gray, somber central office, a dimly lit building that would not seem out of place in Moscow's Red Square. By letting directors at each individual park have greater leeway in making decisions, Claypool sought citizens' input in how their park was managed. He listened to city residents and asked Friends of the Park for advice on how to run the parks better.

"It's an old concept," he said, "as old as Jeffersonian democracy. The notion that the closer a government is to the people it serves, the more accountable it will be. It's a 200-year-old principle. We're not doing anything new here. We try to put that power and authority close to the people that are served."

Claypool made evident his drive to institute accountability in the list of goals he printed and distributed to employees. Goal No. 1: "To create safe, inviting and user-friendly parks and facilities that attract increasing numbers of Chicagoans and visitors." In case the message got lost, Goal No. 2 read: "To create a park system that inspires pride in the community and its employees."

The results were impressive. Friends of the Park, which two years earlier gave the district a D-plus, wrote that "new management has accomplished a tremendous amount in a short period of time through the creation of a management structure to replace the 'dysfunctional' one that existed."

"Forrest Claypool is the perfect symbol of the difference between the elder Daley and his son," former U.S. senator Adlai E. Stevenson said. "He's politically nimble, but that's not all. He's an accomplished public manager as well. He's got the technocratic side down. Claypool has done a great job making the city work once again."

Making the park system accountable to city residents shocked the old system of accountability. Many park employees didn't see the changes coming. Said Claypool: "It was the equivalent of storming the Bastille."

EVERY FEW years, elected officials have a very public referendum in which they are held directly accountable to the people. It's called an election. But if that's the only time public officials listen to citizens, they are doomed. A long time passes between elections. And appointed officials, like Forrest Claypool, never directly face the voters.

The widespread distrust of government has been documented by nightly newscasts, daily papers, and books. The feeling runs so deep that many candidates, to gain public favor, run against the government they wish to join. Because government is not responsive to its concerns, citizens are disgusted.

The anecdotal evidence of public officials that forgot for whom they work is endless.

In May 1996, a discarded metal umbrella hit an electrified rail of the New York City subway during evening rush hour and sent the system into chaos. The high-voltage explosions sounded and felt like bombs. Fire started under one train and panicked passengers, with memories of the World Trade Center bombing filling their heads, poured into the dark, damp tunnels and hiked their way out. With riders on the tracks, power was shut down.

"I was screaming 'Run! Run!'" one passenger said. "I thought I was going to get burned up."

Said another: "Everybody thought the worst."

Everybody, that is, but subway chief Joseph E. Hoffman. He stayed home in New Jersey for some two hours—leaving midlevel staffers at the scene—after being told by employees that the problem was fairly routine. That delay kept emergency workers from fixing the problem.

Mayor Rudolph Giuliani was outraged. "When there are three thousand New Yorkers in that subway, they'd damn well better have a high-level person there," he said. "There's no excuse, and it should never happen again."

But Hoffman had an excuse, and amazingly, it was the passengers. If they hadn't gone on the tracks, power wouldn't have been shut off. Forget that Hoffman arrived at the scene two hours late. Forget the unseemliness of blaming scared passengers.

Riders were furious.

"Even if you're right, you don't shift the blame for problems to someone else," one New Yorker said. "Maybe if people were instructed what to do, if someone responsible was there to tell them what to do, they wouldn't have gone on the tracks."

Said another: "In business, the customer is always king. If government is ever to become efficient, it's going to have to take that mental step—that and accountability. Without accountability, it's total nonsense."

Citizens, of course, are not customers. They are owners and deserve an even higher degree of accountability. Making government remember its citizens is easy to say, difficult to do. It's a constant battle. Public officials must regularly check that employees are delivering what the program promises.

In Chicago, Claypool constantly reminded his staff that they worked for city residents. His goal was to let citizens enjoy their parks again. To monitor his staff's progress, he implemented regular audits. Using interviews, regular spot checks, and even taking Polaroid photos of the parks, he kept track of improvement.

Not every government official goes to such lengths. But the good ones find specific ways to ensure they are doing the work voters requested.

Making the Grade

The way Beverly Stein saw it, it was more than just another government takeover. After giving up her Oregon state legislature seat in 1993 to run against eight candidates for Multnomah County chair, her inauguration swearing-in ceremony was a chance to send a message of how she would run county government as its chief executive.

She had two choices for the festivities—inside or outdoors. Given that Multnomah County surrounds Portland, one of the country's rainiest cities, the choice would seem simple. And to Stein it was. Despite suggestive clouds filling the August sky, the inauguration would be outside. That put government in its proper place—"where the public can see it."

To Stein, government service comes down to a series of straightforward questions:

" 'Is government providing good service?' is too narrow," she said. "It avoids the question, 'Is government advancing democracy?' Are we creating a democratic commons for helping citizens and communities to help themselves? Is government serving as a catalyst to bring resources, people, and plans together to accomplish our common goals?"

In other words, is government accountable?

"Citizens," said Stein, "want government to assure personal and community security and protect basic freedoms."

For Stein, the question was how to do it. And she had little time to find the answer. Stein was elected to fill a term left vacant when the previous county chair died. She faced reelection—and possibly those eight former opponents—in just ten months. Stein quickly implemented a program to guarantee the accountability she desired, no matter who would serve as county chair.

Benchmarks was a program based on an award-winning initiative of the Oregon state government. Stein brought it to the local level. At town meetings, citizens identified what they wanted their government to achieve, such as reducing violent crime and increasing visitors to local parks. Then Stein and her staff identified numerical progress indicators—or benchmarks—to measure the government's progress, to make sure they were accomplishing the work people wanted. Examples of benchmarks might include "murders per one thousand citizens" or "park visitors per month."

The people had spoken. Benchmarks gave Stein the bottom line that government lacks—specific indicators to grade her progress along the way. Now she had to fulfill her responsibility.

"Sadly, some politicians offer simple slogans as solutions to the crime problem. 'Three strikes and you're out' and 'remand all juveniles to adult court' are the latest rallying cries," Stein said. "I do have my own simplistic campaign slogan for fighting crime: 'No simple solutions to complex problems.'"

For example, citizens decided in town meetings that their priorities included aiding first-time juvenile offenders, supervising repeat criminals, and expanding domestic violence services. To meet these benchmarks, Stein's only option was sure to make enemies—cutting twenty-three sheriff's deputies and moving them to Portland's jurisdiction in order to free up money. Stein felt that her responsibility was to achieve the goals the community had established. She would be measured by her progress toward meeting them.

Not surprisingly, objections followed, led by the county sheriff who would lose one-fourth of his staff. "There are several new untested programs being started," he said, "and frankly my contention is that six of 10 people on the street would say their highest priority is safety in their neighborhood."

But Stein stood by the citizens' choices. And setting benchmarks helped her win the battle against the sheriff. The community had ranked goals and, with limited resources, knew it would be impossible to meet them all. Stein fought for their decision and moved the deputies to the Portland police department, freeing up $2 million for her crime-stopping plans.

The result was to increase monitoring of juvenile offenders—to "get serious" after one offense, not four or five—and expand adolescent drug and alcohol programs. Just ten months later, county voters got to render their own judgment. If they didn't like the shift of twenty-three deputies, or any of her other choices, they had specific benchmarks against which Stein would be held accountable.

And they did hold Stein accountable. She won the general election unopposed; nobody dared run against her.

AT THE LEAST, elected officials get input from constituents every four years. But for effective public officials like Beverly Stein, that's not enough. For example, Stein not only promised to give people the government they wanted, she installed measurement techniques to ensure it happened.

Without a clear bottom line in government, benchmarks provide one. The process works like a midterm election, giving officials direction for the future and hard figures against which to measure their performance.

But while waiting for voting time is unwise for elected officials, it presents no solution for appointed officials. After all, no one elected them.

Robert Reich, who served in the Carter and Ford administrations early in his career and the Clinton team more recently, questions whether public officials have enough information to determine what the public really wants. After elections, officials typically rely on legislators to understand the will of the people. But Reich notices:

> The statutes that authorize them to take action are often written in vague language, unhelpful for difficult cases of a sort the legislative drafters never contemplated or did not wish to highlight for fear that explication might jeopardize a delicate compromise. The legislators may have had conflicting ideas about how the law should be implemented and decided to leave the task to those who would be closer to the facts and circumstances of particular applications. Or they may simply have wanted an administrator to take the political heat for doing something too unpopular to be codified explicitly in legislation. Or the legislators may have felt that the issue was not sufficiently important to merit their time and resources.

In other words, public officials—elected or appointed—have wide room in which to navigate a course. They are not merely executors of clear legislative will. They must seek public input.

"Sometimes higher-level public managers have an obligation to stimulate public debate about what they do. Public deliberation can help the manager clarify ambiguous mandates," Reich observes. "Thus the public manager's job is not only, or simply, to make policy choices and implement them. It is also to participate in a system of democratic governance in which public values are continuously rearticulated and recreated."

Children are taught in elementary school that American government is "of the people." That's mostly true. The United States has a representative government; voters elect people to represent their needs and views, from the school board to the Senate to the electoral college. Citizens do not directly vote for bills any more than they directly vote for their president. They elect representatives who cast the actual ballots that count.

But in the end, no election explains the public's desire on every issue. Many problems an official faces during a term never come up during the campaign. Benchmarks helped Beverly Stein understand the public's will on issues facing her county. Community forums helped generate public discussions and prioritize goals.

Now technology promises to change American democracy even more. Using the information superhighway, voters are telling their governments what to do. It works similarly to Beverly Stein's forums, only at cyberspeed, and not just on election day, but every day. Former NBC News chief Lawrence K. Grossman sees a transformation toward an "electronic republic," with Americans moving away from the current representative government toward the pure democracy of the Greeks.

This is the first generation of citizens who can see, hear, and judge their own political leaders simultaneously and instantaneously. It is also the first generation of political leaders who can address the entire population and receive instant feedback about what the people think and want. Interactive telecommunications increasingly give ordinary citizens immediate access to the major political decisions that affect their lives and property.

For today's public officials, accountability goes beyond the public's right to know. Government managers now have an obligation to know what the public thinks.

Electronic Democracy

Santa Monica, California, is known essentially for two things: world-class surfing and grassroots politics. So perhaps it's not surprising that the nation's first governmental on-line service, called the Public Electronic Network (PEN), began there. Now, to contact their government, citizens use PEN and a personal computer instead of pen and paper.

Jory Wolf built the on-line system. When he started the project in 1987, it generated considerable excitement. PEN promised to expand access to Santa Monica government, an important concept in a city where government accountability was imperative. It also promised to move information not just in one direction—from government to the people—but in two.

"It had to be universally accessible," said Wolf, warming at remembering his grand experiment. "This was something that we needed to allow everyone who had a computer to have access to. We felt it was important not just to provide 'pets for adoption' and 'how to secure your home while on vacation.' We wanted to have something people could participate in."

The problem was, of course, that nothing like it had ever been built. The Internet was still a Pentagon experiment to link a bunch of universities and military offices. It took two years, several citizen surveys, and dozens of equipment donations before PEN was ready to go. Citizens could read city council minutes, make on-line transactions, communicate with council members, and participate in open conferences with other citizens.

The time came to make the council members—who had suggested the project in the first place—aware of their new responsibilities. Wolf recalled the reaction:

"We had the city manager's office saying, 'What are you telling us we need to do? We need to respond to the public through electronic mail within twenty-four hours? We need to participate in on-line discussions about heated local issues? You want us to be visible to the public and available twenty-four hours a day?'

"And we said, 'Absolutely. That's what our role is as government.' "

The council agreed. Technology had changed the link between the public and its government.

"They took the challenge," he said. "They said, 'Let's do this. We're going to be the risk takers. And we're going to make it work.' We had a lot of people who were doubtful, and a lot of people who said, 'Boy, this is different.' But everybody became real positive—if this works, we're going to go down in history as the people who showed that there could be open government."

The experiment caught on quickly. Wolf hoped to sign up one thousand applicants the first year. He got one thousand the first month. The staff placed terminals and modems around town for easy access: from libraries to nursing homes to public parks. Soon, people were logging on the network approximately four thousand times each month.

There were problems, of course. While PEN became more popular, it also grew slightly out of control. One city council member complained that some of the on-line conferences, such as ones that dealt with TV, movies, or sports, drifted too far from the topic of city government. In addition, the city confronted "flamers"—users who took the anonymity of on-line correspondence to engage in scorching personal attacks. Free speech represents a basic tenet not only of Santa Monica's beliefs but also of on-line culture. Still, something needed to be done.

"The flamers came in and trashed everybody," said Judy Abdo, Santa Monica council member who also served as the city's mayor. "I was specifically targeted in attacks. They would raise inconsistencies from something I said in, like, 1982 and tried to provoke me to use things against me in the next election. It was very upsetting. I couldn't just be a person."

As a result, PEN authorities suspended some people from the system and implemented a user agreement.

But PEN's primary goals—including greater government accountability to the citizens—have been realized. The network led directly to the passage of several initiatives, including a new homeless shelter. And people get the information they want, no matter how small. When one writer, wanting to know how far he ran during his daily jogs, asked at 9:43 P.M., "What is the distance around the outter rim walkway at Clover Park? Do you have any other walking/running dimensions for Clover?" By 8:24 the next morning he was thanked for the message and told, "The Clover parcourse is 4,757 feet, approximately 9/10 of a mile."

"People use PEN like they use their government," said Keith Kurtz, a PEN manager. "So people may log on once a year, every day, once every two months, four months, once every two years. Once someone's got an account, they can stay on."

"The Public Electronic Network has changed the culture of this organization," Wolf says excitedly. "When I talk to people in other governments, I really don't get the sense that I do from our staff. Our staff seems to have developed a new mindset for being available to the public. For being a partner with the public. Instead of being an entity that governs, I've seen that the staff really sees themselves as facilitators.

"It gives us a better sense of how we're doing."

THE ELECTRONIC republic has arrived. On-line services, fax machines, talk radio, and the like have shortened the distance between people and their government. They have also added a new sense of accountability, changed since the days of the Boss, Mayor Richard J. Daley. Success will come to those officials and governments that respond.

Imagine a government official saying the following about Congress:

> Such an institution may be sometimes necessary as a defense to the people against their own temporary errors and delusions. . . . There are particular moments in public affairs when the people, stimulated by some irregular passion, or some illicit advantage, or misled by the artful representations of interested men, may call for measures which they themselves will afterwards be the most ready to lament and condemn. In these critical moments, how salutary will be the interference of some temperate and respectable body of citizens, in order to check the misguided career and to suspend the blow meditated by the people against themselves, until reason, justice and truth can regain their authority over the public mind?

Today, voters would likely send this official into early retirement. Most citizens will not vote for candidates who think they know better than the voters. But that comment was made by James Madison in the *Federalist Papers* in 1788 as the nation struggled to define democracy.

That such a statement today would no sooner be uttered by most public officials than they would take back women's right to vote demonstrates how American democracy has evolved.

The Founders believed there existed a class of people better suited to making big decisions than the American people. Times have changed. Ordinary Americans no longer feel that elected representatives are superior citizens. The new information sources available to voters have shown the political class to be quite fallible. Many simply abuse their authority. From Watergate to Whitewater, few presidential administrations seem to escape scandal. From Speaker Jim Wright's resignation to Speaker Newt Gingrich's reprimand, the legislative branch has its problems, too. Public officials seem as capable of dishonesty as the common voter. While this may have been just as true in the past, citizens are more aware of it today.

Not all public officials can be expected to do the right thing. As a result, citizens must exercise their authority—act as a check on the other branches of government—to make sure their government serves society well. Today, many citizens feel the answer lies in giving more decision-making authority directly to the people. Direct democracy means government officials can no longer squirrel themselves away, not having to answer fully for their decisions until the next campaign.

"The stakes are too high for government to be a spectator sport," the late congresswoman Barbara Jordan said. Indeed, direct democracy means involving people more in government. It means that if all people are considered equal under the law, why do most stand by for four years, either doing nothing or letting anger simmer? That is not true democracy.

The way to accomplish a fuller democracy, proponents suggest, is through increased voice and input from voters. Mostly, this entails more referenda, putting certain issues directly to the voters for decision. But it also means calling upon citizens to help the executive branch implement laws, serve on commissions, and testify before the legislature. Electronic town meetings, once just a gimmick, are used more seriously by government officials.

Needless to say, many people do not support the concept of direct democracy. Citizens are too easily swayed by emotion, naysayers argue. Citizens won't take the time necessary to weigh serious issues. Citizens could be swept up by lies. It's inefficient for citizens to waste their time on multiple issues; the job should be left to people who consider them full-time. Citizens are not specialists (also known as the "if you're sick, call a doctor" theory). Citizens already do not vote regularly in elections. Citizens are too splintered and too interested in single issues to see the big picture. The list of criticisms goes on.

The two most persuasive arguments against direct democracy involve voter choices. First, opponents fear that in referenda, voters will act solely in their self-interest. One imagines choices like: "Should your taxes be raised to help the poor?" Backers of representative government say, of course people can't vote on such issues, because they will undoubtedly behave selfishly.

On the Internet "there's alt.politics.greens, alt.politics.libertarian, alt.politics.radical-left, alt.fan.dan-quayle, alt.politics.nationalism.white, alt.fan.g-gordon-liddy, alt.rushlimbaugh.die.a.flaming.death," reported *Time* magazine. "In a nation that has trouble fixing its attention on the public good and is facing increasingly bitter cultural wars, this is not a wholly encouraging glimpse of the future. There's no alt.transcendent.public.interest in sight."

Not exactly. Many examples exist where Americans, warned about impending problems, give up individual benefit for the public good. The most obvious is recycling. Individually, recycling does nothing except cause headaches—separate this garbage here, put that trash there. Yet people continue to separate, categorize, and recycle, not for individual gain, but for a perceived public advantage—everyone doing their little part to create greater good.

In addition, the experience of other countries proves the point. Switzerland has moved toward direct democracy more than just about any other country. And in 1993 its voters made two decisions that one would think would have gone the other way. The first was to reject a proposal to forbid the military from purchasing any new aircraft for the rest of the century. In peace-loving Switzerland, this cost-saving measure would appear to be a shoo-in. It lost. The same year, the Swiss voted, against conventional wisdom, to increase their gas taxes.

America has seen similar results. One study collected thousands of polls taken front 1935 to 1990 to determine the competence of public opinion in America. The 1992 report, *The Rational Public*, found that "public opinion as a collective phenomenon is stable, meaningful, rational and able to distinguish between bad and good." Other studies of voter initiatives in Oregon, South Dakota, New York, and California showed similar results.

The second most persuasive argument against direct democracy is what is called the "tyranny of the majority." Leave decisions to a simple majority, opponents argue, and that creates room for all kinds of racist or discriminatory regulations. Indeed, American history is littered with examples of outside authority (usually the feds) coming in to clean up locally created messes. The civil rights disputes of the 1960s are most apparent.

But protection against abuse of the minority exists. It's called the Bill of Rights. And judges regularly strike down laws that unfairly discriminate or infringe on the necessary conditions for democracy such as equality and freedom of speech. This system may not be perfect, but it is more than adequate to protect against this possible, though unproved, fault with direct democracy.

In 1996, the *Economist* devoted an entire section to a survey of the move toward direct democracy:

> The defenders of the old-fashioned form of democracy have to face the fact that the world has changed radically since the time when it might have seemed plausible to think the voters' wishes needed to be filtered through the finer intelligence of those "representatives." The changes that have taken place since then have removed many of the differences between ordinary people and their representatives. They have also helped the people to discover that the representatives are not especially competent. As a result, what worked reasonably well in the 19th century will not work in the 21st century. Our children may find direct democracy more efficient, as well as more democratic, than the representative sort.

The debate has broken down into two main camps: One fears too much democracy; the other fears too little.

Ted Koppel of ABC News captured the concerns of those who dread excess democracy: "It promises to be a fiasco. . . . Imagine an ongoing electronic plebiscite in which millions of Americans will be able to express their views on any public issue at the press of a button. Surely nothing could be a purer expression of democracy. . . . Now imagine the paralysis that would be induced if constituencies could be polled instantly by an all-but-universal interactive system. No more guessing what the voters were thinking; Presidents and lawmakers would have access to a permanent electrocardiogram, hooked up to the body politic."

Larry Grossman brushes aside these criticisms. "Our political system has shown itself to be remarkably resilient in accommodating the nation's expanding democratic impulse. The two-hundred-year-old Constitution has survived vast geographical expansion, multiple population increases, and enormous demographic transformations among the nation's citizens," he says. "Now it will have to withstand still another great transformation."

Santa Monica's Jory Wolf considered the question of too much democracy a practical problem. "We see it from the standpoint that you can never have too much information," he said. "There's no way that you're trying too hard. And we like to think that there will always be factions and there will always be public debate, but without that discourse, you don't have an end result that meets the needs of everyone."

As for too little democracy, the argument goes that access will be bought out by big companies. These telecommunications giants will then have undue influence over public opinion and public debate, limiting the free flow of ideas.

This threat seems more worrisome than the concern of too much democracy. Each of the major television networks is owned by a huge corporation of which the networks are just an operating division and the news-gathering operations a mere unit. Consolidation has reduced the number of companies owning cable networks, on-line services, and radio stations as well.

Still, while the number of big news outlets will dwindle, the ease of desktop publishing, the simplicity of publishing information on the Internet, and the ability directly to contact public officials in more ways than ever makes it unlikely that citizens' voices will go unheard.

Public officials must understand the evolving democracy. That's because, like it or not, direct democracy has made its move, from dozens of initiatives in Oregon to mail-in voting in North Dakota to voting by phone in New Mexico to using the Internet to rethink tax codes in Texas. The question, as Grossman puts it, "is not *whether* the new electronic information infrastructure will alter our politics, but *how*."

Takeover Tips

Any new public official must understand the changes that democracy is undergoing. Bluntly stated, this is not your parents' democracy. To ignore the ramifications of such change, to avoid public comment, is to invite disaster.

This does not mean, however, that public officials must govern by polling data. The changes are more complex and more subtle than that. Indeed, the lack of a core set of values has earned more than one public official extreme public ire. In addition, polls can be made to say virtually anything one wants them to say. That's part of the reason there exist both Democratic and Republican pollsters. Instead, a fine line must be walked, between listening to what constituents want and being true to oneself.

Some public officials can listen closely to constituents, and implement their requests, without violating their core set of beliefs.

When Thomas M. Davis III took over as chairman of the Fairfax (Virginia) County Board of Supervisors in 1992, he was not afraid to make decisions certain to upset people on all sides of the spectrum.

"You have to ruffle some feathers," he said.

But ruffling feathers didn't mean ignoring people's concerns. Not only did Davis organize brown-bag lunches with county employees, he also invited special interest groups once a month for a "chairman's roundtable."

"I was real impressed with him," said one county activist who met with Davis on race issues. "Each of us went in very stern in what we wanted. We didn't go in with rose-colored glasses. But we came out pretty pleased."

Said the school superintendent, who had a "frosty relationship" with Davis: "He's straight. I may not like everything he tells me, but I trust him."

The question becomes how to walk that fine line. Here are some answers.

Tip #1: SET GOALS AND ANNOUNCE THEM.

When Arne Carlson took over as Minnesota governor in 1990, he knew how to measure results. His previous twelve years were spent as the state auditor, where he created, for the first time in Minnesota history, uniform accounting for cities, counties, townships, and special districts.

But Carlson knew that accountability went beyond accounting. For the state's chief bean counter, knowing where money was spent was a relatively simple question. As chief executive, however, his job depended on results. It was not enough just to spend state money and determine by chance years later whether the spending was productive.

"Historically, government has done a poor job of measuring results," read one state document. "It does an excellent job of measuring how much activity occurs: how much money is spent, how many forms are filed, how many reports are prepared, how many permits are issued. But government is less successful at measuring results of those activities—whether they resulted in a safer or cleaner environment or a better life for Minnesota's citizens."

Carlson decided to answer this problem by setting measurable goals and announcing them. Minnesota voters would know by a simple score sheet whether he was getting the job done or not. He would create a bottom line where one previously didn't exist.

Carlson began Minnesota Milestones, a report card that included twenty measurable goals and seventy-nine milestones to determine progress toward those objectives. Goals included "sustaining above-average economic growth" and "emphasizing advanced education so Minnesota will become a global economic leader." Some related milestones were Minnesota per capita gross state product and college graduation rates.

The goals were determined by surveying thousands of Minnesotans at more than forty-five statewide meetings and through mail-in questionnaires. To keep the program up to date, new surveys are periodically conducted.

"Monitoring progress will help us know if our programs are working the way they are intended and accomplishing the results we want," said Linda Kohl, who helped run the project. "If the measurements show that our programs are not working, it will allow us to redirect our efforts."

Said Carlson: "Minnesota Milestones has enabled us to better identify the needs and goals of Minnesotans. Today we can rally our limited resources around these key priorities."

The *St. Paul Pioneer Press* applauded the system's ability to "ensure that politicians make progress toward meeting those goals."

The voters agreed. In 1994, they reelected Carlson by the largest margin in state history.

Tip #2: LISTEN TO THE PEOPLE.

Anyone passing through Reno, Nevada, with more than a quarter in their pocket would kill for a hot tip from Harrah's, the world-renowned casino. However, the last people one would expect to profit from such inside information would be the Reno police. And it was all above board.

When the number of car accidents swiftly rose in the early to mid 1980s, Reno police took action. They bought twenty-one new radar guns, stationed themselves around the biggest little city in the world, and waited for speeders. They got what they asked for. Suddenly, Reno cops wrote more than twice as many traffic tickets as before. Speeding stopped.

Amazingly, however, the accident count remained the same. The number of radar guns was up; the number of tickets was up; but the numbers that really mattered—deaths and injuries—hadn't moved. The people were furious. And even in those heady days of ever-increasing police budgets, voters turned down two initiatives to increase police funding.

Then the Reno police hit the jackpot. Acting on a Harrah's hint—and copying the casino's old trick—police officials surveyed more than a thousand citizens and asked for their advice. Where are the city's worst streets, they asked? Which are the most dangerous?

The police got answers—and results. They shifted resources to the places that needed them. And while the total number of tickets written dropped, the accident rate fell 20 percent. Moreover, some 90 percent of Reno citizens approved of their police department, up from 40 percent in 1988.

The cops took a hint, made the call, and won the big prize.

Tip #3: USE THE IMUS EFFECT.

Technology allows much greater interaction today between those who govern and the governed than ever before. Political scientists can debate for hours whether new communication tools, polls, and electronic town halls will bring great benefit or harm to our government (and they do). But successful public officials must understand that like that long-lost relative who shows up for holiday dinner only to announce he's staying indefinitely, this change is permanent. Call it the Imus Effect.

Don Imus is an extraordinarily popular New York radio host. His show, one of the original homes of "shock jock radio," became famous for its guest list; despite Imus's caustic, sometimes insulting wit, he never found himself without a top government official for a morning political chat, from Senator John McCain to Governor William Weld. Before the 1992 New York primary, Arkansas governor Bill Clinton even called the show from his hotel room to chat with a man who insisted on calling him "Bubba." Imus later took credit for helping elect President Bubba.

However, Imus made the most headlines for a series of supposedly tasteless jokes he told at a 1996 roast of President Clinton. After the roast, "official" Washington was aghast, with politicians and establishment media almost climbing over one another to denounce the humor. But more significant than whether the jokes actually were tasteless—and where the Imus Effect becomes clear—was in what happened to Imus's guest list for his radio show afterward.

Nothing.

Despite the outrage, despite the calls for apology, virtually no one stopped showing up at Imus's studio. Why? They couldn't. If these public officials wanted to reach voters and influence public opinion, they had to visit Imus. Because as fewer Americans read newspapers and get their information from the traditional television networks, a greater number of outlets have gained importance. And Imus is one of them.

"The success of democracy depends on the enlightenment of its people," New York Mayor Fiorello La Guardia said. "The people should know what's going on, and public officials should keep the people informed."

To do so in this new world, public officials must actively seek out new ways to reach citizens. For example, many residents did not attend Beverly Stein's public hearings. But she still had an obligation to understand their views.

That a significant number of Americans might have their political opinions formed by Don Imus rather than through traditional news outlets mirrors, indeed drives, the shift in American democracy and defines the Imus Effect. As new technology has grown and fax machines have multiplied and the Internet has expanded, a million

Don Imuses have blossomed and democracy has changed. Public officials must understand this change, and then employ it to ensure greater accountability.

Tip #4: STAY AHEAD OF THE TIMES.

Since Santa Monica, California, put its government on-line, many other public officials have sped onto the information superhighway. These systems have become a vital way to know what citizens want in this new age of democracy. They allow information to flow from citizens to public managers—not only the other way. Some of the best include Hawaii FYI, which has created access to public records and linked the state's diverse cultural groups, and UtahNet, which ties local and state information services together.

The systems don't have to cost a lot. In the early days, Virginia Beach, Virginia, took a spare computer and modem to serve some 1,200 users a month for less than $1,000 in equipment and system upkeep fees. Most jurisdictions now use the Internet to make their information easily accessible.

Bruce Kirschner designed interactive systems in Colorado and recommends certain basics to make a system work. The first, of course, is to focus on users; the system must be user friendly. It should also be kept simple and flexible; getting overwhelmed by technical issues can turn off officials and users. Public officials should also plan an evolving system; it should adapt as user needs change and new technology develops. Finally, a little research goes a long way; investigating other governments' successes and failures can save time.

Kirschner also warns of possible obstacles from key decision makers who know little about computers. They must understand the benefits to appointed and elected officials, or the project could be sunk before it begins.

Tip #5: KEEP TRAFFIC MOVING.

It's a familiar scene. On the way to work, drivers notice a nasty accident ahead on the other side of the road. Even though their own traffic is not blocked, most drivers slow down and peer out their windows to inspect the wreckage. Before long, a full-blown traffic jam exists. What started as a fifteen-minute commute takes much longer. Had each driver considered the cumulative effect of his actions, no one would have stopped for the five-second glance that ended up costing much more time.

In a direct democracy, there will be more drivers, more novices. And these novices, unfamiliar with the rules of the road, will create more traffic jams. So instead of arguing about whether we'll have more drivers, it's better to find ways to keep the traffic of government moving.

This evolution of American democracy would seem to imply that public officials will become less important. The opposite is true.

Like democracy itself, the public official's job will evolve under the new system. To keep the traffic moving on increasingly crowded streets, public officials will be like traffic cops trying to prevent gridlock. Far from being irrelevant, public officials will be the key to making government work.

Public officials will also have to encourage greater public participation. The disgrace of today's general elections—where fewer than half of all eligible voters make it to the polls—cannot continue in direct democracy. Too many issues will be determined at the ballot box for voters to ignore. To ensure fair, representative votes, government officials will have to do more to get the vote out.

Public officials also must clearly spell out their own views and more energetically understand the views of their constituents. Direct democracy will thrive on the free flow of ideas. The better public officials realize what the voters want, and the better they make voters realize where they stand, the better the system will work.

Conclusion

This book began with a simple idea: Only through better governing will America get better government. Instead of reinventing government or embracing the next hot management fad, public officials must look in the mirror for answers. They must admit that public service is unlike any other job they've held. They must learn how to govern.

The people we profile bring life to governing. Their stories provide basic lessons for getting something done in government. They give an inside look into why some public officials succeed and others fail. Many of their lessons run contrary to today's conventional wisdom. Others simply provide common sense that too often is ignored. Woven together, these insights prepare any new public official for the takeover.

The help is needed. Nationwide, government seems unable to complete its most elementary tasks, from filling potholes and fixing crumbling bridges to educating children and housing the homeless. Candidates promise change, then find they cannot deliver it once in office.

When a politician enters public office, citizens entrust their government to that person's judgment, skill, and honesty. When the elected official staffs senior jobs, the trust extends to those appointees. All public officials, not just elected representatives, must prove the confidence is merited.

Few aspects of the American experience are as exciting—or as inspiring—as the peaceful government takeover. It embodies American democracy. It differentiates our leaders from dictators and our nation from many others around the world. That's because for more than two centuries, American government officials have willingly given up power to a new team of citizens that voters selected on election day.

But few aspects of the American experience are more frustrating than a government of novices stumbling along and never achieving goals promised to voters. Our democracy's strength is also its major weakness. We celebrate a system that allows ordinary people to serve in government, and then we become frustrated when these novices don't get the job done.

By learning from those who have served effectively before, new public officials can flourish. Citizens will once again see that their election day choices are meaningful, because those choices translate into real actions after the takeover. The challenge is only made tougher when newcomers confuse governing with their previous jobs.

Many new public officials confuse governing with managing. But what business people consider as management—motivating workers, overseeing product lines, and controlling costs—represents but one facet of governing. Successful public officials must also master political management—negotiating the minefield of special interests, listening to citizens, and responding to other powerful officials. In addition, they must understand communications management, with citizens, the media, and other branches of government.

Many public officials also confuse governing with campaigning. Democrats and Republicans may disagree on government's proper role, what services it should provide, and how they should be funded. Facing the same facts, liberals and conservatives draw vastly different conclusions about appropriate public policies. These are important debates. They also define elections. The public chooses between ideologies and determines in which direction the country, state, or town should move.

This does not mean successful public officials shed their beliefs once in office. Ideology is frequently why private citizens put their lives on hold and delve into public office; like a birthmark, it subtly lends character to the overall person. A political philosophy can inspire a clear vision for one's agency or department.

But after a takeover, most public officials find that ideology affects only a fraction of their job. It can't clear snow or collect garbage or ensure airline safety or inspect meat or approve drugs. It has a negligible effect on the herculean task of getting the little things done. Despite this, from political talk shows to talk radio to campaign ads, Americans are bombarded with ideology. If Americans don't feel their government works anymore, it's not because too little ideology exists.

Governing is more complicated than that. It's about implementing the agenda voters approved at the ballot box. It means following through on promises. Yet it's also the part of our democracy that gets the least amount of attention. Scores of books, television shows, and radio programs focus on the art of campaigning. The same is true for the politics of government. But by ignoring the difficulties new public officials face in the takeover, our democracy suffers.

The takeover is the most difficult period of governing. We elect, after all, a government of novices, rookies to the sport. How can they be expected to know how to begin? How can they know what to do next?

The Takeover Checklist

Through real stories of success and failure, we documented eight traits of effective public officials. To reverse the trend of Americans' diminishing confidence in their government, newly elected and appointed officials must make a takeover work the way it was designed more than two centuries ago. This checklist summarizes the key points made in the book.

Public officials succeed because they:

Recognize government is not a business. Many of the principles that guide business—profits, risk taking, secrecy, and speed—simply don't work in government. To force government into a business structure is to jam a square peg in a round hole. To govern successfully, public officials must:

- Recognize that businesses seek to maximize profits; governments seek to maximize voter satisfaction.
- Understand that business leaders are compensated for risk taking; politicians are reelected for avoiding risk.
- Treat citizens as owners, not customers.
- Make decisions in public.

Rethink government's main purpose. If government can be run like a business, perhaps it should be one. Over the years, many government agencies have ventured beyond their basic mission. Some activities may be more appropriate for the private sector, some should be done by other agencies, and others disbanded. This allows officials to concentrate on the core tasks that truly matter. To succeed, public officials must:

- Take advantage of the honeymoon period to rethink government.
- Look in obvious places to cut duplication.
- Beware of election year politics.
- Use public-private partnerships to get work done that can't be privatized and government can't do alone.

Know what they want to accomplish. The number of public officials who take office without a clear vision is shockingly high. Elected and appointed officials should know what they want to do once in office. To succeed, they must:

- Develop a clear and understandable vision.
- Communicate their vision throughout the agency or department.
- Create a sense of urgency around their vision.
- Put employees who embrace their vision on a pedestal. Step back and remember the big picture.

Change the old guard, the old culture—or both. Public officials are handcuffed by strict limits on hiring and firing. Still, new officials must surround themselves with the right people—not "yes men" or "yes women" but able, loyal staffers who can help attain their vision. In addition, once the bodies are in place, the minds must follow. As a result, public officials must:

- Choose experience before political connections.
- Fill key positions with loyal staffers.
- Recognize the value of career employees.
- Resist the temptation to criticize predecessors.
- Resign if they find they cannot morally and effectively do their job.

Take control of the bureaucracy. Nearly everyone tells new public officials they must "empower" the bureaucrats who work for them; then they take office only to find they are not "empowered" themselves. Public officials must find ways to free themselves from bureaucratic constraints. To be effective, public officials must:

- Replace traditional management structures with new ones.
- Find new ways to communicate with bureaucrats.
- Create incentives beyond pay raises and bonuses to invigorate workers.
- Use common sense to override useless rules.
- Avoid wasting time trying to deal with "deadwood" employees.

Juggle many balls at once. At its essence, government is about dealing with crises. Not only do more pressures come from more directions than in the private sector—legislators, constituents, media, underlings, supporters—but the game clock that marks a public official's term counts down quickly. To handle these crises, public officials must learn to tackle many issues at once. To prevail, they must:

- Govern like a one-termer.
- Understand the consequences that decisions made today will have tomorrow.
- Be prepared for crises by running fire drills.
- Act quickly to defuse crises.
- Turn crisis into opportunity.

Manage their message. Communication skills frequently get overlooked for public officials. Not just elected officials, but even appointees and staffers must get their messages across to the public. The alternative is for their political rivals to do it for them and

frame the issue in an unflattering way. To successfully manage
their message, public officials must:

- Make the story easy to report.
- Make the story easy to understand.
- Make the story personal.
- Make the story symbolic.
- Tell the truth.
- Find new ways to get the message out.

Seek feedback from citizens. Just as government has changed over
the years, so has the concept of accountability. No longer can public officials sit, hermetically sealed in government offices, inac-
cessible to the public except during campaign season. Democracy
has changed, and public officials at all levels must continually
give citizens information and, perhaps more important, seek
information and direction from citizens. As a fuller democracy
becomes a reality, public officials must:

- Set clear goals and announce them publicly.
- Listen to the people.
- Use new media to reach out to citizens.
- Stay ahead of the times with the latest technology.
- Make sure that government evolves smoothly as a fuller
  democracy takes hold.

The list is long, but no one said public service was easy. Demands
on public officials rank among the sternest of any profession. Long
hours with low pay, lack of recognition, bureaucratic in-fighting, and
the risk of getting into a career-damaging scandal command tremendous sacrifice from public leaders.

Even under the best of circumstances, public officials' work can be
exasperating. Those who govern will make mistakes. Getting something
done in government requires persistence rarely needed in other organizations. Still, citizens—rightfully—remain very demanding.

After Connecticut governor Lowell Weicker rammed the state's
first income tax through the legislature in 1991, angry protesters
chased the heavyset public official after he left his car to go to the
opera. Others waved signs that read "Cut the fat out of government.
Start with Lowell Weicker." After the opera, Weicker escaped out the

theater's back door for his own safety. Although Weicker later won the Profiles in Courage Award from the John F. Kennedy Memorial Library for taking the unpopular income tax stand, the decision ultimately ended his political career.

On the federal level, Bush cabinet official Manuel Lujan lamented: "Being Interior Secretary is like being in a sack full of cats clawing at each other." And that was after only two years on the job.

In addition, the prickly relationship with the media tries even the most patient official. Honestly criticizing public officials over issues or rooting out cheating and deceit makes democracy stronger. But it only makes a public official's job more difficult when even the smallest mistakes appear in the morning newspaper.

For many citizens, the rough-and-tumble of government service makes it increasingly hard to attract outstanding people for important public service jobs. Many public officials—from Robert Bork to Gary Hart to Zoe Baird; from Borking to Monkey Business to Nannygate—have seen the vitriol rise in step with their careers. A new, dark spirit exists, and many of our wisest, most capable people want nothing to do with public office. It's not worth the hassle.

This book's goal, at its most basic, is to restore nobility to public service. It's a challenge. On the eve of President Clinton's second inauguration, the American public had to sift through the public dirt of *Paula Jones* v. *William Jefferson Clinton*, staggering campaign money and influence-peddling revelations, the Newt Gingrich House ethics battle, and the Jim McDermott ethics battle (he was the Washington congressman investigating Gingrich who allegedly turned transcripts of surreptitiously taped cellular phone calls over to the media). And that's not to mention the Whitewater, travel office, and FBI file-gate scandals. "Bunting and Dirty Laundry Hang Side by Side in Capital," is how a *New York Times* headline depicted the state of the union.

To explain the pervasive American cynicism, President Clinton declared in his second inaugural address that "Government is not the problem; government is not the solution."

We believe Clinton was wrong. Government is the problem *and* the solution. Public officials can make the problem go away with better governing.

Despite the vast amounts of energy required, many (including Clinton) find public service extremely rewarding. Government jobs can be far more satisfying than successes in other professions because the impact is so much greater. The local health director who immunizes school children changes history if only one child avoids a fatal disease. The governor who eliminates an unneeded department frees scarce resources to build a needed highway that boosts his state's economy. The ambassador who uses diplomacy to prevent war in some faraway land prevents needless bloodshed.

Though Clinton battled Bob Dole fiercely for the presidency, he would surely agree with what the former senator said after Clinton gave him the Medal of Freedom, the nation's highest civilian distinction, in 1997: "I have found honor in the profession of politics. I have found vitality in the American experiment. Our challenge is not to question American ideals or replace them but to act worthy of them . . . The moral challenges of our time can seem less clear, but they still demand conviction and courage and character. They still require young men and women with faith in our process. They still demand idealists captured by the honor and adventure of service."

Public service can be a valuable part of every American's life. Whether as a full-time elected official, part-time appointed commission member, or simply as an informed voter, the average citizen can make a difference in his or her community. But for elected and appointed officials in government, it was never intended as a permanent job.

"Politics, like theater, is one of those things where you've got to be wise enough to know when to leave," Richard Lamm said after three terms as Colorado governor.

America's democracy was designed to allow citizens to take over their government after regular elections. The ruling class was not meant to be permanent. The lessons in this book will help any new citizen servant survive what will surely be the experience of a lifetime.

THE AUTHORS WELCOME YOUR COMMENTS.
You can send email to
Taegan D. Goddard at TDGoddard@aol.com
and to
Christopher Riback at CRiback@aol.com.

Selected Bibliography

Andrews, Robert. *The Concise Columbia Dictionary of Quotations.* New York: Avon, 1989.

Birnbaum, Jeffrey H. *Madhouse: The Private Turmoil of Working for the President.* New York: Times Books, 1996.

Blumenthal, Sidney. *Pledging Allegiance: The Last Campaign of the Cold War.* New York: HarperCollins, 1990.

Califano, Joseph A. *Governing America: An Insider's Report from the White House and the Cabinet.* New York: Simon & Schuster, 1981.

Caro, Robert A. *The Power Broker: Robert Moses and the Fall of New York.* New York: Vintage, 1975.

———. *The Years of Lyndon Johnson: Means of Ascent,* New York: Alfred A. Knopf, 1990.

———. *The Years of Lyndon Johnson: The Path to Power,* New York: Alfred A. Knopf, 1982.

Citizens Transition Project. *Changing America: Blueprints for the New Administration.* New York: Newmarket, 1992.

Clift, Eleanor, and Brazaitis, Tom. *War Without Bloodshed: The Art of Politics.* New York: Scribner, 1996.

Dallek, Robert, *Hail to the Chief: The Making and Unmaking of American Presidents.* New York: Hyperion, 1996.

Dionne, E. J., Jr. *Why Americans Hate Politics.* New York: Simon & Schuster, 1991.

Donald, David Herbert. *Lincoln.* London: Jonathan Cape, 1995.

Drew, Elizabeth. *On the Edge: The Clinton Presidency.* New York: Simon & Schuster, 1994.

Eggers, William D., and O'Leary, John. *Revolutions at the Roots: Making Our Government Smaller, Better, and Closer to Home.* New York: The Free Press, 1995.

Ehrenhalt, Alan. *The United States of Ambition: Politicians, Power and the Pursuit of Office.* New York: Times Books, 1991.

Eigen, Lewis D., and Siegel, Jonathan P. *The Macmillan Dictionary of Political Quotations.* New York: Macmillan, 1993.

Fallows, James. *Breaking the News: How the Media Undermine American Democracy.* New York: Pantheon, 1996.

Gore, Al. *Creating a Government That Works Better and Costs Less: Report of the National Performance Review.* Washington, D.C.: Government Printing Office, 1993.

Grossman, Lawrence K. *The Electronic Republic: Reshaping Democracy in the Information Age.* New York: Viking, 1995.

Haass, Richard N. *The Power to Pursuade: How to Be Effective in Government, The Public Sector, or Any Unruly Organization.* New York: Houghton Mifflin, 1994.

Hamilton, Alexander; Madison, James; and Jay, John. *The Federalist Papers.* New York: Mentor, 1961.

Hart, Gary. *The Patriot: An Exhortation to Liberate America from the Barbarians.* New York: The Free Press, 1996.

Heifetz, Ronald A. *Leadership Without Easy Answers.* Cambridge: Harvard University Press, 1994.

Holtzman, Elizabeth, with Cooper, Cynthia L. *Who Said It Would Be Easy?* New York: Arcade, 1996.

Howard, Philip K. *The Death of Common Sense: How Law Is Suffocating America.* New York: Random House, 1994.

Katz, Jon. *Virtuous Reality: How America Surrendered Discussion of Moral Values to Opportunists, Nitwits, and Blockheads like William Bennett.* New York: Random House, 1997.

Kelman, Steven. *Procurement and Public Management: The Fear of Discretion and the Quality of Government Performance.* Washington, D.C.: The American Enterprise Institute Press, 1990.

Maraniss, David, *First in His Class: A Biography of Bill Clinton.* New York: Simon & Schuster, 1995.

Matthews, Christopher. *Hardball: How Politics Is Played Told by One Who Knows the Game.* New York: Simon & Schuster, 1988.

McCullough, David. *Truman.* New York: Simon & Schuster, 1992.

McGinniss, Joe. *The Selling of the President 1968.* New York: Trident Press, 1969.

McNamara, Robert S. *In Retrospect: The Tragedy and Lessons of Vietnam.* New York: Times Books, 1995.

Micklethwait, John, and Wooldridge, Adrian. *The Witch Doctors: Making Sense of the Management Gurus.* New York: Times Books, 1996.

Neustadt, Richard E. *Presidential Power and the Modern Presidents: The Politics of Leadership from Roosevelt to Reagan.* New York: The Free Press, 1990.

Nixon, Richard M. *Six Crises.* New York: Touchstone, 1990.

Noonan, Peggy. *What I Saw at the Revolution: A Political Life in the Reagan Era.* New York: Random House, 1990.

Osborne, David, and Gaebler, Ted. *Reinventing Government: How the Entrepreneurial Spirit Is Transforming the Public Sector from Schoolhouse to Statehouse, City Hall to the Pentagon.* New York: Addison-Wesley, 1992.

Pinkerton, James P. *What Comes Next: The End of Big Government and the New Paradigm Ahead.* New York: Hyperion, 1995.

Rauch, Jonathan. *Demosclerosis: The Silent Killer of American Government.* New York: Times Books, 1994.

Reich, Robert B. *Locked in the Cabinet.* New York: Alfred A. Knopf, 1997.
———. *The Resurgent Liberal (and Other Unfashionable Prophecies).* New York: Times Books, 1989.
———., ed. *The Power of Public Ideas.* Cambridge, Mass.: Harvard University Books, 1988.

Richardson, Elliot. *Reflections of a Radical Moderate.* New York: Pantheon, 1996.

Rosenstiel, Tom. *Strange Bedfellows: How Television and the Presidential Candidates Changed American Politics, 1992.* New York: Hyperion, 1993.

Royko, Mike. *Boss: Richard J. Daley of Chicago.* New York: E. P. Dutton, 1971.

Safire, William. *Safire's New Political Dictionary: The Definitive Guide to the New Language of Politics.* New York: Random House, 1993.

Savoie, Donald J. *Thatcher, Reagan and Mulroney: In Search of a New Bureaucracy.* Pittsburgh, Pa.: University of Pittsburgh Press, 1994.

Bibliography

Seidman, L. William. *Full Faith and Credit: The Great S&L Debacle and Other Washington Sagas.* New York: Times Books, 1993.

Stockman, David A. *The Triumph of Politics: Why the Reagan Revolution Failed.* New York: Harper & Row, 1986.

Woodward, Bob. *The Agenda: Inside the Clinton White House.* New York: Simon & Schuster, 1994.

Notes

The accounts described came primarily from interviews in 1995, 1996, and 1997, speeches and testimony by public officials, personal observations, and from reporting in various newspapers and magazines. Major sources included *The New York Times, The Washington Post, The Los Angeles Times, The Wall Street Journal, The Philadelphia Inquirer, The Chicago Tribune, The Economist, Time, Newsweek, U.S. News & World Report, The Atlantic Monthly, The New Yorker, Slate, Weekly Standard, The New Republic, Governing, National Journal,* and *Government Executive.* Other useful sources included ABC News, NBC News, CBS News, PBS, National Public Radio, and CNN. All quotations not attributed in the text or in these notes are from interviews or correspondence with the authors.

Chapter 1: A Government of Novices

21: Opening quote: Clark Clifford, interview with Bill Moyers, PBS, 1981.

23: "You get burned out very quickly": Stuart Eizenstat, quoted in Lewis D. Eigen and Jonathan P. Siegel, eds., *Macmillan Dictionary of Political Quotations* (New York: Macmillan, 1993), p. 574.

24: "another part can only be attained": James Madison, *The Federalist Papers, No. 53* (New York: New American Library of World Literature, 1961), p. 332.

25: "Getting people elected": Quoted in Todd S. Purdum, "Tracking the North Campaign, from Dirt to Ashes," *The New York Times,* June 16, 1996, p. H17.

26: "The only problem with running for office": J. Marshall Coleman, quoted in *Macmillan Dictionary of Political Quotations,* p. 573.

26: "We campaign in poetry": Mario Cuomo, speech at Yale University, 1985.

26: "There are very few people": Quoted in John Harwood and Michael K. Frisby, "This Year's Odd Race Pits Legislator vs. Campaigner," *The Wall Street Journal,* July 19, 1996, p. A1.

26: "To be elected to public office": Ed Eilert, quoted in *Macmillan Dictionary of Political Quotations,* p. 573.

26: "The first duty of any campaign": James Fallows, "Issues—Or Politics?" National Public Radio, Apr. 19, 1996.

26: Only twenty-five years ago, three-quarters of the public said: Joseph Nye, "Visions of Governance in the Twenty-first Century," keynote speech, John F. Kennedy School of Government Spring Symposium, 1996.

26: When ABC News polled citizens in 1993: David Brinkley, *Everyone Is Entitled to My Opinion* (New York: Alfred A. Knopf, 1996), p. 148

27: Even at Harvard's John F. Kennedy School of Government: *Outreach Notes,* John F. Kennedy School of Government, Jan. 1997.

27: "There is a very deep public frustration": Quoted in Jennifer Warren, "Promises, Promises," *The Los Angeles Times,* Aug. 2, 1995, Life & Style, p. 1.

27: Money is "the mother's milk of politics": Quoted in R. W. Apple, "Pushing the Envelope on Favors for Donations," *The New York Times,* Feb. 26, 1997, p. A18.

28: "The basis of effective government": John F. Kennedy, "Message to Congress on Ethical Conduct in Government," April 27, 1961.

28: "This country faces all kinds of problems": Anthony Lewis, "Hating the Government," *The New York Times,* Sept. 6, 1996, p. A27.

28: "There is a difference between healthy skepticism and mistrust": Nye, "Visions of Governance in the Twenty-first Century."

28: The idea that public officials are inept: Sam Howe Verhovek,

"Political Briefs: Arkansas, North Carolina, New York," *The New York Times*, Oct. 15, 1996.

29: "Everybody believes in democracy until he gets to the White House": Quoted in "Thrills, No; Discipline, Yes," *The Economist*, Nov. 16, 1996, p. 26.

29: "If the political process keeps running down government": Nye, "Visions of Governance in the Twenty-First Century."

29: "The most difficult job is being a manager in government": Ed Rendell, speech, Reason Foundation Conference, Philadelphia, Pa., Sept. 18, 1995.

30: "The right people can make a poor organizational structure work well": Donald Rumsfeld, testimony before the House Committee on Government Reform and Oversight, Subcommittee on Government Management, Information and Technology, June 6, 1995.

31: "Imagine a small dinner party": Jonathan Rauch, "The End of Government," *National Journal*, vol. 28, no. 36.

Chapter 2: Reinventing Government Again (and Again)

33: Opening quote: Governor Lawton Chiles, inaugural address, Tallahassee, Fla., Jan. 3, 1995.

33: "Mr. President, if you want to know why government doesn't work": Al Gore, speech, Washington, D.C., Sept. 7, 1993.

34: "For too long government has been an obstacle": Ibid.

34: "To accomplish any of these goals": Bill Clinton, speech, Washington, D.C., Sept. 7, 1993.

34: More important to Clinton, the review promised: Ibid.

35: "We have excellent, hardworking, imaginative workers": Al Gore, speech, Washington, D.C., Sept. 7, 1993.

35: "It's old-fashioned, outdated government": Ibid.

36: In fact, the administration's budget director: Elizabeth Drew, *On the Edge: The Clinton Presidency* (New York: Simon & Schuster, 1994), p. 295.

36: Gore had five taxpayer-financed offices: "Speaking of Waste: The Vice President Should Take His Own Advice," *San Diego Union-Tribune*, Sept. 17, 1993, p. B6.

36: Peter Drucker ridiculed the Gore effort: Peter F. Drucker, "Really Reinventing Government," *The Atlantic Monthly*, Feb. 1995.

36: For example, as proof of "radically changing government": Al Gore, "The Best Kept Secrets in Government," Government Printing Office, Sept. 1996.

36: In the administration's first two years, opinion polls indicated:

Robert Siegel, *All Things Considered*, National Public Radio, Dec. 26, 1994.

37: When asked if the Clinton administration had made progress: *The Washington Post*, poll, Sept. 13, 1994, p. A6.

37: "We will stop making so many decisions in Washington": Quoted by Robert Siegel, *All Things Considered*, Dec. 26, 1994.

37: A 1996 GAO report reviewing Gore's progress: Stephen Barr, "GAO Report Details Quiet Efforts of Gore's 'Reinvention Labs,' " *The Washington Post*, March 25, 1996, p. A15.

38: One Gore report declared: Al Gore, *Common Sense Government*, Government Printing Office, September 1995.

38: "The crime," an editorial at the time stated: Quoted in "Reinventing Government, 1882," *American Heritage*, Feb./Mar. 1994, 45, 1:20.

39: "When I came into power": Benjamin Harrison, qouted in *Macmillan Dictionary of Political Quotations*, p. 17.

40: "grown up without plan or design": Quoted in James K. Conant, "Executive Branch Reorganizations in the States, 1965–1991," *The Book of the States 1992–93* (Lexington, Ky.: The Council of State Governments 1992), p. 65.

40: "a responsible and effective chief executive": Quoted in ibid.

40: "Our struggle now is against confusion": Quoted in Donald Kaul, "Yet Another Shot at Fixing Government," *Kansas City Star*, Sept. 14, 1993.

41: "a very revolutionary system": Lyndon Johnson, quoted in "Re-re-re-re-re-inventing government," *Time*, Sept. 13, 1993.

42: "It's simple and it works": Jimmy carter, quoted in ibid.

42: In the next decade, more than twelve thousand auditors: Paul Light, "An End to the War on Waste," *Brookings Review*, Apr. 1, 1993.

42: "work like tireless bloodhounds": Quoted in "Re-re-re-re-re-inventing government," *Time*, Sept. 13, 1993.

42: "I honestly believe that this is the only way": George Bush, quoted in ibid.

43: "Make no mistake about this": Bill Clinton, speech, Washington, D.C., Sept. 7, 1993.

44: Over the past 75 years, more than 170 attempts were launched: Conant, "Executive Branch Reorganizations in the States, 1965–1991," *The Book of the States 1992–93*.

44: the average "germination time" was a staggering forty-five years.: Ibid., p. 67.

45: After a wave of new governors: Alliance for Redesigning Government, Internet web site (http://192.156.133.18/Alliance/clusters/rd/regoscan.txt).

45: "When a family goes shopping": Pete Wilson, State of the State Address, Sacramento, Calif, Jan. 9, 1995.

45: "We can make our government work . . ." Parris N. Glendening, State of the State Address, Anapolis, Md, Jan. 26, 1995.

45: "cuts obsolete spending": Mel Carnahan, State of the State Address, Jefferson City, Mo, Jan. 18, 1995.

45: "Above all else, citizens said they want": Edward T. Schafer, State of the State Address, Bismark, N.D., Jan. 3, 1995.

45: "Is this all that can be done": Angus S. King, budget address, Augusta, Me, Feb. 1, 1995.

46: "to let us build a government": Evan Bayh, State of the State Address, Indianapolis, Ind, Jan. 10, 1995.

46: For example, Vice President Gore's suggestion: Peter Drucker, "Past Efforts Aside, Here's How to Really 'Reinvent' Government," *San Diego Union-Tribune,* Feb. 19, 1995, p. G1.

47: "Reinventing government is nonsense": William J. Janklow, State of the State Address, S.D., January 10, 1995.

47: "There is no Republican way to collect garbage": Quoted in Christopher Matthews, *Hardball* (New York: Harper & Row, 1988), p. 16.

47: "Al Gore talks about reinventing government": Chap Hurst, quoted in Patrick Scott, "Lancaster Administrator Aims to Rein in County Costs," *Charlotte Observer,* Jan. 16, 1994, p. 1Y.

47: "Many elected officials": Elizabeth Holtzman with Cynthia L. Cooper, *Who Said It Would Be Easy?* (New York: Arcade Publishing, 1996), p. 99.

48: "Whenever people get frustrated with substance": Dan Glickman, *CNN Newsmakers,* July 3, 1988.

Chapter 3: Reinventing Government Officials

51: Opening quote: John Adams, quoted in *Macmillan Dictionary of Political Quotations,* p. 387.

51: "They threw tons of staff time": Steve Silver, quoted in Jonathan Walters, "Fad Mad," *Governing,* Sept. 1996, p. 48.

52: "I was naïve in thinking": Ibid.

52: "In the 1960s politicians who wanted to appear": "Leviathan Re-engineered," *The Economist,* Oct. 19, 1996, p. 67.

52: "TQM, managing for results": Walters, "Fad Mad," *Governing,* Sept. 1996, p. 48.

53: "In states where a 're-' initiative is underway": Frank Luntz, "KPMG Peat Marwick's Better American Government Survey," July 1995.

54: "the problem with Osborne and Gaebler's book is": John Mick-lethwait and Adrian Wooldridge, *The Witch Doctors* (New York: Times Books, 1996), p. 86.

54: "It reads like the Cliff's Notes version of *Reinventing Government*": Walters, "Fad Mad," *Governing,* Sept. 1996.

55: "Most government managers know": Quoted in Larry Reynolds, "Can Government be Reinvented?" *Management Review,* Jan. 1, 1994.

58: handing in "inaccurate, incomplete and unreliable information": Newt Gingrich, quoted in David E. Rosenbaum, "Middle Ground on Ethics," *The New York Times,* Dec. 25, 1996, p. A1.

Chapter 4: It's Not a Business

61: Opening quote: William S. Cohen, testimony beofre the Senate Committee on Government Affairs, May 13–14, 1986.

61: The top executives from Time-Warner, Viacom, Walt Disney, and Capital Cities/ABC attended: Ken Auletta, "Awesome," *The New Yorker,* Aug. 14, 1995, p. 28.

62: "I literally passed Tom Murphy on the street": Michael Eisner, quoted in Bernard Weinraub, "For Disney Chairman, a Deal Quenches a Personal Thirst," *The New York Times,* Aug. 1, 1995, p. 1.

62: "Everything I speculated on was wrong": Quoted in Michael A. Hiltzik and Claudia Eller, "Chemistry Made Talks Quick, Quiet," *The Los Angeles Times,* Aug. 1, 1995, p. A-1.

62: In the one-share-one-vote: Floyd Norris, "Disney's Stock Defies Usual Rules of the Game," *The New York Times,* Aug. 1, 1995, p. D1.

63: "$600 hourly rate": *Current Biography,* Apr. 1995, p. 39.

64: "I have a successful, twenty-year career in the private sector": Quoted in Edwin Chen, "A Lifetime of Pushing the Limits," *The Los Angeles Times,* June 1, 1993, p. A1.

64: "a highly structured process": Quoted in Adam Clymer, Robert Pear, and Robin Toner, "The Health Care Debate: What Went Wrong? How the Health Care Campaign Collapsed—A Special Report. For Health Care, Times Was a Killer," *The New York Times,* Aug. 29, 1994, p. A1.

64: What started as a twelve-member task force: Clymer, Pear, and Toner, "The Health Care Debate: What Went Wrong?".

65: "a cross between Ph.D. orals and the Spanish Inquisition.": Quoted in Michael Duffy and Dick Thompson, "Behind Closed Doors: The Inside Story of How Bill and Hillary Clinton Fashioned the Heath-Care Plan," *Time,* Sept. 20, 1993.

65: "The secrecy . . . angered consumer advocates": Robert Pear, "U.S. Decides Not to Prosecute Clinton Health Plan Architect," *The New York Times*, Aug. 4, 1995, p. A22.

65: The White House hadn't released any photographs: "Do You Know These People? The First Lady's Task Force on Health Care Reform," *The Wall Street Journal*, March 24, 1993, p. A14.

66: "misleading, at best": Quoted in Pear, "U.S. Decides Not to Prosecute Clinton Health Plan Architect," *The New York Times*, Aug. 4, 1995, p. A22.

66: "I'm used to company environments": Quoted in Edwin Chen, "A Lifetime of Pushing the Limits," *The Los Angeles Times*, June 1, 1993, p. A1.

67: "They came over and saw us all the time": Quoted in Clymer, Pear, and Toner, "The Health Care Debate: What Went Wrong?."

67: "We don't speak the same language": Quoted in Gloria Borger, "Poor Diagnosis, Bad Prescription," *U.S. News & World Report*, Oct. 3, 1994.

67: "Mr. Magaziner acted like a parody of a consultant": "Gurus in Government," *The Economist*, May 20, 1995, p. 21.

68: "They ought to make Ira Magaziner the Ambassador to Kazahkstan": Quoted in Robert Pear, "High-Level Dispute on Who Will Redo Health Care Policy," *The New York Times*, Oct. 13, 1994, p. A1.

68: "Working in the federal government is everything": *Current Biography*, April 1995, p. 42.

69: "Making decisions and issuing orders": Elliot Richardson, *Reflections of a Radical Moderate* (New York: Pantheon, 1996), p. 6.

70: "Fewer than half of the city's residents finish high school": Testimony of Bret Schundler before the U.S. House of Representatives Committee on Economic and Educational Opportunities, Jan. 12, 1995.

70: more than 14 percent are on welfare: William D. Eggers, "Righting City Hall," *National Review*, Aug. 29, 1994.

70: In a town where two-thirds of the population are black: "Radicals at Work," *The Economist*, Nov. 6, 1993.

70: 68 percent of the vote: William D. Eggers, "Righting City Hall," *National Review*, Aug. 29, 1994.

70: "Wielding corporate-style tactics": John F. Dickerson, "Waste Not, Want Not," *Time*, May 20, 1994.

70: In fact, fewer than 1 percent of homeowners: William Claiborne, "Jersey City—Rich in Democratic Traditions—Switches to GOP Portfolio," *The Washington Post*, July 4, 1993.

70: Schundler attacked the situation: Tom Groenfeldt, "Jersey City Sells Off Tax Liens," *The New York Times*, Sept. 19, 1993.

71: "We took dormant assets": Ibid.

71: Schundler put an additional sixty police officers: "Radicals at Work."

71: the newly elected Republican governor: Evelyn Nieves, "Driving Home a Point Against a Popular Mayor," *The New York Times*, Aug. 22, 1995.

71: "I spent my first year": Quoted in Iver Peterson, "The Garden State's Iron Horse of Politics Rolls Again," *The New York Times*, Feb. 4, 1994.

71: "politically counterproductive": Quoted in "Radicals at Work."

71: Schundler reduced the city workforce nearly 10 percent: John H. Fund, "Reform Mayor May End Political Machine," *The Wall Street Journal*, May 11, 1993.

72: In a city that was only 6 percent Republicans: Ibid.

72: The mayor invited residents to the . . . Armory: Lally Weymouth, "Jersey City's New Broom," *The Washington Post*, Jan. 10, 1994.

72: "We want those directly affected by services": "The Leadership Fifty," *Time*, Dec. 2, 1994.

72: "the height of hubris": "Radicals at Work."

73: "I'm not a conservative": George F. Will, "Cleaning Up After Boss Hague," *The Washington Post*, July 4, 1995.

73: "They stressed how the constantly changing": Donald J. Savoie, *Thatcher, Reagan and Mulroney: In Search of a New Bureaucracy* (Pittsburgh: University of Pittsburgh Press, 1994), p. 29.

74: "People say the city should be run": Quoted in Thomas White, *The New York Times*, June 10, 1991 (*Macmillan Dictionary of Political Quotes*, p. 398).

74: some 8,500 workers expected to lose their jobs: Chart, *The New York Times*, Sept. 21, 1995, p. A1.

77: "In the corporate world": Quoted in *Regardies*, Jan. 1991 (*Macmillan Dictionary of Political Quotes*, p. 395).

77: "He was an extraordinarily successful businessman": George Shultz, quoted in *The Washington Post*, March 19, 1989 (*Macmillan Dictionary of Political Quotes*, p. 396).

Chapter 5: Rethinking Government

79: Opening quote: Richard Daley, Reason Foundation Conference, Chicago, May 10, 1994.

79: "a leafy oasis of 75,000 people": David Osborne and Ted Gaebler, *Reinventing Government: How the Entrepreneurial Spirit is Transforming the Public Sector* (New York: Addison-Wesley, 1992), p. 2.

80: "It was a real test-tube situation": Quoted in Dennis J. McGrath, "A City's Visionary Plan Unraveled with Its Own Zeal," *Minneapolis Star Tribune,* Jan. 12, 1993, p. 1A.

80: "appraised at $6 million after putting in more than $27 million": "Residents Blame Innovative Government for Bad Times," National Public Radio, *Morning Edition,* July 7, 1994.

80: "Government was competing with the private sector": Ibid.

81: "We've struck any reference to it": McGrath, "A City's Visionary Plan Unraveled with Its Own Zeal."

82: "The private sector is better": Quoted in William D. Eggers and John O'Leary, *Revolution at the Roots,* (New York: The Free Press), p. 40.

82: "The winner brought down our costs by 44 percent": Speech by Stephen Goldsmith, Reason Foundation Conference, Philadelphia, Sept. 18, 1995.

82: "The golf courses were awful": Stephen Goldsmith, Reason Foundation Conference, Chicago, May 10, 1994.

82: "The legitimate object of government": Quoted by Pete Wilson in *Competitive Government: A Plan for Less Bureaucracy, More Results,* Sacramento, Calif., April 1996, p. 14.

83: "We don't need another efficiency study": "Rethinking Government," *Philadelphia Inquirer,* editorial, August 10, 1993.

83: "No one would ever design such a system from scratch": Donald Riegle, *Congressional Record,* Nov. 8, 1993.

84: "We have the most bizarre, entangled regulatory system": William Proxmire, quoted in ibid.

84–85: "If one wants to talk about 'reinventing government' ": William Seidman, quoted in ibid.

85: "I seriously underestimated the depth": William Proxmire, quoted in Taegan D. Goddard, "To Reinvent Government Don't Neglect Bank Reform," *Sacramento Bee,* Dec. 3, 1993.

85: "All the bank regulatory agencies . . .": Ibid.

85: "was in keeping with both the substance and the spirit": Al Gore, statement from the Office of the Vice President.

86: "Generally, and not surprisingly, our analysis illustrates": General Accounting Office, "Government Restructuring: Identifying Potential Duplication in Federal Missions and Approaches," June 7, 1995, p. 2.

86: "Many departments and agencies were created in a different time": Ibid.

87: "The taxpayers of Texas are demanding 'fat free' government": Press release, "Whitehead & Sharp Applaud Senate Vote on Abolishing State Treasury," March 16, 1995.

89: "This transition has been what pilots call a 'soft landing' ": Press release, "Sharp to Hire Management Firm to Help Conduct Comprehensive Performance Review of Newly Acquired Treasury Division," Sept. 3, 1996.

89: "Today, Texans have agreed that": Press release, "Whitehead & Sharp Applaud Senate Vote on Abolishing State Treasury."

89: "The fact is that another bureaucracy": Press release, "Sharp to Hire Management Firm to Help Conduct Comprehensive Performance Review of Newly Acquired Treasury Division."

91: "The first task is to decide what your core business is": Donald Rumsfeld, testimony before the House Committee on Government Reform and Oversight, Subcommittee on Government Management, Information and Technology, June 6, 1995.

91: "No major political thinker": Peter Drucker, "Really Reinventing Government," *Atlantic Monthly*, Feb. 1995.

92: "The highest priority of the Administration": Originally stated in press release, "Governor Cayetano Announces Reduction of 1,294 in State Work Force, as State Begins Government Restructuring," Aug. 1, 1995.

92: "Like many of you": Benjamin J. Cayetano, State of the State Address, Hawaii, Jan. 23, 1995.

92: "We have taken the lead to eliminate duplication": Press Release, "Governor Cayetano Announces Reduction of 1,294 in State Work Force."

93: "After only 45 days in office": Benjamin J. Cayetano, State of the State Address, Hawaii, Jan. 22, 1996.

95: "Election year politics can unravel": Patricia C. Watt and Kenneth I. Rubin, "Privatization Tips and Traps: Illustrations from the DC Village Nursing Home Initiative," *Government Finance Review*, June 1995.

95: "Closing that facility means no more crimes": Timothy L. Takas, "Elder Law Fax," Sept. 2, 1996 (From http://www.nashville.net/~ttakacs/prior/960902.html).

Chapter 6: The Vision Thing

97: Opening quote: "A Model of Christian Charity," a sermon delivered by John Winthrop on board the *Arbella* in 1630.

98: "We had lost the plot to the story": Speech by James Pinkerton to the Log Cabin Republicans National Convention, Aug. 26, 1995.

98: "If Bush didn't care": James P. Pinkerton, *What Comes Next: The End of Big Government—and the New Paradigm Ahead* (New York: Hyperion, 1995), p. 10.

99: "an idea man": Norman Ornstein, "Big Idea Man," *The New York Times,* Oct. 15, 1995, p. 28.

99: "I survived": James P. Pinkerton, *What Comes Next,* p. 7.

100: "Oh, the vision thing": Quoted in Sidney Blumenthal, *Pledging Allegiance: The Last Campaign of the Cold War* (New York: Harper Collins, 1990), p. 52.

100: "I'm following Mr. Reagan—blindly": Ibid., p. 51.

100: "When I worked in the Reagan White House": Quoted in Douglas Jehl and James Gerstenzang, "The Mind of the President; In Making Policy, George Bush Relies on a Group of Comfortable Managers and Shies Away from Grand Ideas," *The Los Angeles Times Magazine,* Oct. 11, 1992, p. 22.

101: Just ten months later, it had been cut in half: John E. Yang, "An Enigmatic President Is a Study in Contrasts; Bush Can Be Commanding and Quirky," *The Washington Post,* Feb. 12, 1992, p. 1.

101: Eight months before the vote: Poll results cited in ibid.

101: one of the least experienced and most poorly prepared men: David Herbert Donald, *Lincoln* (New York: Simon & Schuster, 1995), p. 14.

102: "he was entirely ignorant": Ibid., p. 285.

102: "It is the duty of the President": Abraham Lincoln quoted in ibid., p. 269.

103: appointees carry a card at all times with his administration's five goals: Michael Barone, "Move to the Middle: Secrets of Popular Democrats," *U.S. News & World Report,* date unknown.

103: "There is ample evidence that": Robert B. Reich, *The Resurgent Liberal (and Other Unfashionable Prophecies)* (New York: Times Books, 1989), p. 261.

108: Green's staff and budget were cut by about one-third: Jonathan P. Hicks, "Public Advocate, Private Battle," *The New York Times,* Feb. 14, 1994, p. B4.

108: "How do I implement anything?": Mark Green, quoted in ibid.

109: "It was a hands-down, no quibble decision": Quoted in Cathi Carr, "Overhaul at Revenue Department Receives National Federation Award," *Tallahassee Democrat,* May 8, 1995, p. 4B.

110: "Americans are working harder for less": Robert Reich, quoted in "Department of Labor Performance Agreement," March 1, 1994.

110: "I've always been on Bill Clinton's short list": Quoted in James Risen, "An Idea Man Flexes His Muscle," *The Los Angeles Times,* June 7, 1993, p. A1.

110: To verbalize his visionhe started calling himself: Ibid.

110: "A generation ago": Robert Reich, "Perspective on Employment; Meet the Nimble New Middle Class; Lifetime Factory Jobs May Be Dead, But the People Who Can Keep Technology Humming Are in the Catbird Seat," *The Los Angeles Times*, March 27, 1994, p. M5.

110: "He is being heard": David Obey, quoted in Kirk Vistor, "Point Man," *National Journal*, Aug. 19, 1995, p. 2094.

111: "I've seen these work before": Thomas P. Glynn, quoted in Frank Swoboda, "Inside: Labor—A Working Agreement; Reich Sets Some Goals for his Employees," *The Washington Post*, March 24, 1994, p. A27.

Chapter 7: Changing of the Guard

115: Opening quote: quoted in *Executive Speechwriter Newsletter*, sample issue, 1996.

116: "I wanted to be part of history": David Watkins, quoted in Peter J. Boyer, "A Fever in the White House," *The New Yorker*, April 15, 1996, p. 60.

116: Watkins, however, felt Cornelius lacked experience: Boyer, "A Fever in the White House."

117: Because of Thomason's closeness: Ibid.

117: "lavish lifestyles, minimal work, kickbacks and missing money": Ann Devroy, "Study Clears White House Travel Office," *Philadelphia Inquirer*, July 2, 1993, p. A1.

118: "In a single week of political hari-kiri": "White House Follies: Did 'Saturday Night Live' Script This Scandal?" *Philadelphia Inquirer*, May 27, 1993, p. A22.

118: "When you add this thing up": Frank Wolf, quoted in "Travelgate Savings? Quite the Opposite," *Philadelphia Inquirer*, March 3, 1994, p. B7.

119: "We need to get those people out": Peter J. Boyer, "A Fever in the White House," *The New Yorker*, April 15, 1996, p. 67. Although Hillary Clinton denies saying this, a memo from Watkins that surfaced nearly two years later said that "there would be hell to pay if . . . we failed to take swift and decisive action in conformity with the First Lady's wishes."

119: "One of the greatest but least utilized tests": Gary Hart, *The Patriot* (New York: Free Press, 1996), p. 151.

119: "I can get 100 bureaucrats who can fill": Michael White, Reason Foundation Conference, Chicago, May 10, 1994.

122–23: "Some moments call out for dramatic change": Richard N. Haass, *The Power to Persuade* (New York: Houghton Mifflin, 1994), p. 109.

123: "You can use the Western movie analogy": Quoted in Jonathan

Walters, "The Perils of Imported Management," *Governing,* July 1993, p. 54.

123: "As is often the case": Haass, *The Power to Persuade,* p. 112.

124: "This day marks more than the orderly transition of government": Mike Foster, inaugural speech, Baton Rouge, La, January 8, 1996.

125: Kopplin read the newspaper headline: As remembered by Andy Kopplin.

125: "If they don't do it constitutionally": Quoted in Carl Redman, "Leaders Plan Quick Start on Controversial Agenda," *Baton Rouge Advocate,* March 24, 1996.

126: "I think 100 days is a metaphor": Quoted in "The People and the Power Game with Hedrick Smith," aired on PBS, September 3 and 10, 1996.

126: "Every day that I'm in office": Lyndon Johnson, *Macmillan Dictionary of Political Quotations,* p. 541.

127: "Competence is achieved through experience": Elliot Richardson, *Reflections of a Radical Moderate* (New York: Pantheon Books, 1996), p. 82.

127: "No executive can succeed without good people": L. William Seidman, *Full Faith and Credit: The Great S&L Debacle and Other Washington Sagas* (New York: Times Books, 1993), p. 95.

127: "We're a small office": William J. Bennett, *Meet the Press,* March 19, 1989.

128: "Currently, FEMA is like a patient in triage": Quoted by Alliance for Redesigning Government, Internet web site (http://www.clearlake.ibm.com/alliance).

128: The agency would live up its new motto: "People helping people": Alan C. Miller and Carla Rivera, "A True Master of Disaster," *The Los Angeles Times,* April 8, 1994, p. A1.

128: "FEMA is now a model disaster relief agency": Quoted in Bill McAlister, "FEMA Chief Given Cabinet Status," *The Washington Post,* February 27, 1996, p. A17.

129: "This is the essence of McCarthyism": Quoted in Elisabeth Bumiller, "The Unbearable Lightness of Being 2 to Pataki," *The New York Times,* June 4, 1996, p. 1.

129: "I have no intention of quitting": Ibid.

132: "I had worked as hard as I could": Peter B. Edelman, "The Worst Thing Bill Clinton Has Done," *The Atlantic Monthly,* March 1997, p. 43.

133: "I could not permit my silence and my inaction": Arnold I. Burns, testimony before the U.S. Senate Judiciary Committee, July 26, 1988.

Chapter 8: Ending Bureaucracy As We Know It

135: Opening quote: George McGovern, quoted in Robert Andrews, *The Concise Columbia Dictionary of Quotations* (New York: Avon Books, 1989), p. 32.

135: it would rank as twelfth largest in the nation and thirty-third largest in the world: Based on 1995 revenues, U.S. Postal Service advertisement.

135: "where good performance is seldom recognized": Carl M. Levin, quoted in Bill McAllister, "On Hill, Runyon Calls for Labor Peace Summit," *The Washington Post*, Dec. 1, 1994, p. A21.

135: "dysfunctional organizational culture": Quoted in ibid.

135–36: Since 1973, postal employees had turned guns: "Postmaster Vows to Improve Work Conditions; Suspect Sought," *Chicago Tribune*, May 9, 1993.

136: "We've got regions, divisions and headquarters": Quoted in "Postmaster Plans Service Overhaul," *Chicago Tribune*, Aug. 8, 1992.

136: "institutional suicide": Quoted in Bill McAllister, "Don't Blame Buyouts, Postmaster Says; Runyon Says Policy Is Not Responsible for Service Collapse," *The Washington Post*, Sept. 29, 1994, p. A21.

137: "My magazines come months late": Quoted in Sharman Stein and Jerry Thomas, "First Class Gripes Greet Postmaster; Mail Woes Tough to Lick, He Says," *Chicago Tribune*, March 22, 1994.

137: Postal inspectors conducted a test: John Kass and Elaine S. Povich, "Daley Fumes About Postmaster—and the Letter's in the Mail," *Chicago Tribune*, March 24, 1994.

137: "This won't be fixed quickly": Quoted in Stein and Thomas, "First Class Gripes Greet Postmaster."

137: "Welcome to the bureaucratic government": Quoted in Kass and Povich, "Daley Fumes About Postmaster."

137: "We needed a surgeon": Quoted in Bill McAllister, "Can Marvin Runyon Deliver?" *The Washington Post Magazine*, July 10, 1994, p. 16.

138: "All government service": Robert Moses, quoted in Robert Caro, *The Power Broker*, (New York: Vintage, 1974), p. 75.

139: "It's as if we said": Speech at Reason Foundation Conference, Philadelphia, Pa., Sept. 18, 1995.

139: "In 60 years, we've gone from a nation": Arne Carlson, State of the State Address, Jan. 18, 1995.

140: "You have to stay with it until": Quoted in Jonathan Walters, "Flattening Bureaucracy," *Governing*, March 1996, p. 21.

145: "Any change is resisted because bureaucrats": Richard M.

Nixon to Peter Flanagan, 1969, quoted in William Safire, *Before the Fall* (New York: Doubleday, 1975).

145: "The personnel and procurement laws": Daniel Beard, speech delivered at the National Conference on Federal Quality, Federal Quality Institute, Washington, D.C., Aug. 1, 1995.

145: "It's a rude awakening when someone": Quoted in Jonathan Walters, "Reinventing Government: Managing the Politics of Change," *Governing*, Dec. 1992, p. 37.

146: "[The] bureaucracy is loaded with worker bees": Quoted in Steve Duin, "Too Many Fires to Light the Eternal Flame," *Oregonian*, Aug. 25, 1994, p. E9.

146: "Vera is not utilizing her talents": Quoted in ibid.

147: "Folks, the truth of the matter is": Zell Miller, State of the State Address, State Capitol, Atlanta, Ga., Jan. 10, 1996.

149: "Universal requirements that leave no room for judgment": Quoted in ibid.

150: "We're trying to change the culture and mindset": Quoted in Charles Mahtesian, "Reinventing Government from the Bottom Up," *Governing*, Nov. 1995.

152: "In too many cases, the incentives within government": Pete Wilson, *Competitive Government: A Plan for Less Bureaucracy, More Results*, Sacramento, Cal., April 1996.

152: "In North Carolina, Governor Jim Hunt gave . . . that saved $1.7 million": Foon Rhee, "Bright Ideas to Save State a Bundle," *Charlotte Observer*, Sept. 20, 1994, p. 1C.

152: "In Seattle, employees at metropolitan water-treatment": Alliance for Redesigning Government, Internet web site (http://192.156.133.18/Alliance/clusters/lm/apend_d1.htm.).

153: For example, Michellee Craddock: Stephen Barr, "A Simple Suggestion Worth Millions; Civil Servant's Idea Expected to Mean Big Savings in Procurement," *The Washington Post*, Oct. 13, 1994, p. A17.

154: "Michellee brought up . . . problems": Steve Kelman, quoted in ibid.

154: "a bureaucratic nightmare": Quoted in Stephen Barr, "Clinton Administration Backs Bill to Overhaul Procurement System," *The Washington Post*, Feb. 25, 1994, p. A19.

154: "All of these things": ibid.

154: One legal secretary at the U.S. Labor Department: Frank Greve, "Wanted: Easy Work, Lifetime Guarantee," *Tallahassee Democrat*, Nov. 29, 1993, p. 1A.

155: "There was an employee who physically attacked someone": Quoted in Wilson, *Competitive Government*, p. 14.

Chapter 9: Juggling Many Balls at Once

157: Opening quote: Henry Kissinger, *The New York Times Magazine*, June 1, 1969.

158: "[Bilandic] thought the snow had been gotten rid of": Bill Granger, "Council's Hot Air Could Melt Snow," *Chicago Tribune*, Feb. 20, 1985.

158: The foul-up cost the city an estimated $75 million: Hugh Dellios and Robert Davis, "Flood Promises Grim Financial Future," *Chicago Tribune*, Apr. 19, 1992.

158: "A little bit of snow is fun": Quoted in James Warren, "Timely Tips on the Unthinkable for Each of You Soon-to-be Losers," *Chicago Tribune*, Nov. 8, 1988.

158: "Other than former Mayor Michael Bilandic": Joel Kaplan, "Francis Degnan, Ex-City Official," *Chicago Tribune*, May 18, 1996.

159: "There always is another crisis": Harry Truman, quoted in *Macmillan Dictionary of Political Quotations*, p. 580.

159: "You can set almost any agenda": Quoted in John F. Harris, "The Man Who Squared the Oval Office," *The Washington Post* (National Edition), Jan. 13, 1997, p. 11.

161: (His successor, Jane Byrne, spent millions on new snow removal equipment): Dick Stahler, "It's a War Out There—Keeping Chicago Streets Clear of Snow Is a Battle That Begins in Summer," *Chicago Tribune*, Dec. 29, 1991.

162: "It was like I was elected doctor to a sick patient": Quoted in Craig R. McCoy, "One Problem Down . . . Rendell Tackled the Budget. The City Isn't Fixed. He'd Like to Keep Trying," *Philadelphia Inquirer*, Oct. 15, 1995, p. C1.

162: "We don't have time to pussyfoot around": Quoted in Dan Meyers, "The Task Facing Mayor Rendell," *Philadelphia Inquirer*, Jan. 5, 1992, p. A1.

163: "We have to break the rules": Quoted in Marc Duvoisin and Tom Turcol, "The New Mayor's Message is Clear: No Pain, No Gain," *Philadelphia Inquirer*, Jan. 7, 1992, p. A1.

163: saving approximately $150 million in 15 months: William D. Eggers, "Three Big City Mayors Show the Way to Survival for Cities on the Brink," *Philadelphia Inquirer*, July 13, 1993, p. A7.

163: Rendell regularly published annual performance statistics: Craig R. McCoy, "One Problem Down . . . Rendell Tackled the Budget. The City Isn't Fixed. He'd Like to Keep Trying," *Philadelphia Inquirer*, Oct. 15, 1995, p. C1.

163: The Philadelphia turnaround made Rendell a celebrity mayor:

Story, including quotes from *The New York Times* and *The Los Angeles Times*, by Matthew Purdy, "Rendell's Heady Days of Glory," *Philadelphia Inquirer*, Sept. 26, 1993, p. A1.

164: "Well, I came in and this boat": Quoted in Ron Scherer, "Mayor Sets New Tone in City Hall," *Christian Science Monitor*, Dec. 24, 1993, p. 2.

165: "I did not come into government to win an award": *Inside Albany*, June 19, 1988.

165: a $52 billion state budget—the nation's second largest: As remembered by Dall Forsythe; $37 billion in state funds plus $15 billion in federal funds.

167: "Too much goes on too fast for the president": Jeffrey Birnbaum, *Madhouse* (New York; Times Books, 1996), p. 40.

168: "Govern like you're going to be": Quoted in Steven Lee Myers, "Government Reinvention: A Seminar with a Master," *The New York Times*, March 6, 1994, p. 35.

168: "Movies and TV shows often feature": James Fallows, "Clinton a 'One-Termer?'" National Public Radio Commentary, Jan. 23, 1995.

169: "I'm just not going to spend a lot of political capital": Quoted in William Greider, *Atlantic Monthly*, Dec. 1981.

170: "The ability to be cool, confident": Richard Nixon, *Six Crises* (New York: Touchstone, 1962, 1990), p. 1.

170: "He's really putting together": Quoted in Cynthia Brown, "Rendell Picnics for Party Unity," *Philadelphia Daily News*, Sept. 3, 1991, p. 5.

171: "We studied literally every cost-saving initiative": Quoted in Ron Scherer, "Mayor Sets New Tone in City Hall," *Christian Science Monitor*, Dec. 24, 1993, p. 2.

172: "Decisive action relieves the tension": Nixon, *Six Crises*, p. 131.

172: "It is axiomatic in politics": Richard Lamm, quoted in *Macmillan Dictionary of Political Quotes*, p. 392.

Chapter 10: Managing the Message

175: Opening quote: John F. Kennedy, quoted in *Macmillan Dictionary of Political Quotes*, p. 404.

175: *Governing* magazine article: Robert D. Behn, "Evaluate Managers—on Page One," *Governing*, Jan. 1995, p. 84.

176: "I challenge [the author] to obtain a real job": E. J. Knittel, "Job Offer," *Governing*, March 1995, p. 12.

176: "Fired Swartara Township Manager Gets Job on Opposite Shore," *Harrisburg Patriot News*.

177: The late Washington governor Dixie Ray Lee so disliked the press: Patricia O'Brien, "The Ladies Auxiliary Is Alive and Well," *Columbia Journalism Review*, Sept./Oct. 1996, p. 61.

177: "Openness allows us to know what our governments are doing": Elliot Richardson, *Reflections of a Radical Moderate* (New York: Pantheon, 1996), p. 14.

178: After all, journalists . . . rate near them: John Carmody, "The TV Column," *The Washington Post*, July 19, 1996, p. B6.

179: "Mainstream journalism has fallen into the habit": James Fallows, *Breaking the News: How the Media Undermine American Democracy* (New York: Pantheon, 1996), p. 7.

179: "Officials and reporters, representing two sides": Marvin Kalb, "A Puzzle for the Press Corps: What's Deeper than Deep?" *Boston Globe*, March 28, 1996.

180: The department published a 200-page book: Gary Lee, "Final Data Released on Tests Involving Radiation Exposure," *The Washington Post*, Aug. 18, 1995, p. A23.

180: established an 800-number for victims: Philip J. Hilts, "Panel Urges U.S. to Apologize for Radiation Testing and Pay Damages," *The New York Times*, Oct. 3, 1995, p. A19.

180: "We ought to go forward": Quoted in Melissa Healy, "Payments Urged for Radiation Test Victims; Energy Secretary O'Leary's Call Is First Indication that U.S. Is Willing to Acknowledge Liability," *The Los Angeles Times*, Dec. 29, 1993, p. A1.

180: "O'Leary has shown she can do it": "The Staying Power of Secrecy," *Los Angeles Times*, Dec. 29, 1993, p. B6.

180: "Far more than her predecessors . . .": Quoted in Matthew L. Wald, "Energy Chief Expresses Chagrin over Monitoring Reporters," *The New York Times*, Nov. 11, 1995, p. A9.

181: The program ran some nine months and cost $46,500: Michael Moss, "Turning the Tables, Energy Department Reports on Reporters," *The Wall Street Journal*, Nov. 9, 1996, p. A1. Note: *The Wall Street Journal* originally reported the cost at $43,500, and this number was picked up in other press stories. The amount was later amended by the Department of Energy to $46,500. The nine months' time frame was reported by *The Los Angeles Times* on Nov. 10, 1995.

181: "The money involved may not sound much": Quoted in Gary Lee, "Energy Secretary Faces Hill Fire on Consultant," *The Washington Post*, Nov. 18, 1995, p. A12.

181: "threatened to overshadow her substantial achievements": "Grading the News—at Your Expense," *The Los Angeles Times*, Nov. 10, 1996, p. B8.

181: O'Leary rebutted: Matthew L. Wald, "Energy Chief Expresses Chagrin over Monitoring Reporters," *The New York Times*, Nov. 11, 1995, p. 9.

181: Senate Majority Leader Bob Dole said . . . a petition calling for O'Leary to step down: Ibid.

181: The local CBS television affiliate in Hartford: Chris Rohrs, WFSB editorial, November 27, 1995.

181: "The Secretary could most effectively": "Energy's Friends-And-Enemies List," editorial, *The New York Times*, Nov. 11, 1995, p. 22.

183: "I absolutely love, and maybe I overdo this": Rudy Giuliani, quoted in John Tierney, "The Holy Terror," *The New York Times Magazine*, Dec. 3, 1995, p. 60.

183: "concentrate on substance": Quoted in Alison Mitchell, "New Mayor Tests Magic of the Airwaves," *The New York Times*, Jan. 12, 1994, p. B1.

183: "his ability to make people think the politically unthinkable": "A Time for Wisdom," *The New York Times*, Oct. 3, 1995, p. A24.

184: One tale began after the 1995 Japan subway bombing: Bruce Weber, "A Press Secretary Under Fire; Giuliani's Spokeswoman Draws Criticism from Reporters," *The New York Times*, Mar. 24, 1996, p. B1.

184: "One night Giuliani's press secretary called a *New York Times* editor": William Glaberson, "Giuliani and Reporters: Disparate Views of Mayor's Image," *The New York Times*, July 4, 1994, p. 21.

184: "Some of the criticism of my press and communications operation": Rudy Giuliani, quoted in ibid.

185: It wasn't the first time: David Gonzalez, "About New York: Paying a Price for Candor," *The New York Times*, March 9, 1996, p. 25.

185: "study the sad list of officeholders": "The Mayor's Censorship Office," *The New York Times*, Feb. 24, 1995, p. A28.

185: "government-by-enemies approach": Quoted in Joyce Purnick, "Sorting Out the Hopefuls to Run Against Giuliani," *The New York Times*, Feb. 19, 1996, p. B1.

186: "The press also has a professional obligation": "The Mayor's Censorship Office," *The New York Times*, Feb. 24, 1995, p. A28.

189: "A lot of reporters don't know anything about economics": Quoted in Howard Kurtz, "Asleep at the Wheel," *The Washington Post Magazine*, Nov. 29, 1992, p. 10.

189: "Recognizing that the public will hear and comprehend": David T. Ellwood, "Welfare Reform as I Knew It: When Bad Things Happen to Good Policies," *The American Prospect*, May–June 1996, pp. 22–29.

190: "These people have no business": Quoted in Robert A. Rankin,

"President Vetoes Ban on Late-Term Abortion; The Bill Would Have Outlawed the 'Partial-Birth' Method," *Philadelphia Inquirer,* April 11, 1996, p. A1.

191: They called it "heroes in the balcony": Peggy Noonan, *What I Saw at the Revolution* (New York: Random House, 1990), p. 198.

191: "Ten years ago a young girl": Quoted in ibid., p. 199.

192: "Whenever we have found any issues": Quoted in Mireya Navarro, "Search Called Off for Survivors of Crash in Everglades; Hope of Rescue Is Swallowed by Swamp," *The New York Times,* May 13, 1996, p. A1.

192: statistics . . . showed that ValuJet had a higher accident rate: Chart, "F.A.A. Files Show Early Lapses by ValuJet," *The New York Times,* May 20, 1996, p. B10.

192: Like many stuck politicians, Pena went on *Nightline* to defend his comments: *Nightline,* May 16, 1996.

193: Just three days later, Senator Trent Lott said on *Meet the Press:* Quoted in Adam Bryant, "F.A.A. Files Show Early Lapses by ValuJet," *The New York Times,* May 20, 1996, p. B10.

193: "Precisely because press secretaries have lied": Mike McCurry, "At the White House Press Podium, Accuracy Is All," *The New York Times,* March 10, 1997, p. A14.

Chapter 11: Remember Who Sent You

195: Opening quote from speech by Ronald Yates, "Total Quality Leadership," at Computing Devices TQM Conference, Minneapolis, Minn., Nov. 1, 1994.

195: "Like the marriage vows": Mike Royko, *Boss: Richard J. Daley of Chicago* (New York: E. P. Dutton, 1971), p. 9.

196: "He brings a list of all new city employees": ibid., p. 17.

196: "The best evidence of American perspective": Elliot Richardson, *Reflections of a Radical Moderate* (New York: Pantheon, 1996), p. 13.

196: "The root of the problem": Jimmy Carter, quoted in *Macmillan Dictionary of Political Quotes,* p. 634.

197: "said to house 'park-barrel politics' ": Charles Mahtesian, "The End of Park-Barrel Politics," *Governing,* Jan. 1995, p. 34.

197: "The system was built originally as a patronage empire": Quoted in ibid.

197: "Twenty years ago when I was a young clerk": Quoted in ibid.

198: "This year marks our 60th anniversary": Forrest Claypool, speech before the Chicagoland Chamber of Commerce, Jan. 27, 1994.

198: "There are a lot of people at the Park District": Quoted in Mahetsian, "The End of Park-Barrel Politics," p. 34.

199: "new management has accomplished a tremendous amount": "The Chicago Park District: A Progress Report on Decentralization," prepared by The Civic Federation and Friends of the Park, Sept. 1995.

200: "I was screaming. . . . Everybody thought the worst": Quoted in Richard Perez-Pena, "Series of Electrical Blasts Under Subway Shuts Down Lexington Line," *The New York Times,* May 2, 1996, p. B1.

200: "When there are three thousand New Yorkers": Quoted in Richard Perez-Pena, "Transit Chiefs Fault Riders in Shutdown," *The New York Times,* May 3, 1996, p. B1.

200: "In business, the customer is always king": Quoted in Clyde Haberman, "In Subway, the Customer Is Blamed," *The New York Times,* May 4, 1996, p. 21.

201: "where the public can see it": Quoted in Nancy McCarthy, "Stein Carries Sunny Attitude Outside for Her Swearing-In," *Oregonian,* Aug. 25, 1993, p. D9.

201: " 'Is government providing good service?' is too narrow": Beverly Stein, speech before the Portland City Club, Jan. 12, 1996.

201: "Citizens . . . want government": Ibid.

202: "Sadly, some politicians offer simple slogans": Ibid.

202: cutting twenty-three sheriff's deputies and moving them: Graphic, *Oregonian,* Apr. 12, 1994, p. B2.

202: "There are several new untested programs": Quoted in Bill McKenzie, "Stein Defends Plan to Transfer Sheriff's Deputies to Portland," *Oregonian,* May 15, 1994, p. B4.

203: "The statutes that authorize them": Robert Reich, *The Power of Public Ideas,* p. 124.

204: "Sometimes higher-level public managers": Ibid., p. 123.

204: "This is the first generation of citizens who": Lawrence K. Grossman, *The Electronic Republic: Reshaping Democracy in the Information Age* (New York: Viking, 1995), p. 4.

207: "Such an institution may be sometimes necessary": James Madison, *The Federalist Papers, No. 63* (New York: New American Library of World Literature, 1961), p. 384.

208: "The stakes are too high for government to be a spectator sport": Quoted in "A Report from the Texas Performance Review," Office of the State Comptroller, Austin, Tex., Dec. 1996.

209: "there's alt.politics.greens, alt.politics.libertarian": Robert Wright, "Hyperdemocracy: Washington Isn't Dangerously Disconnected from the People; the Trouble May Be It's Too Plugged In," *Time,* 1995.

209: Switzerland has moved toward direct democracy . . . the Swiss voted . . . increase their gas taxes: Brian Beedham, "A Better Way to Vote: Why Letting the People Themselves Take the Decisions Is the Logical Next Step for the West," *The Economist,* survey, Sept. 11, 1993.

209: One study collected thousands of polls: Grossman, *The Electronic Republic,* pp. 65–67.

210: "The defenders of the old-fashioned form of democracy": "It Means Government by the People, and We Are the People," *The Economist,* survey, p. 4, Dec. 21, 1996.

210: "It promises to be a fiasco": Ted Koppel, "The Perils of Info-Democracy," *The New York Times,* July 1, 1994, p.A 25; as quoted by Grossman, *The Electronic Republic,* p. 147.

211: "Our political system has shown itself": Grossman, *The Electronic Republic,* p. 147.

211: "is not *whether* the new electronic information infrastructure": Ibid.

212: When Thomas M. Davis III took over as chairman: Peter Baker, "Tom Davis, Still the Consensus-Builder . . . But Not Always," *The Washington Post,* July 5, 1992, p. B1.

213: "Historically, government has done a poor job": "Introduction to Minnesota Milestones 1992," State of Minnesota web site (http://www.state.mn.us/).

213: "Monitoring progress will help us know if our programs are working": Quoted in "What Is Minnesota Milestones? 1994," State of Minnesota web site (http://www.state.mn.us/).

213: "ensure that politicians make progress toward meeting those goals": *St. Paul Pioneer Press,* Aug. 8, 1992.

214: The police got answers . . . up from 40 percent in 1988: Don L. Boroughs, "Bureaucracy Busters," *US News & World Report,* Nov. 30, 1992, p. 49.

215: "The success of democracy depends": Fiorello La Guardia, quoted in *Macmillan Dictionary of Political Quotes,* p. 636.

216: "The systems don't have to cost a lot . . . to make their information accessible": *The Public Innovator,* No. 2, Apr. 14, 1994.

216: "Bruce Kirschner designed interactive systems": Ibid.

Conclusion

225: "Being Interior Secretary is like": Manuel Lujan, quoted in *Macmillan Dictionary of Political Quotes,* p. 577.

225: "Government is not the problem; government is not the solution": ABC News, Clinton inaugural address, Jan. 20, 1997.

226: "I have found honor in the profession": Quoted in James Bennet, "With Ballots Still Warm, Clinton Pays Homage to Dole," *The New York Times*, Jan. 18, 1997, p. A12.

226: "Politics, like theater, is one of those things": Richard Lamm, quoted in *Macmillan Dictionary of Political Quotes*, p. 577.

Index